A HISTORY OF VERNHAM DEAN

A village in Hampshire

by G.L. Palmer
assisted by
J. Garbutt and J. Cobbold

This book is dedicated to

Leslie Le Mottée (1913-99)

without his help this history would not have been recorded

ISBN 978-0-9557322-0-1

Published by	G.L. Palmer
Copyright	G.L. Palmer
Printed by	Bulpitt Print Ltd
	Unit P Hunting Gate
	East Portway
	Andover
	SP10 3SJ

The publication of this book was assisted by a grant
from Hampshire County Council.

Hampshire
County Council

Contents

FOREWORD

"A History of Vernham Dean" – a careful title. How to begin to thank all those people who have contributed to the work? Leslie Le Mottée was the prime researcher, spending many hours in the Hampshire Record Office and in the offices of the Andover Advertiser, peering over ancient manuscripts and noting the results in his meticulous handwriting. Sadly he has not lived to see the project come to fruition, but his work formed the basis of all that came after.

Millie and Bruce Seward – without them we would not have known so much about the village. They both worked for many years in the shops and gave us a full picture of the village economy. It is they who provided so much about the chapel, as well as many tales of the characters who supported that side of village life.

Other sources: official publications helped us with a framework, specific publications were drawn to our attention by Tony Jackson. The Hampshire Record Office could not have been more helpful, particularly Suzanne Foster who produced countless archives from Winchester College for our perusal. The HRO also reproduced a fascinating map, much used by John Garbutt in his work on agriculture and the land. Joe Scicluna of the Andover Advertiser gave us permission to quote at length from old copies of the newspaper. We had help from the Andover History and Archaeology Society – we listened to lectures given by the Hampshire Field Club which guided us to resources of particular importance. We have to thank Thelma Cobbold for proof-reading the finished product before we submitted it to Diana Coldicott for her guidance as to the historical content. Mrs. Coldicott had generously contributed her lecture notes on Friendly Societies which facilitated our work to a great degree.

Who else? Betty Mills for her knowledge of the Manor, and Vernham Mills in the early years for his many tales. Jon Fairbrother, who kindly waded through the prehistoric content and gave advice and permission for us to use his map of the village in 1776. Tony Vincent, for his long knowledge of the village. Michael Harley, a previous vicar, for useful bits and pieces. David and Eileen Sullivan, for checking the "Mission Hall" chapter and contributing an update. David Vining and Michael Whittingham for their reminiscences. The "old boys" in the pub, for their many patient reminiscences over the years and not least our many Email correspondents from all corners of the earth – Peter Dawkes in Germany, and his brother Wilfred among others - and parishioners who have submitted their memories. Eric Levell gave us permission to quote freely from his "Country Ways" and from notes we took on a village walk he conducted. And finally, Harry Paris and John Marchment, wonderful characters, whose notes and pictures greatly facilitated the overall result … …... and all those other people whose names we have not recorded – we owe you our heartfelt thanks.

Just for the record, there are many versions of the spelling of Vernham Dean – Fernhamsdean, Fernham, etc but for simplicity the modern day 'Vernham Dean' will normally be used. Vernham Dean applies to the village in the valley bottom; Vernham Street takes in many of the houses at the top of Bulpit's Hill up to Littledown, and Vernham Row encompasses the houses up Bower's Lane towards Henley.

Man first appeared in the Hampshire area about 700,000 years ago, but as you walk along a track in Vernham Dean you could go much further back in time and pick up a 60 million year old echinoid (sea urchin) and then light on a Ski School Medal (3rd class) dropped by an Italian prisoner of the Second World War. There are artefacts from prehistoric times and all ages since – Roman, Saxon, medieval and later.

The area around Vernham is on the boundary between the Middle and the Upper Chalk, which is responsible for the landscape of rolling downland and steep valleys of this section of the North Wessex Downs. The valleys, mainly dry today, were cut by rivers when the water table in the chalk was higher. Complacent householders can still be taken by surprise when the bournes flow and the River Swift comes to life. In 1995 the bourne flowed strongly from Upton, fields were flooded, water rose in the Bury Dene in Vernham, and wells in Upton, unused for many years, scoured themselves free and re-appeared. Gardens laid over the old watercourse had to be traversed with duckboards. Springs came up through living room floors, and sewage created a problem.

Clay with flints appears to the north of the parish, the lower valley regions being covered with valley gravel. Soil shows considerable variation from one area to another, agricultural quality on the chalk being mostly Grade 3, with small localized pockets of Grade 2.

There are extensive areas of woodland around Vernham, some of it semi-natural in origin, and important remnants of ancient woodland can be found. Blessed with steep slopes and scarps which have escaped the ravages of agriculture, the occasional unimproved chalkland habitat can be found, as at Rushmore, Conholt and Kiblet Down. There is a mix of arable and pastoral farming, and the valley is surrounded by three estates on which game is a vital resource. Estate management has a different flavour from the farm and valley mix, and the estates themselves have played an important part in the development of the Vernham area.

During the Pleistocene era, two million years ago, it would have been cold, damp and uncomfortable in the area, and man would only have come over the land bridge from the continent during the summer to follow herds of game. No evidence of Pleistocene activity has been found in Vernham Dean, but the rapid rise in temperature towards the end of the Palaeolithic era (700,000 years ago) meant a more stable soil surface could develop, so vegetation could advance – forest trees. Flint implements from this time have been found in parts of the Test Valley. Mesolithic man (7000 – 4500 BC) seems to have had a preference for the Greensand areas around the edge of the Weald, but it is known to be a time of forest growth, with the appearance of woodland fauna and red deer, roe deer, pig, cattle, elk, beaver, pine marten, lynx and wolf. Again, the existence of Mesolithic man in Vernham cannot be proved, but one would have to travel no further than Oakhanger, (near Alton, Hants): Marsh Benham (off the A4 Newbury-Hungerford): Thatcham (A4 Newbury-Reading) and Greenham Dairy Farm (near A339 Newbury-Basingstoke) to know that he was "about".

In the Neolithic Age (4500-2500 BC) there are more distinct signs of man. There was woodland clearance, exposed soil would be impoverished, and perhaps the first heathlands developed. Man hunted red and roe deer, wild cattle and pig, and searched for nuts – the hazel nut was very important. The Vernham area may have seen Mesolithic man who was very much on the move, seeking game, but Neolithic Man was of a different calibre. He began to form settlements, and established and developed cultivation of land. He kept oxen, sheep, pigs and dogs. Work at Boxgrove, near Chichester, has shown that very early man was much more advanced than was thought, and Neolithic Man in his turn was quite a sophisticated gentleman. Trading began, objects are found which could only have come from a considerable distance. About 4,000 years ago there was a definite trade in stone axes. Over in Wiltshire axes made from igneous rock from Penmaenmawr in North Wales have been found, showing that appearance was as important as utility. Around Vernham, Chute and Fosbury stone axes have come to light, shafted by being bound into a cleft of a forked stick. One particularly smooth beautiful axe was found in the hedge at Sargents Farm, at the west end of the village. Besides axes, there were other artefacts, pottery sherds, flint and stone tools, worked antler and bone implements. With Neolithic man's improved farming techniques he grew cereals, domesticated animals, cleared much of the forest cover, and coppiced or pollarded the remains of the trees. Modern research reveals that much of the land was cleared before the Bronze Age (2500-750 BC) and in these early years man began to dominate the landscape. He also created funerary monuments, several can be seen to the west of the Chute Causeway, and one only has to go to Stonehenge and Avebury to see Neolithic man's monuments. Though there are few remains in the parish, the landscape to the west of the Chute Causeway is littered with smaller examples of burial mounds – earthen long barrows – elongated, ovoid, rectangular or trapezoidal in shape, with length varying between 30 and 95 metres. Ditches may be found down the long side and sometimes around one end. Burial places, to be sure, but also used for other purposes, perhaps socio-religious, a focus for communities or even territorial markers. They are always on the chalk, not all in prominent landscape positions but nevertheless visible over a large area. The "Kenward Stone" was found at the Conholt end of the Chute Causeway, not far from the turning south to the Chutes, and has markings similar to those found in prehistoric rock art in many parts of the world, notably in the work of the Bushman in South Africa. There is a tale that the Kenward Stone marks a Saxon Moot site, others say the markings are merely the work of vegetative roots. For all that it is a striking sight and many are the tales of accidents which have befallen anyone attempting to move the stone from its resting place.

The Bronze Age (2500-750 BC): a survey of Sarsen Stones records one at Hurstbourne Tarrant before the river bridge, and three surrounding the church at Tangley, but the highlight in Vernham's history also stems from this time. The Vernham Treasure, found at Kent's Copse (SU331597), indicates Bronze Age man in Vernham. The first of the Bronze Age palstaves were found by John Herriott of Upper Row(e) Farm before 1920, on the edge of Kent's Copse, and the remainder by Mr. Ken Whatley, then of Horns Farm, in 1988. Mr. Whatley had been an avid searcher for artefacts for many years. His collection gave ample evidence of the existence of man in considerable numbers in the Vernham area since earliest times. The following description of the 1988 discovery is by Mr. Andrew Lawson, of the Trust for Wessex Archaeology, an expert on Bronze Age metalwork, and is reproduced, in attenuated form, by kind permission of Andover Museum.

"The Vernhams Dean hoard is a valuable addition to the record of Middle Bronze Age metalwork in Hampshire, and is striking in that it contains solely palstaves of a wide variety of forms. The axes, no two of which are alike, are predominantly un-looped, only one is looped, and with broad blades, although one is distinctively narrow. In two examples the blade is short and the cutting edge splayed as if frequently reworked. Decoration varies from a simple median rib through poorly executed trident motifs to strongly contoured shapes. A shield pattern is infilled with internal ribs, while others have multiple rib decoration only ..... individually these palstaves can be paralleled in Middle Bronze Age hoards throughout southern England ...... which serves only to confirm the interchange of bronze products in a widespread zone of contact during the Taunton phase of metalworking in the 14th and 13th centuries BC. Many of the forms also bear comparison with the Normandy series of Northern France, which demonstrates long distance exchange networks in the Middle Bronze Age ...... although the closest physically to Vernhams Dean is the ornament hoard from South Wonston, all others lie within twenty miles of the south coast. Geographically the hoard is relatively isolated on the upland north of the county, the closest contemporary hoards being those in the River Avon catchment of Wiltshire, or in Oxfordshire (Hagbourne and Wantage) ...... the deposition of the hoard in a flat based globular vessel is similar in practice to those of the Birchington, Kent, hoard. Such associations form rare and valuable links with the normally separate ceramic tradition of the Middle Bronze Age and indirectly with the contemporary social activity."

The Vernham Dean Hoard can be seen in the Andover Museum, where it is displayed by kind permission of the finders.

Bronze Age sites were sometimes overlaid by later Iron Age (750 BC – 43 AD) occupation. Early fields often stem from the Bronze Age, but may be much earlier, and in turn they were often re-used in the Iron Age and in Roman times. Such fields are very clear on the south-facing slopes of the fort near Fosbury at Knollys Down, high above the road to Hippenscombe. The fields were straight-sided, square or rectangular, between 0.1 and 0.4 hectares. (0.25-1.00 acre). Fields formed on slopes tended to have their upper and lower limits defined by scarps (lynchets) formed by the build-up of soil from ploughing, the height varies with the steepness of the slope and how intensely the areas have been ploughed since Bronze Age times. Early fields can also be distinguished in other parts of the area and, as mentioned previously, there are just a few sites in the area which are recorded as being genuine chalk grassland: Kiblet Down, Conholt Down (south), two sites in 17 ha, Rushmore Down (21 ha) and Conholt Down (north) 1.5 ha. OS references to the exact sites are given at the end of the chapter.

In chalkland Hampshire a linear or 'ranch' boundary is often seen, whose origins may be Bronze/Iron Age – a single ditch and bank of 3-6m across often extending for many miles. It could be a divide between adjoining blocks of early fields, or field and pasture. "Grim's Ditch" is very visible both on the map and the ground, particularly if looked at from the south slope of the Romano/British fort at Knollys Down, over towards Conholt. Information gleaned from the National Monuments Record at Swindon goes as follows: *"SU287559 to SU 326554 – a bank or ditch nearly three miles long just north of Chute Causeway and for most of its length coincident with the parish boundaries of Chute, Tidcombe and Fosbury. The ditch is on the southern uphill side suggesting a boundary rather than a defensive work, field work by Bonney leading him to suggest Iron Age date. 14th century documents ascribe the name Grim's Ditch to the work. On the 6" sheet the ditch and bank are for the most part clearly defined and little damaged. There seems no doubt that they were associated with the field system, possibly as a boundary droveway, and a pre-Roman date is confirmed by an aerial photograph which clearly shows an extension to the west beyond the Roman road. The latter extent is not visible on the ground. SU300551 – SU 325554 – for most of the distance the earthwork has been reduced through silting and erosion to two downhill facing scarps each averaging 1.5m in height with an overall width of 15m. Across Little Down (SU300551 – SU 306554) the bank reappears visible in air photographs and is up to 1.0m in height, but the ditch is silted and faint: it has been eroded by surface quarrying for about 175m in area SU 302551. The work is now fully covered by bushes and gorse."* (Note: there are also other areas of Grim's Ditch in the parish around SU 366567).

Iron Age man continued to clear more of the forest, and larger areas of open country appeared on the chalk. Wind and weather eroded the soil but man may have used the area for agriculture where it is no longer possible today. Division of labour had appeared, they produced practical and ornamental metal objects, and trading or barter was common. In the early Bronze Age it was drier and warmer than today, but climate deteriorated towards

4

the Iron Age and although the fort at Knollys Down near Fosbury is not strictly within the parish of Vernham it is too spectacular a feature to leave out. Again, a visit to the National Monuments Record Centre in Swindon produced details as follows:

"(The fort) occupies the south side of a prominent E-W ridge and commands extensive views in all directions. It measures some 430m E-W by 330m transversely and comprises a rampart, ditch and counterscarp bank, all of massive proportions: additionally a quarry ditch which can be recognised within the rampart along the majority of the south side. The area enclosed is 26 acres, and Iron Age sherds were found within the camp by Grinsell and Meyrick, but no sustained excavation has ever taken place. There is a fine interned entrance at the east end of the work but of the other four 'entrances' none can be positively identified as original. The interior of the fort has been ploughed at some time but is now permanent pasture. Over much of it, but especially the southern half, innumerable pits and hollows are recognisable ranging from 1m to about 4m in overall diameter and up to 0.5m in depth. They obviously represent settlement (storage pits, threshing and winnowing pits etc) but no huts can be identified. None of the features can be recognised as encroaching upon the quarry ditches." The fort is above the 250m contour line, and a visit in a blizzard was a challenging experience.

Forts arose from an organised community, and often developed into towns with houses and streets. This was not the case here, but the fort would have had extensive grain storage capacity in the form of beehive shaped pits. Pits in chalk are very efficient methods of storing grain, and such forts perhaps housed specialised craft workers, including metal workers. Forts may have been the centre of a large agricultural area including settlements, trackways and field systems – all to be found around Vernham. It is estimated that there was more arable land farmed in the Iron Age than in the 17th century. Wheat (emmer and spelt) was grown as well as spring sown barley: wheat dominated but barley became popular later, whereas oats were not much favoured. The cattle were small shorthorn breeds, the sheep like those found on Soay. The farmers manured the fields and used chalk to break down the heavier clays. From 750BC onwards iron was developed, a hard material suitable for ploughshares and tree-felling so woodland clearance could take place on the heavier clay areas on the lower slopes of the downs and in the river valleys. There was a decline in population from the later Iron Age to the 2nd century AD, after which the area appears to have had a considerable number of Romano-British farms.

The Romans – AD 43 onwards.

The Romans must have been somewhat disconcerted to find they had to construct the longest bend of all Roman roads to form the Chute Causeway. This is a five mile deviation in the Andover-Cirencester road to avoid the steep valley of Hippenscombe. The road is composed of straight sections and, in spite of being on dry chalk, is built up in true Roman fashion. Eric Levell's grandfather told the story that the surveyor had been seconded from road-making in the Fens, and followed the same rules: build it up to avoid the marsh found in the Fens. The road is constructed of layers of rammed chalk, flints and soil, and covered with layers of gravel. J.P. Williams-Freeman said *"It showed the definite regulation way in which Roman work was done, as on this hard dry chalk ridge such an embankment could not have been necessary. Red tape is not a modern invention."*

The Romans were around for about 400 years, and Vernham is not far from the important road mentioned above. 'They' say that the Romans used to picket their horses in the fort at Knollys Down. It is an easy journey from near Five Lane Ends/Scot's Poor on the Causeway to the fort over high ground. 'They' say there is also a Roman villa not far from the village but to date no definite information has come to light. There is also a legend that the south-facing slopes above the Hippenscombe road held a Roman vineyard. After all, if evidence of a Roman vineyard can be found near Wollaston, Northants, in the Nene Valley *(Ian Meadows, Current Archaeology No: 150)* why not near Vernham Dean? Ken Whatley was firmly of the opinion that there was "something Roman" in a field near Horns Farm, on the outskirts of the area, although subsequent investigation by the Andover Museum could not substantiate this. There is also a site in the field just to the left hand side of Hatch Lane in the direction of Church Lane. It is called, vaguely, 'Iron Age Romano British settlement – site of. It is a nearly circular enclosure c. 95m N-S and 103m E-W enclosed by a bank averaging 0.3m in height, entrance to the SE.' This was partially ploughed out at the time of the field investigation, and there were no finds apart from a few unidentified sherds of coarse ware close by. At SU339569 there were a number of lynchets, probably contemporary with the settlement, but almost ploughed out. Near Upton Manor (SU359558) there is an Iron Age/Romano British 40m Banjo enclosure (i.e. shaped like a banjo) just within the eastern boundary of Farm Copse on the crest of the west-facing slope, a near-circular earthwork comprising a ditch some 8m in width and 12m in depth with traces of both an inner and outer bank, the east side of the earthwork destroyed by ploughing. The interior is level, entered by a fieldway on the south west. At SU 360557 a cropmark 30m in diameter was noted from aerial photography, but no trace could be seen on the ground. A scatter of coarse Romano-British potsherds may be associated. At SU 355537 three fragments of an Iron Age rotary quern bearing signs of repair with an iron band were found in 1945 by O.G.S. Crawford on the eastern bank of the Upton-Andover road. They had obviously been found in an adjoining field and were thrown aside. They are now in the Winchester Museum. At SU 348540 there is an enclosure, probably Iron Age/Romano-British with soil and shadow marks of a sub-rectangular enclosure and possibly an associated field system. The earthwork comprises the remains of an extremely strong rampart and ditch enclosure, occupying a summit ridge which commands extensive views in all directions, with sub-rectangular rounded corners. Probably 100m sq. overall, ploughing has completely destroyed the SE side and reduced the rampart elsewhere to a height of 0.2m above the enclosure area, and the ditch to about 0.7m in depth. The overall measurements of the rampart and ditch reach 25m and a slight causeway at the northern corner of the work is the only visible remains of an entrance. It has the appearance of being Roman or sub-Roman, and although occupying the fringe of an early field system, the exposed position, apparent strength and complete absence of surface finds makes it a doubtful habitation site.

The Romans did not have an outstanding effect on Iron Age culture, but tended to superimpose where they thought fit. During their sojourn the ploughs improved, heavier soils were cultivated and longer narrower fields appeared. Early upland sites decayed and the farms became dependent on the richer soils of the valleys. Perhaps due to a deterioration in climate which favoured wheat there was more wheat production in the 4th century. Also, the introduction of the low-cutting scythe enabled hay to be gathered and stacked for winter fodder, so the cattle could be kept in the farmyard during the winter months and did not need to be slaughtered.

The Romans introduced many new plants: vine, mulberry, walnut, fig, sweet chestnut, plum, medlar, pea, radish and culinary herbs (fennel and dill). Perhaps the spectacular row of chestnuts at Conholt, close to the Chute Causeway, the medlar at Lower Conholt and the walnut at Upton Manor might just owe their origins to Roman influence?

After the Roman army was withdrawn in 410 AD there were further incursions. It was by no means the blaze of pillage and bloodshed commonly depicted, rather a complicated pattern of settlement and assimilation with the native population. The "Saxons" took over little from the Romans: villas fell into disuse, although sites could have been covered over with subsequent buildings. The Roman roads tended to be avoided, some said the long straight lengths looked like snakes. The Saxons did, however, establish many of the local settlements and the tracks leading to them. It is worth looking at the map to see how the Tangley and Hatherden roads wiggle around, compared with the now disused section of the Roman road. Slowly rural settlements began to look more like villages, farmsteads became large, hamlets appeared, located mainly in river valleys and the lower slopes of the chalk downs. Most modern villages are known to date back to the 10th century. Vernham's church is known to be 12th century, but that one was built of stone and it could be that there was an earlier foundation built of wood. Churches were being established as early as the 6th century and the present system of parishes had its origin in the mid to late Saxon period. Further research may well take Vernham's church to a pre-12th century foundation. A study of an old parish map showed several variations from today's parish: there are islands belonging to Vernham Dean parish in Hurstbourne, and vice versa. This indicates that land is being farmed by a farmer from the adjacent parish and is counted as belonging to the parish of the person who farms it. Banks and ditches often reflected boundaries of late Saxon estates, possibly even earlier land units. Work for this history is carried out on the 19th century boundaries, well marked on the maps, but in earlier times a perambulation (i.e. a walk around the parish boundaries in order to establish them in people's minds) was a yearly event in some places.

The *Winchester College Muniments* (5611 p 261) speaks of a dividing line between the townships of 'Fernham' and Upton thus: (16th century): ...... *thence to Fernham; thence to foot of lane by Abbot's messuage where a cross formerly stood. The cross has fallen down, but the pieces of it are there. Thence to Lord's wood called 'Wylstraw' along road by Abbot's grange; then to 'Holeway' by way that lies btw sd wood and 'Ryecroft' belonging to Abbot; thence N along way that lies betw sd wood and 'Uptonesheth' that lies to E; hence to Grim's Ditch a way leading to Faccomb ......"*

It would seem that boundary disputes were often settled by custom and hearsay, but in the Vernham area ponds were a very valuable landmark. Often mentioned and essential from the earliest times for watering livestock and people, some were natural hollows, deepened and then puddled. This involved alternate layers of straw and clay. The pond at Vernham Dean was puddled until modern intervention was thought appropriate. By the time it fell into disuse (1950s) it was only fed by run-off from the road, and no longer potable, due mainly to a fall in the water table and reduced run-off from the surrounding fields. Knyghtes Mere and Rockmoor Pond are used as boundary markers still, and were invaluable for watering animals being driven to market. For centuries the Vernham Dean pond was a regular watering hole for cattle and sheep. Knyghtes Mere (SU 336443) is a pond where Conholt (or Ankers) Lane enters Wiltshire and is a boundary mark of the parish of Vernham Dean AD 1410. It is a circular pond embanked on the north east and probably formed by artificial deepening of a natural hollow. Rockmoor Pond (Throcmere SU 350590) is at the present meeting place of three counties and four parishes and was encircled by a high artificial bank. It occurs in the boundary charter as Throcmere (AD863) and Th(o)rocomere (AD 961) It is called Trokmere in 1410, now designated as a 'stagnant pool situated in the bottom of a deep quarry-like pit. No trace of encircling bank is visible.' It was certainly not stagnant in the 1990s, and benefited from a 'good clean out' by a villager, with resultant new growth and much pond life. Subsequent applications of pesticides to the surrounding fields resulted in draining and leaching into the pond and by 1996 it was again a dull, stagnant, lifeless pool.

SU 331564 is Goudyses Gate – a boundary mark in 1410. It now applies to the point where the county boundary crosses the road, but occurs in several forms in charters. In 863 the old 'Aescmere' referred to the whole or part of the lands of Linkenholt and Vernham Dean and names can still be identified: 'Maple Combe – Facca's Combe – Rough Barrow – Lilla's pond – Throcmere' i.e. Mascombe, Faccombe, Limber and Throcmere. Mascombe is a field and woodland name in the southern part of Vernham, near to Lower Conholt. It probably referred to the whole of that valley. Throc Mere means 'drain pond'.

In the charter of 961 50 hides at Hisseburn, which King Edgar granted in that year to the Abbey at Abingdon, included Vernham Dean and Linkenholt, and are included in the Hurstbourne Tarrant survey. 'Hisseburn' 'Esseborne' (Hurstbourne Tarrant) was later designated the Pastrow Hundred for administrative purposes, but 'Aescmere' disappears, and by the mid 10th century Linkenholt, Vernham Dean and Upton can be recognised as included in Hurstbourne Tarrant: indeed Vernham Dean was a chapelry of Hurstbourne until 1871. Linkenholt, however, had an association with St. Peter's of Gloucester and was independent of Hurstbourne, possibly by the 12th century. By the end of the medieval period Vernham Dean, Vernham Street, the Manor, Lower Conholt and Mascombe were known, and the earliest mention of Vernham Dean says it contained 1580 hectares: '*A valleyed situation, main E-W valley with branches to North*'. *It had a Manor House and church, with common fields to the east and north of the Manor.* Mascombe was mentioned in 863, Vernham Dean 1410, Vernham Street 1324, Lower Conholt 1334 – all of which are in valley situations. There are no obvious signs of settlement around the Manor House, and an archaeological survey has yet to substantiate the legend that the village was moved down to the valley in time of plague.

The Normans in the 11th century would have found a farmed landscape with the pattern of the villages almost complete. The level of farming was equal to that of later centuries. Defence was important in many areas, but that would not have been the flavour of Vernham. Land was given by the Normans as rewards for services, was made over to abbeys as penance or service to God, was divided, amalgamated, squabbled over – so in the next chapter it will be appropriate to place Vernham Dean in relation to general history and to gain the wider view.

SOURCES

National Monuments Record, Swindon

Andover Museum

General oversight, and maps by kind indulgence of Mr. Jon Fairbrother.

Winchester College Muniments

Eric Levell

Grid references:

OS Pathfinder 1202: Ludgershall & Hurstbourne Tarrant.

Early fields:	SU324563 and 319562
	SU354543: SU363537: SU359525: SU378520: SU 387548
	SU396534.
Kiblet Down	334554
Conholt Down (s)	340544
Rushmore Down	350545
Conholt Down (n)	347554

contributed by John Cobbold

As seen from the previous chapter, Vernham Dean as a separate entity did not really exist until the late Middle Ages. There is no mention of it in the Domesday Book, and William's tax collectors did not miss much. People living here would be included within Hurstbourne Tarrant, which does figure.

However, this does not mean nothing was happening. In the wider area, quite a lot was taking place. This chapter details some of the events that occurred within an approximately 50-mile radius of Vernham Dean.

THE PALAEOLITHIC ERA (Old Stone Age) 700,000 to 7,000 BC

Some authorities do not start the period until 500,000 BC: however as little or nothing has been discovered in the area from this period, it seems academic. There have been some flint and hand axe finds in Hampshire, mainly near rivers close to the south coast and on the Basingstoke Downs, so it is not impossible that early man passed through the area.

England was still connected to Europe at this time, making travel easier. However, there were several periods of extreme cold, so the population is never likely to have been large. Man would have existed mainly by hunting. Towards the end of the period there was a significant rise in temperatures, the ice retreated, and forests grew.

Although outside the 50-mile radius, about 200 miles away, on the coast at Pakefield in northern Suffolk, 32 pieces of worked flint were discovered on the shoreline. These have been dated to approximately 700,000 years BC, right at the start of the Palaeolithic era. It is thought at this period the climate was quite balmy, lions, hippos, elephants roamed the area, and early humans lived along river banks, moving in and out as the climate changed.

THE MESOLITHIC ERA (The Middle Stone Age) 7,000 to 4,500 BC

In this period tree cover increased significantly, and mankind began to change the environment by burning, tree felling etc. The way of life was still that of a hunter gatherer. There is little evidence of human activity in the local area, but at Foxcotte, Andover, and near Basingstoke some flint works have been recorded. On the coast, near Havant, evidence of huts has been discovered.

At Romsey a deer's antler with engraved rows of chevrons has been discovered, dating to this era. Carbonised hazelnut shells have been found in several areas, together with deer, pig and cattle bones, but nothing significant close to Vernham Dean.

11

THE NEOLITHIC ERA (The New Stone Age) 4,500 to 2,500 BC)

The hunter gatherer way of life gave way to more settled arable and pastoral farming during this period. Pottery and stone tools from this era are frequently found. Animals – goats, sheep, cattle, pigs and dogs – were domesticated, and cereals grown. At South Street, Wiltshire, cross-ploughed furrows dating to about 3,500 BC have been discovered.

There is little evidence for settlement in the area, however a ditched enclosure has been excavated near Winchester. Also in that area were two burial pits, one containing human bones and some grave goods. Flint mining took place at Martin's Clump, Over Wallop. This is also the era of the long barrow. There are a large number in the area, over 40 in Hampshire, many more over the border in Wiltshire and further west. The Nutbane barrow, near Weyhill, has been dated to circa 3,500 BC.

Stone axes have been found in the area, some originated in Dorset, some in Cornwall, and others from Langdale in Cumbria. Long distance travel and trade were common in this era, with trackways running across the county in all directions. The Ridgeway is quite close to Vernham Dean

THE BRONZE AGE (2,500 to 750 BC)

There is little evidence of Bronze Age settlements in the area, however use of the long barrows continued from the earlier era. The lack of archaeological evidence could be because there never has been anything, or that later settlers have effectively destroyed most of what there was to find. As well as the field patterns mentioned in the previous chapter, an example can be seen at Stockbridge Down. In this area are several linear boundary ditches; these consist of a single V-shaped ditch with a bank, two to three metres across, and about two metres deep. Although partially destroyed by later ploughing, some of these extend for miles.

During the construction of the M3 at Twyford Down, early Bronze Age cremation burials were discovered. These were found within an enclosure, and contained pottery. No evidence of long term settlement was discovered, although a number of postholes indicate some occupation of the site.

At Chilbolton, more burials have been located. These consist of a pit with a wooden mortuary chamber alongside. Beaker pottery, golden earrings, stone beads and a copper dagger were also excavated, along with the remains of two bodies, both adult. These can be seen in the Andover Museum.

At Walworth, near Andover, a pair of round barrows was excavated in 1987 ahead of some industrial development. Much had already been destroyed in earlier times, but a child had been buried there, together with two adults and a complete skeleton of a cow.

During the early part of this period, the climate was drier and warmer than it is today, but later in the period rainfall increased, something that continued into the Iron Age. Forest clearance continued, and some of the heathland we know today came into existence.

Although there is little evidence of settlement in the local area during this period, there were many people living in the wider area, and they have left their mark: Stonehenge, Woodhenge, Avebury, Durrington Walls and Silbury Hill. There were people here in considerable numbers over very long periods of time. Settlements have been found at Winterbourne Stoke, only a few miles from Stonehenge.

(Henge: a circular enclosure surrounded by a ditch, which is surrounded by a bank, with one or more causewayed entrances i.e. it is designed to keep people in, rather than keep them out.)

THE IRON AGE (750 BC to AD43)

This is the age of the hill forts. In Hampshire alone there are over 30, but they are found throughout southern England. Many, like Danebury or Fosbury are sited on top of hills and are visible for many miles around. Others are on lower ground, for instance Buckland Rings near Lymington. Some have impressive concentric rings of ditches and mounds, with complex entrances. The best example of this is Maiden Castle in Dorset but Danebury and St. Catherine's Hill near Winchester are nearer examples. Others such as Fosbury only have a single ditch and bank. Danebury has been excavated, the banks surround over 16 acres of land. Within the 12 acres which have been fully excavated were 10,000 postholes, 500 rectangular structures, 73 roundhouses, 2,300 storage pits and over 150,000 pottery sherds. This was a considerable settlement.

Some hill forts were never completed, Ladle Hill, near Newbury, for instance. Woolbury on Stockbridge Down was only occupied for a relatively short period. Roman records and archaeological evidence record an attack on Maiden Castle by troops under Vespasian in AD45. The battle appears to have been ferocious and ended in victory for the invaders (according to Roman sources).

Hill forts were the centre of extensive agricultural territories, with field systems, trackways and smaller scattered settlements. Many show evidence of specialised craft working, pottery and metal. Bury Ring, Upper Clatford, has produced a collection of horse harnesses. The smaller settlements come in various shapes and sizes. A 'banjo' enclosure can be found at Blagden Copse, at Hurstbourne Tarrant, and there is another in Micheldever Wood and one at Abbotts Ann.

The use of iron tools and weapons identifies this period. Ploughshares and axes enabled the clearing and cultivation of larger fields. Animals were still being domesticated, early Roman writers describe manure being spread on the fields to break down the chalk.

THE ROMAN ERA (AD43 to 400)

In AD43 the Romans arrived intending to stay, and for nearly 400 years they did. Landing on the south coast, they rapidly moved north and Hampshire became the base camp for the Roman army as the conquest of the rest of Britain, except for the Celtic north, continued. The Roman army not only fought the Britons, it was also expert in the construction of forts, towns, ports and roads. There are over fifty known Roman sites in Hampshire. Winchester (Venta Belgarum) was a major Roman city. There was a small villa at Stockbridge and (recently excavated as part of the Danebury Environs Project by Sir Barry Cunliffe) villas were found at Thruxton, Grateley and Abbotts Ann. In Andover a burial of nine skeletons in coffins, together with funeral goods, was discovered in the 1980s.

Towards the end of this period the climate deteriorated and became much wetter. Roman farmers tended to concentrate in the lowlands, allowing the higher land, such as that around Vernham Dean, to revert to scrubland or forest. Woodcutting continued, rather more to provide fuel than to open up land, so an increase of heathland acreage occurred during the era.

In 410 Emperor Honorius wrote to the cities of Britain telling them to look after their own defences, and ordering his legions to leave Britain and return to Rome, thus the country was no longer subject to central Roman government and its tax demands.

THE SAXON ERA (AD400 to 1066)

After the Roman army left Britain, various Germanic tribes moved into eastern England. They gradually moved westwards, but there is little evidence of significant fighting, rather of gradual assimilation. Except at the very top of society little changed, there was plenty of land to go round. There is very little archaeological evidence of Anglo-Saxon building. While the Romans built in stone, the Anglo-Saxons built almost exclusively in wood. At Portway Saxon graves have been found, and some building foundations at Cowdery's Down, Basingstoke. Small huts have been excavated at Old Down Farm, Andover.

By the middle Saxon period (640-850) Winchester had become a major ecclesiastical and political site. In the ninth century, the House of Wessex became dominant rulers of Southern England. Starting with Alfred the Great, they went on to become the Kings of England. Alfred's grandson, Athelstan, was recognised as King of Britain by most of the other minor kings of England and Scotland. At the end of the 920s, he issued an important code of laws at Grateley, which included the establishment of just one coinage throughout the kingdom.

In 871 the Vikings defeated the Wessex army at Basing, the Saxons retreated westwards past Andover, pursued by the Vikings. King Alfred soon reversed this defeat.

Up until this period, the woodland area was being steadily reduced, but in the 8th century laws protecting the forest were passed. This started a period when most of Hampshire was subject to Forest Law. The areas affected reached their greatest extent in the 12th century. Chute Forest encompassed Vernham Dean. This forest was huge and spread over three counties: Hampshire, Wiltshire and Berkshire. The Hampshire portion was divided into Digerley Forest and Finkley Forest.

In 950 King Edred built a hunting lodge in Savernake Forest, and in 962 King Edgar held a council at Andover. In 1008 King Ethelred (The Unready or, alternatively, ill-advised) held a parliament (Witanegemot) at Enham. Ethelred, despite the unfortunate nickname which was given to him posthumously, actually reigned for 38 years in an era when a decade was considered a considerable achievement. The Enham parliament was a major lawmaking assembly, attempting to reform ship tax and ultimately the military capability of England. The Vikings were still raiding the southern part of the country, having conquered most of the north and east. The Enham legislation also included major reform of the Church, the monasteries, and the rules governing the observance of saints' days; vows of chastity and obedience were reinforced. This was a major secular and religious reformation and it all happened just down the road from Vernham Dean. In 994 King Ethelred came to Andover to attend the confirmation of Olaf Tryggvason who became king of Norway soon afterwards. In 1011 Ethelred signed a treaty with the Viking Thurkill at Andover.

After Ethelred's death, the two rival kings of England, the Viking Cnut and the Saxon Edmund Ironside, fought the Battle of Andover in 1016. It was a draw. A few months later they agreed a treaty: each recognised the other as his successor, and split the country between them until one died. Edmund died first, and Cnut went on to rule until his death in 1035.

There is still no hard evidence for any settlement at Vernham Dean, however, place names ending in 'ham' indicate Saxon settlements.

THE MEDIEVAL PERIOD (1066 – 1485)

In January 1066 Edward the Confessor died, and in the autumn of the same year the last English King, Harold II, died at the Battle of Hastings. William I (The Conqueror) became king.

This invasion was different from the previous invasions. Only a few thousand Normans arrived with William, but the king's hold over the country was soon complete. They took over, killed or married the Saxon nobility, but for the majority of the population nothing changed – as long as the army had not swept through their district - except taxes went up.

Castles started to appear in the landscape: locally Ludgershall, Basing House and Old Sarum. Sarum Cathedral was built in stone, before the clerics moved down the hill to Salisbury.

The Saxon field system continued, but many wealthy landowners created deer parks. Much of Hampshire was still subject to the Forest Laws. Rabbits had been introduced, initially farmed, but some escaped. Now look how many there are. In 1266 twenty buck carcasses were sent from Chute Forest to Windsor, and twenty more to Kenilworth. In the reign of King John, Windsor Park was restocked with deer from Chute Forest on several occasions. In 1231 twenty oaks were sent to Amesbury Priory from Chute Forest and a further twenty went in the same year to a mill in Newbury, and more to Winchester. In 1251 Henry III gave twenty oaks each from Digerley and Finkley to repair Salisbury Cathedral. In 1320 sixty oaks went from Chute to Old Sarum to repair the King's water mills. All this shows that quite a number of people lived and worked in the forest. There is archaeological evidence of metalworking in this period at Faccombe.

In Romsey, the Abbey was built in stone. Andover had several stone houses, the foundations being unearthed in the Chantry Street area, while others have been found in Winchester Street and Newbury Street. Wherwell Abbey, another great Benedictine nunnery, had been founded at the end of the 10th century, but became the site of a battle in 1141: forces loyal to King Stephen besieged John Marshal, a leading magnate in the area, and the Empress Matilda, in the abbey. It was set on fire, however Matilda managed to escape to Ludgershall. John Marshal was eventually rescued from the burning abbey but lost an eye in the fight. Stephen's men went on to burn down Andover in celebration of their victory. John Marshal was the father of William (the) Marshal. William was a drinking friend and right hand man to the future Henry II. He then became Marshal of England some years after Henry became king, holding this post under both Richard I and King John. Finally he became Regent of England in the early years of Henry III's reign. Not a bad record for a local lad, who was born near Devizes into a minor landowning family, especially as he was one of the younger sons. Wherwell Abbey was finally destroyed after Henry VIII's Dissolution of the Monasteries, although some buildings remain.

Winchester was the capital of England during the Saxon period, although during the reign of the Confessor London started to replace it. The royal treasury remained at Winchester until late medieval times, the Bishop of Winchester often doubling as keeper of the treasury. He was a major political and ecclesiastical figure, sometimes the former being more important than the latter. Winchester's political importance can be seen in 1100. Immediately following the 'accidental' death of his brother King William II in the New Forest, the future Henry I went directly to Winchester to secure the support of the monastic chapter. Winchester did not have a bishop at the time, owing to William II's policy of not replacing deceased or retiring bishops, but leaving the post vacant, thus enabling the Crown i.e. William, to pocket the revenues of the Diocese. Henry gained the support of many of the English magnates who had also headed for Winchester. Then Henry went to London to be crowned king. The bones of William II finished up in one (or more) of the burial chests stored in Winchester Cathedral, along with Cnut and several Saxon kings and queens.

The Black Death appeared in 1349 and there were subsequent outbreaks between then and the 17th century. Nearly half the priests in the diocese died (recorded in The Register of William Edington, Bishop of Winchester) Two rectors of Linkenholt died in 1349 (Hants Record Services Vol 7 Nos; 485, 703.) Andover burned down for the second time in 1435. .... still not a lot happened in Vernham Dean.

In 1485, far away in the Midlands, King Richard III was betrayed and killed at the battle of Bosworth Field. The Welsh Tudors took over, which seems a good place to end this chapter and turn attention to the Manor.

There is no mention of the manor of Vernhams Dean in the Domesday Book, but as in the 13th century it was still a member of the neighbouring manor of Hurstbourne it is probably included in the entry under 'Esseborne'. It continued to form part of that manor until circa 1177, when it was granted by Henry II to Henry de Bernevall and his heirs to hold by the service of one knight. This grant was confirmed by King Richard I and by King John, the latter confirmation being dated 25th August 1203.

The following information is taken from the Victoria County History, Vol IV, pp 329-330 and should perhaps have a health warning attached, or rather "boredom warning". For those deeply interested it is fascinating, for those who would prefer easier meat it is suggested judicious skipping is in order. The editor is indebted to Jon Fairbrother, who transcribed the original into simpler format, and to the proof-reader who pointed out, in no uncertain terms, that the passage is "a bit indigestible".

In 1213 Roger de Bernevall, nephew of Henry, undertook to pay the king 200 marks for lands of his uncle in Hampshire. Perhaps he fell into arrears, because Henry III granted the manor to Thomas the younger to hold during the royal pleasure. Roger regained possession and held the estate until his death in battle in 1226. Custody was then granted to Robert Haget, his wife's brother, but on the 2nd October 1232 the sheriff of the county was ordered to give seisin (possession of the manor) to Reginald de Bernevall, Roger's brother, on condition he recompense Robert for the loss of his chattels and pay him £5 a year for the support of the heirs of Roger until they attained their majority. However, Robert Haget recovered his right of custody on 27th October, after which the manor stayed in the Bernevall family until 1277. When Gilbert de Bernevall died it was divided between his daughter Cecily and his grandson Gilbert de Cundy, son and heir of his other daughter, Aubrey.

Cecily married Gilbert de Nevill who claimed, in 1280, to have the fines of the assize of bread and ale in Vernhams Dean. She died in 1300, having survived her husband by six years, and her moiety (half) of the manor passed to her son and heir, John Nevill, aged 26. The latter died in 1334, leaving his moiety of the manor to his son Gilbert. Gilbert died in 1359 and willed his estate to his heir, his daughter Elizabeth, wife of Simon Symeon. Soon after the death of Simon without issue in 1387 Elizabeth married John de la Warre, and in 1389 the moiety of the manor was settled on them in fee-tail (Fee-tail – a limited inherited estate, as opposed to fee-simple which means unlimited) with contingent remainder to feoffees (group of trustees appointed to manage an endowed institution e.g. a charity school). There were no children from this marriage either and so after their deaths (Elizabeth predeceased her husband in 1395) the moiety of the manor passed to the feoffees who in 1399 obtained licence to grant it in free alms to Winchester College. This was done by fine in 1401, and in 1428 the Warden of Winchester College was returned as holding half a fee in Vernhams Dean. Thereafter the governors of Winchester College were the Lords of that portion of the Manor.

Now back to Gilbert de Cundy (son of Aubrey, daughter of Gilbert) – the other moiety: West Vernham or Botes. By an undated charter Gilbert de Bernevall granted this manor to Gilbert de Botes in consideration of homage and services and a white palfrey and 1d. yearly rent, and a pair of white gloves at Easter. Probably Gilbert de Botes – who gave his name to West Vernham was Gilbert de Cundy and in 1303 called Lord of the Botes Manor. In 1303 Gilbert de Cundy obtained a licence from the king to grant it to Walter de Romsey on condition that Walter pay Gilbert an annuity of two marks and should board respectably (honorifice) in his own or a religious house Gilbert's brother, Geoffrey. He should allow Gilbert every year a furred gown such as Walter himself wore as 'valet' and if Walter should be dubbed a knight he should allow Gilbert 20/- or a gown of that price and in alternate years a gown of cloth and fur like that worn by his own wife, or 2/- in lieu.

Soon afterwards Gilbert and his wife Eleanor acquired from Walter de Romsey a life interest in the moiety. But it was then seized by the Crown, since it was said to have been acquired without licence. In 1318 Eleanor was pardoned and received permission to retain the premises for life in return for a fine paid by her second husband, Thomas Heryngawd. However, before 1333 it had reverted to the Romsey family, Walter de Romsey (son of the previous Walter) who died in possession of it in that year, 1333. His son John, died soon afterwards, but John's son Walter, who had become a knight, obtained licence in 1381 to convey his moiety of the manor of Vernhams Dean to his son Thomas and Eleanor his wife in fee-tail. Thomas died in possession of the moiety in 1400, during the lifetime of his father, leaving son and heir, Thomas, who died 20 years later, in turn leaving infant Joan as heir. Thomas' wife was also Joan, she died in 1440, in possession of a third part of the moiety, which she had held in dower. The next year the whole moiety was settled on daughter Joan and husband Thomas Payne. On Joan's death the estate was divided between her two next heirs, which were her father's cousin, Joan, wife of Roger Wyke, (and a granddaughter of Sir Walter Romsey through his daughter Mary Byngham), and William Horsey, son and heir of her father's cousin Eleanor, sister of Joan Wyke.

The moiety of Vernhams Dean was assigned to cousin Joan. In 1461 Joan and Roger Wyke dealt by fine with half the manors of Vernham, Vernhamgreen and Botysplace. Joan had married as her first husband Thomas Keileway, whose descendant John Keileway in 1517 granted a 40 years' lease of the manor of East Vernham and Botes to Thomas Hellier, husbandman. John died in 1547, in possession of half of the manor of Vernham Dean. His heir was son William, who in 1567 in conjunction with his son Francis and wife Anne convened to George Burley premises described in the fine as the manors of Vernhams Dean and Botes. In 1570 Thomas, son and heir of Francis, gave up all the rights in the premises to George Burley, who in turn alienated them (i.e. transferred ownership) to Thomas Larke, John Attwood and Roger Watton in 1575, probably trustees for Winchester College. The manor from time to time was conveyed to new feoffees. The two Manor Farms mark the sites of the moieties of the original manor of Vernhams Dean, while Botes Copse, to the south of the village in the extreme west of the parish still preserves the name of the Manor of Botes, and the name is further immortalised in the 20th century development of 'Botisdone Close' near the centre of the village of Vernham Dean.

When William of Wykeham became Bishop of Winchester in 1366 he *'desired to revive and improve the education and administration of a country disrupted by plagues which had severely depleted not only the population but also the civil service which was drawn from the educated clergy.'* (Phillimore). Winchester College was founded in 1382, opening with a warden and 70 scholars in 1394, the provision for its endowment being made in the acquisition of properties throughout Southern England – hence the purchase of land at Vernham, always referred to in the college archives as 'Fernhamsdean'.

Eventually most of the land in the area became the property of Winchester College, to whom it belonged until quite recently. A hefty amount of research is required to bridge the gap between the 16th century and the present day, which is readily accessible in the *Winchester College Muniments* ed. Himsworth (3 vols).

In 1998 it became possible to view in the Hampshire Record Office letters written from Vernham inhabitants to the Bursar at Winchester College, and it is from these letters that we are able to flesh out some of the shadowy characters from the 19th century.

In the church of St. Mary the Virgin at Vernham Dean are plaques to the Bull family, and John Bull was granted tenure of the Manor in 1796. In 1831 Hiram Bull, Darius Bull and Thomas Hawkins were acting as Executors for John Bull. In 1838 the Manor went to William Child, who had five sons and one daughter: Criswick, Thomas, John, Robert, Edwin and Sarah Ann. William was born in 1803 and came to Vernham Manor from 'Uphurstbourne' i.e. Hurstbourne Tarrant. After the Child family, Edwin Quick took the tenancy. By all accounts the Manor was uninhabitable when he took it over, Criswick had boarded up the windows, there were repairs needed throughout, rats were rife. The College allowed it to be taken rent free for the first two years in recognition of this. Edwin's sister, Kate, married John Mills and a son, Edwin John Vernham Mills was born on the 2nd December 1909. Vernham's tales are worth repeating:

"William Child was an old-fashioned squire. All the children were very frightened of him and would hide in the hedges if they saw him coming on his horse, as he would give them a crack with his whip if they got in his way. He would go down to the George Inn and if he had a disagreement with the landlord his whip cleared the bar of its glasses and then William would say how much the landlord had to pay for the breakages.

William enjoyed visiting his neighbours, sometimes staying over seven days, or even longer. When they got tired of him they would get his horse and have their men put him in the saddle, as he would be very drunk by that time. As soon as William was in the saddle the horse was told to go home. In his drunken state William would fall to one side or the other. The horse knew what to do, and would sidestep to catch him, getting him home safely. On arriving at the front of the Manor, loud shouts would come. Two men would come with a chair with poles each side. They would get him off the horse, sit him in the chair, and carry him up the front steps into the front hall, where Miss Child was standing ready to lecture him.

One day William was riding down the Linkenholt Road towards Pond House Cottage (that was on the corner of the Upton-Linkenholt Road at the junction with the road going down to the Manor). *Passing the cottage he saw the smoke pouring from the chimney. He sniffed – it was the smell of cooking. 'Ha', he thought, 'my game' so turning his horse, he tied it to the gate and walked to the cottage door, rapping it with his whip. The woman opened the door. 'Mrs – what are you cooking?' 'Some soup, Sir', the woman replied. He walked to the pot on the fire and took off the lid. Turning to the woman he said 'You are a liar, Mrs. It is one of my hares. Your husband will have the sack and you will go.'"*

The story goes that Miss Child, who 'had a fondness' for the Curate, asked him to lunch, but before going to church had locked the wine cupboards and cellar doors, so that her father could not get drunk and disgrace her. But as they came from church and turned up the drive she could see, to her horror, what her father had done. He was so angry at her locking the wine cupboard and cellar doors that he went to her bedroom, took her bedclothes and threw them out of the window onto the lawn. He then went to her chest of drawers containing her underwear. First to go was her nightdress, then corsets, bloomers, petticoats and all the undergarments he could find. When he had emptied the wardrobe and chest of drawers of all her undergarments he turned and saw her chamber pot. He picked it up and threw it as far as he could. It landed in the middle of the lawn in full sight of the returning couple. William then went and stood on the front door steps and as they approached he stamped his stick on the stone steps, and in an angry loud voice said 'Look', pointing to the lawn. 'That will larn 'ee, my girl'. No doubt lunch was a very sober affair.

The curate was so scared at what he saw on the lawn plus William's rage that he got himself removed to a distant parish.

William Child, as Churchwarden and School Manager, heard the schoolmistress had attended a chapel service. He went to the school and told her that as the school was Church of England she could not go to a chapel service. He then sacked her and told her to go.

After William's death affairs at the Manor appear through letters from both Criswick and John Fielder Child to the Bursar at Winchester College. Agriculture was in a sad state in the last quarter of the 19th century (due in some case to the importation of American wheat) and various comments in the letters bear out the difficulties.

14th December 1882. Criswick to Mr. Kirby (the Bursar). .... *'long protracted harvest .... some of my neighbours not yet finished and such bad wet weather since we have been unable to thrash to realize from our crops as we usually do ......all the quit rents have not been paid though applied for and more land in the neighbourhood going out of cultivation ....'*

In 1883 Criswick sent £33.7s.6d. for Corn Rents and fees due to the College *'grateful for credit allowed me.'*

When offered the tenancy of the farm Criswick writes to the solicitors, Pink and Arnold 04.02.87: *'Tis not the rent but the outgoings and working expenses of this hilly stony heavy wear and tear land coupled with the present prices which so cripple the prospect. Yesterday at Andover after trying for the three successive weeks I made 28/- per qr of our first thrashings of our Vernham wheat crop. Of barley 29/- per qr and of oats 14/- to 15/- per qr. Such prices would ruin any farmer. Could I see any chance of succeeding I would certainly not refuse but take the farm and remain here in our old home of 50 years standing. Believe me I very very reluctantly decline your kind offer. Our walls here are terrible shook about with the late severe weather lots down in several places ..... the lease I gave to Mr. Ellan yesterday to return to you.'*

And 17th February 1887 to Pink and Arnold again: *'.......... I would willingly do all I could to oblige you and Mr. Kirby but as you know only staying here on sufferance to thrash out our crop to pay the rates etc. and then in a few weeks to quit would make it a dear stay. My beneficial interest expecting the least cannot be much as one can only do their best to keep the place up for a new face. Cannot plant the garden or keep the fences up having no underwood. This weather as you have dried the walls the bricklayers have another fortnight's work and the carpenter has been on a fortnight it is a large place and needs constant keeping up ....'*

Edwin Quick had things no easier. On the 18th July 1890 he is asking to pay tithe after the harvest because he is waiting for a higher price for the hay. 16th January 1892: *'struggling to pay tithes by the end of March. Corn damp on account of wet harvest and not fit to thrash, prices is very low at present.'* In 1892 the Tithe Rent charge payable to the Ecclesiastical Commission (Vernhams Dean Rectorial) was outstanding from James Hughes (Poplars Farm) £1.3s.10d., Edwin Quick £3.8s.8d. and Walter Strange £4.7s.4d. The turning point seems to have come for Edwin Quick in the shape of John Mills for on the 19th May 1892 he writes to the Bursar: *'willing to carry on farm until September 1893, come to terms for a longer time, since writing to you last I have had an offer from a farmer near here by the name of Mills who would like to take about 70 acres of the land ….. it would be a help to get some of it round again into cultivation as most of the grass is now worn out.'* Indeed, by 10th April 1893 Edwin Quick writes to accept the offer of the farm till Michaelmas '94, and then wants a longer term. The College offers him the farm for another year, but Quick considers they ought to take £20 off *'and then I could meet payments and pay off old accounts.'* It must have been a dry season, for he says they had to feed oats to the sheep and could not sow 20 acres because it was dry. There had been wind damage to thatched roofs and not much profit from the shooting. He writes on the 19th April 1894 that he *'cannot see the way to pay off whole of arrears of tithe by Midsummer as it had been a bad season, although it is now looking better. The paint is so bad it will need doing twice and needs 100 lbs of chocolate and 100 lbs of white and some putty ……'*

At last in a letter dated 21st January 1895 he accepts the College's offer and writes (27th April 1896) *'the farm looking better than for many years …. have put down some land to sainfoin, now busy with turnip land.'* He wishes prices were better.

There seem to have been some legal mix ups between the late tenants and Messrs. Quick and Mills, and in 1897 Quick is writing *'The Lease does not include the small wood – Hill Coppice, No: 176'*. He wants this put on, and also a Statement of the Tithe account. A fascinating detail emerges – *'price of wallpaper for bedroom 6d. – 9d per roll – 6 rolls will do. Paint 6d per lb'*. John Mills writes thanking the College for the Lease and on 6th September 1897 Edwin Quick states *'the farm divided between Mr. Mills and myself, and no part to be taken away – we need the wood for repairs.'*

Vernham Manor stayed in the family and in 1977 Vernham Mills purchased it from Winchester College. During the 20th century the College gradually divested themselves of the properties in the parish. Vernham and his wife retired to Manor Farm Cottages, the Manor was sold, the Lordships being retained by the family.

by John Garbutt

Introduction

It is clear to the naked eye that the North Wessex Downs, of which the Vernham area is part, is an ancient landscape, with high arable and grazing lands, sheltered woodland, heath and common land. The influence of the agricultural efforts of man is for all to see and no doubt led to the beauty we see today. This is now manifest in the designation, in 1972, of the down land and valleys as an Area of Outstanding Natural Beauty (AONB).

The geology of the area has played a crucial role in establishing the communities that sparsely populate the AONB. First, the overwhelming influence is the chalk deposit, laid down in the Cretaceous period, some 130 million years ago. Overlying the chalk is usually a thin, well drained soil but with limited nutritional value. It is likely that large areas of higher ground were forested, probably until the Neolithic age (see below). At this stage, forest areas would have been cut down (for food, shelter, tools, weapons) to give way to grassland. This open land would then have been used initially for arable purposes, but later for grazing. The result is the distinctive, close-cropped grassland where grazing takes place. However, in more recent times, particularly since World War II, modern farming methods have enabled cereal and other crops, demanding regular artificial fertilisation, to be grown. Much of the ancient down land grazing has been lost to these more intensive uses, so that the dominant feature now is the large scale open arable field with only a few hedges and small woods. In the Vernham Dean area only in a limited way have the valleys retained sufficient of the clayey soil to provide significant lowland pastures and arable land, such as may be found elsewhere in Hampshire and Wiltshire. Indeed the local soil is much affected for its workability by heavy flints.

Only in special wet weather conditions is there any surface water, and this drains quickly. The one river in evidence usually reaches no further up the Bourne Valley than Upton and quite often no water at all is seen in the winterbourne (River Swift) throughout the year. The chalk acts as a massive sponge, capable of providing a natural storage reserve for summer use via wells and pumping stations.

The need for wood for a variety of construction, tool and fuel uses has resulted in the survival of swathes of small local woodlands, but these have declined in the 20th century as alternative sources have been used. Now the woodlands provide mostly amenity uses and shelter for game birds, (further described by Michael Whittingham later in the chapter).

The development of agriculture in Wessex.

With the retreat of the Ice Age, human activity began to be apparent in the area so that by 8500 BC hunting for food was probably seen on the higher ground while in the valleys plants, fish and wildfowl were available. By 5000 BC there was a major transformation in that the hunter gatherer had given way to significant food production. Modern research indicates that in the Bourne Valley area woodland was cleared for grazing animals, their domestication and the introduction of organised cultivation of crops.

By the end of the Neolithic period and the start of the Bronze Age (c. 2500 BC) man was sufficiently organised both to build the dramatic monuments such as Silbury Hill and Avebury, and to expand pasture and arable uses. Field systems began to appear at this time. In the late Bronze Age an ordered landscape had developed in the Vernham Dean area. A field system is apparent at Fosbury (OS ref 322564), no doubt protected by the nearby hill fort. At about this time cattle would be likely to have been grazed in the valley, where water sources were available, while sheep, needing less water, would have been grazed on the hillsides. Such development, particularly of settled farmsteads of some permanence, was sustained by the strength of centralised control which was a feature of the Roman period, extending into the Anglo-Saxon timescale. The Roman occupation also brought a much enhanced transport era, with roads such as the Chute Causeway. All this helped toward improved trade for local farmers.

Little changed until the Norman Conquest brought quite different French speaking nobility. The result was that land came under the ownership of the Crown, the nobility and, most importantly for this area, the Church. Features from the 10th-13th century were large hunting (deer) parks, settlement of the river valleys with only scattered hamlets on the hills, strip cultivation, with rectangular buildings with their own yards for animals lying along the established roads. Villagers enjoyed common rights to woodland and open areas where grazing was very important. Rabbits were managed in artificial burrows. The large current population of rabbits on the eastern slope of Conholt Hill (around O.S. Ref 333555) suggests that this was a site where burrows were established. Warren Cottage, on the opposite slope of the Hippenscombe valley, is to be noted.

Harvest failures and famines of 1315 to 1322, and the Black Death, in 1439, changed a great deal of local agriculture. Population losses were reported to be 40-50%, villages were abandoned and there was a great reduction in serfdom, caused by the sheer lack of available labour to service the agricultural needs of the landowners. Nonetheless, towns such as Marlborough, Newbury and Whitchurch continued to thrive, relying on the success of large sheep flocks, leading to the intensification of textile production, particularly based on wool. The emergence of the rich merchant farmer was a feature of the 16th-18th centuries. His needs for more land led to the tendency to enclose common and other land. Larger farm units resulted. Enclosure became a statutory reality in the 18th and 19th centuries.

The rise of the larger farm unit was inexorable and continues today as industrialisation and efficiency result in the dramatic reduction in the numbers employed in agriculture. Today it is rare to find village houses occupied by those engaged in agriculture and even farmsteads will be owned by those with more urban occupations.

The Eighteenth Century

Enclosure

The word "enclosure" has two meanings in the context of land ownership and rights. The more common refers simply to the act of fencing, hedging or walling of any given area of open land. However, there is a related but more legally technical meaning. It is the process whereby land passed from communal control into individual ownership. While much enclosure was authorised by Act of Parliament (both general and local statutes), the more usual means in North Hampshire was by agreement or even by unilateral annexation, often because common rights e.g. of pasture, might have fallen into disuse. The main periods of enclosure arose in 1700-1900. No Act of Parliament appears to affect Vernham Dean directly but there is clear evidence of an enclosure by agreement in about 1734. (Winchester College Muniments 9126). The Agreement refers to enclosure of the "Common Mead". A substantial map appears in 1748 (Winchester College 9127a), clearly linked to the Agreement, and seems to show the consequences of an Award, which mentions Rudgefield, North Field, Middle Field, Gulls Field and Merr Field and Heath having been enclosed by 1748. The legal processes were often overseen under the authority of Enclosure Commissioners, of which there were many in Wessex (over 200 are recorded in Hampshire). They were usually appointed from local yeoman farmers and landed gentry, with the occasional clergyman. The Commissioners for Vernham Dean were a Roger Gater/Geater (Senior) and others. They were supported by clerks, surveyors and others, and of course all those with actual or potential interests in the land would have taken part in the inquiry that led to the Award. The Award concerned some 1012 acres which were allotted to 36 persons, one of whom, Roger Geater/Gater received over 10%. Gater (or Geater) is described as a yeoman, from Barton in Kingbury Eagle, Berkshire. He is said to have been active from 1719-46 but only one other enclosure award is attributed to him (jointly with others), at Dummer and Kempshot.

The importance of enclosure to the development of agriculture was significant as communally controlled field systems were swept away and into the hands of smaller numbers of landowners. However, Vernham Dean could be said to be atypical of this trend, largely because of the comprehensive ownership of Winchester College. The imperatives for enclosure would have been less apparent, given the extensive management control by tenancy and copyhold, not only in terms of occupation but also of the use of individual holdings.

A document produced by Winchester College refers to Roger Geater Senior, responsible for a survey in 1734 which it appears is the precursor to the enclosure activity some years later. The document is described thus:

"A Survey of the General Tenants lands in Common (And some Inclosed Lands agreed to be Exchanged) with the Manor of Vernhamsdean in the County of Southampton in order for a Generall Inclosure with the Generall Allotments Alloted to each Tenant.

Delivered into me by Mr. Roger Geater Senior, who took it himself with great exactness, in order to have had the fields enclosed, if the Tenants could have been brought to an agreement therein. 1734"

There are a large number of references to Rudgefield and it appears that this exercise was very much concerned with this area, which we have earlier described as *"extended from the Dean to the north of William Dench's Coppy Hold i.e. the land north of Littledown"*. A further document dated 1748 provides another clue as to the enclosure activity affecting the Rudgefield, clearly common land prior to this date. A document is described as:

"1748. The account of the Several Inclosures and Pieces of Land belonging to the Several Coppyholds in ffernham-dean in the County of Southton which has had any Alteration or Addition by reason of the late Inclosure of all the Common Fields etc and Mentioned in A Indenture of Award relating to the same".

There follow references to John Flower, John Herriott and Roger Geater; clearly the property involved is the Rudgefield area. William Dench died in 1808, aged 87, having survived his wife, Elizabeth, (d.1798). Both graves are at St. Mary's, along with those of three daughters, all of whom seem to have pre-deceased their parents.

It is clear that Roger Geater was an influential yeoman farmer with a large family in Vernham Dean. His burial in St. Mary's churchyard is recorded, as are the burials of eight family members, between 1770 and 1826.

The Importance of the Woods

Almost throughout history, man has been reliant on wood for a variety of essential uses. In the absence of organised transport, with limited building materials and lack of readily available metals, wood use was pre-eminent in the eighteenth century. Michael Whittingham, whose family farmed in the area, has contributed the following:

The Woodsman

While the role of the woodsman was important throughout history, it is helpful to our understanding of his role in the context of the Eighteenth Century. The traditional woodsman had greater and more specialised markets than today. He would supply charcoal, wood for cooperage (barrels), bark for tanning, wood for furniture, hurdles, crates, shipbuilding, transport, construction of buildings, fuel, weapons, clogs, garden ware and other tools and a host of other essential uses. All types of trees were capable of use and the skills of one man might extend from planting and husbandry of standing timber through the whole cycle of felling and utilisation of the right wood for the product required. As market demand changed, so the woodland species might be altered and managed differently. Thorneycombe and Botes (Boates, Botis – take your pick) *are ancient woodlands, continuously managed since the Middle Ages i.e. before 1600. There is clear evidence that they have been coppiced ever since.*

Dale Wallis, who has worked in the woodland around Vernham Dean for some considerable time, contributed the following:

"Thornycombe and Boats Copse:

Traditional ancient woodlands, continually wooded since the Middle Ages, known as Coppice with Standards. Mainly Hazel with oak and ash, other species include beech, white beam, wych elm and sallow. There is a scattering of recently planted cherry, sycamore, beech and oak, but largely the woodland is natural and 'natural regeneration' is encouraged whereby a sapling that has germinated naturally will be protected to grow on as a 'standard' rather than an introduced planted 'whip'. These woodlands have always been coppiced on a 7-30 year cycle, hazel at 7, and ash at 30. The oak standards would be felled at approximately 80-100 years, but selectively to ensure continuity. The woods are managed for three primary objectives: conservation, which is important for the locality, timber production and sporting activity, all of which run hand in hand to produce revenue to ensure the continued management.

Latterly all coppiced areas have had to be deer-fenced to protect the resultant regrowth from a large migratory population, which will quickly eat all the coppice regrowth. Largely, all deadwood is preserved within the woods as habitat and the objective when coppicing is to try to cause minimal disturbance to both ground and trees that are to remain. The work is usually carried out in the winter months and no cutting would take place during the nesting period".

The role of the modern woodsman, also contributed by Dale, runs as follows:

"To understand the role of the modern 'woodsman' it is necessary to draw on the comparisons with the traditional 'woodsman'. This endangered species has had to adapt to both an economic and material change in man's need for wood. Due to the limited markets for wood in modern society, coupled with suppressed prices across agricultural activities, the modern woodsman needs to be a shrewd, penny-pinching individual who can sell his materials to a far smaller customer base but at the same time be able to adapt to constant change within consumerism. The sell-off of and division of once large estates have over the years taken their toll on the labour force: rarely to be found in the Jobs Section is 'woodsman required, cottage available, within rural community' – more likely 'contractors required, piece-rate, short contract'. The demise of the estate where now houses are rented out to mostly non-land-based occupational people is the norm, producing greater revenue for both landlord and tenant.

Essential differences between the modern and the traditional woodsman:

1.   Traditional woodsmen had greater markets and more specialised ones such as charcoal, barrels, bark for tanning, chair backs, hurdles, crates, ship-building, transport, building, fuel, weapons, clog makers, garden ware. Modern woodsmen have limited markets: furniture, building, pulp for newsprint and packaging, fuel sources.

2.   The traditional woodsman could utilise all trees and branches. He had a market to fit the individual species and he and his family could fell a tree and turn it into an array of products. Modern woodsmen cannot do this. Modern industrial machinery requires more precise specifications to operate and obviously the lack of opportunities in markets dictates the size and shape of wood to be processed.

These factors have altered the shape of the landscape and bank balances to manage it. Far more commercial forests have been planted where yield and uniformity have taken priority, thus reducing the surface area for the traditional woodman's activities. Today's woodsman has undergone radical change into a highly-skilled chainsaw operator who fells uniform conifers at knockdown prices competing with cheap imports. He is in danger of being superseded by large forestry influences and large purpose built machines capable of felling much more for much less.

Nevertheless the modern woodsman is a craftsman continuing old practices which comprised knowledge of and care for the ecology of a wood. Woodlands such as Thornycombe and Botes are ancient woodlands continuously wooded since the Middle Ages. They have been coppiced ever since. Even though there is a limited market for the produce cut, the cycle of cutting is continued. This is obviously expensive to manage but it has great rewards as the rich flora and fauna could never be replaced – it is original, not a copy. For example, nightingales require largely coppiced woodland and prefer nesting in dense hazel coppice. If there is no market for hazel then there is no work for the woodsman and in turn no hazel and then no nightingales. The mechanics of woodland management rely on utilisation and consistency with no radical change which would destabilize the ecology and the economy within the system.

Both modern and traditional woodsmen have much in common: both are itinerant and have to be to survive. Both look after woods for future generations as these operations are long term – work today, reap the rewards in the future. Both need to understand more than trees: flowers, plants, birds, animals, when to work, when to refrain to keep impact to a minimum. They evolve a harmony with the produce. As ever, the modern woodsman must understand his markets, be capable of filling them, utilise all his materials and work sympathetically with small ancient woodlands. He must develop a network of people who aspire to his modernised approach to woodland management and supply everything from beansticks to laths. He has a niche in the modern world and his knowledge is vital."

The Influence of Winchester College

The parish of Vernhams Dean is particularly fortunate in that much of the area was effectively in the ownership and control of Winchester and accordingly there are many college records which provide a very valuable insight for social historians, particularly for the 18th century. Perhaps the highlight is the 1776 document entitled:

Map and Survey of the Manor and Tything of Fernhams Dean in the Parish of Hurstbourne Tarrant in the county of Southampton with the proper distinctions between the Freehold Copy Hold and Lease Hold Lands & Messuages and Tenements therein etc. Taken for the College of Winchester Anno Domini 1776.

This map and survey provides an almost complete record of ownership and other interests. Whilst the names of the properties are only infrequently defined, nonetheless the properties are identifiable. Among the farms which may be discovered from the local map are the following:

- Beeches Farm – copyhold held by William Lawrence who also farmed land fronting the Fosbury Road and the Conholt Hill area, but interestingly not the land behind Beeches Farmhouse itself. This was held by John Wheeler up to and including Botesdown and Thorneycombe Woods.

- Conholt Farm was held freehold by Sir Henry Gould, probably the same person who at that time was a judge in the Court of Common Pleas.

- Parsonage Farm (now known as Poplars) was held as copyhold by Hannah Geater.

- The occupation of Hannah Geater is described by the valuer thus: *"This being kind Land and Good Buildings and also in a Convenient situation is worth ...£10"*.

- Sargent's Farm was held freehold by "the late John Wheeler" (see above) but apparently only as to the field immediately above the farmhouse, extending to and including what was then Bower's Cottage (now Bower House). Although the name Bower is a well established one, extending through the 18th and 19th centuries, the College map appears to show only one allocated freehold field, identified as north of Bank Cottage.

- Bank Farm, together with land on the east and west sides of Vernham Row, appears to be farmed by Thomas Bunny.

- Box Farm was described as the freehold of Thomas Webb. Webb was also recorded as in control of isolated fields extending as far as Vernham Street. The graves of Thomas Webb (d.1822) and his wife, Mary, who died four months later, are in St. Mary's churchyard.

- Ankers Farm is shown in the ownership of Daniel North together with land either side of what is now Ankers Lane. There is a valuation of this property said to comprise 83 acres and having a value of £33.12s. per annum. The valuer comments: *"This is a pretty little convenient farm"*.

Coloured areas on the College map (now faded and not providing reliable accuracy) refer to the inclosure award (see above), thus:

"Before that time there were five common fields viz Middle Field, North Field lying on the north east side adjoining to the Manor Farm now mostly belonging to Hooper, Andrews, Durford and Mrs. Bower. The North Field to Hooper Wheeler, the Vicar, Mr. Mills' freehold and John Fowler. The Rudge Field extended from the Dean to the north of William Dench's copyhold."

The Dench land lay immediately north of Littledown, as does Hooper, Andrews, Durford and Mrs. Bower's land.

The College map also shows that Roger Geater was a large landholder of freehold and copyhold land extending from the boundary with Fosbury lands to the west, eastwards to the boundary with Buttermere. The names that crop up most regularly on the map are Herriott, Hall, Flower, Fowler (whose lands included the site of the former Boot public house at Littledown). It will be appreciated that these names have persisted into the 21st century. By far the most dominant name as shown on the map is Joseph Mills, leaseholder of Manor Farm and of other lands. The College map also shows that much of the Upton land was in the ownership of John Poore, comprising 78 acres of Copyhold, including both Ambley and Rushmore (then known as Rishmore) Farms.

Nineteenth Century

Hard Times for Hampshire Agriculture

With the ending of the Napoleonic Wars, the decline in the demand by the Army and Navy for food presented the countryside with some harsh realities. No demand meant reduced food production and less need for labour. Whilst the landed gentry and yeoman farmers were not immune from these effects, the labourer was hard hit. By the end of the 18th century a system of Poor Rate was in place. This was intended to bring wages up to subsistence level but the effect was all too often to result in a reduction of wages. Poor Rate payments continued after 1834 when the Poor Law Amendment Act brought in many changes, including a system of indoor relief in one of the dreaded new Union workhouses, reducing the amount of outdoor relief which enabled paupers to stay in their own homes. Those who had to contribute to the Rate grew resentful of this increasing burden. Rates continued to be levied well into the 20th century. That Poor Law continued until 1930, although the Ministry of Health was responsible from 1919. Local Court records give very revealing snapshots of the plight of the rural poor and the sternness with which the well-to-do would respond. Derek Tempero's records of evidence before local courts in his work *"They Simply Stole to Live"* tell many sad stories of Vernham Dean.

Benjamin Farr brought a case against William Booth and Thomas Gibbs for trespassing in search of game. Evidence was given on behalf of Mr. Farr, gamekeeper to Mr. Bevan. *"On 22nd September 1831 at about half past 5 o'clock in the morning while I was watching some wires, which were in a gap leading into a field belonging to Mr. Alexander, in the parish of Vernhams Dean, I saw both defendants come into the field in my direction and go to the gap where the wires were. Thomas Gibbs took up a wire and added it to other wires he had with him. Defendant Gibbs then said to Booth something to the effect that somebody had been about them and asked Booth if he had returned to them. Booth replied that he had not. I know both defendants well, they were both in company together when the wire was removed."* Both men were fined £5 each. Not shown if the fines were paid or whether the men went to prison, probably the latter.

On 24th March 1832 the court heard the case of James Fermor v. Ann Annetts, Gina Alderman and Jane Annetts for malicious injury to growing wood. James Fermor gave evidence. *"On 12 March I saw the defendants in Moats* (probably Boats) *Coppice in the*

32

Parish of Vernhams Dean. I saw Jane Annetts with a bill in her hands cutting underwood and the others were breaking it up and putting it into bundles. Damage done amounted to more than one shilling and the wood was the property of Mrs. Mary Sargeant." Cross-examined: *"I am sure that the bundles of wood they had had been freshly cut as I saw Ann Annetts cut some of it. The wood was not dead wood that they had picked up off the ground."* Each defendant was fined 2/- plus 1/- damage and 5/- costs.

The welfare of animals features in some cases, no doubt as a reflection of the value of working animals. In one case George Hooper brought proceedings against Edward Bevan for cruelty to a mare. Charles Hillier of Vernhams Dean, ploughboy, said *"I am employed by Mr. Hooper of Vernhams Dean and drive a plough under the directions of the defendant. I was at the stable on that Sunday, when the defendant said 'That one mare had worked and he would try and make the other do so' and kicked it several times very severely."* Bevan was fined 4/- which he paid into court.

A different case involving horses is a forerunner of road traffic offences. On 25th November 1845 police superintendent James Marks prosecuted Henry Williams for riding on a wagon drawn by three horses without holding the reins. Plea: Guilty. The evidence of the superintendent was: *"On Sunday 19 November, I was on duty at Vernhams Dean when I saw Williams with a wagon and three horses. Williams was riding on the shaft of the wagon and was not holding the reins."* Fined 5/- with 2/6 costs. Paid.

In the case heard on 6 October of the same year, of PC Joseph Hibberd v Charles Weeks, the defendant was charged with killing a hare without a certificate. Witness Alfred Hilliard said: *"I live at Vernhams Dean. On 24 September I saw Charles Weeks shoot a hare in a field occupied by Mr. William Clarke at Vernhams Dean. He stood in the track outside the field in Mr. Bevan's liberty. I was watching him for about an hour. When he killed the hare my dog brought it to me.*

"Weeks, when he killed the hare went into the field to collect it and when up to 15 yards of where the hare had been I called out 'Master Weeks'. As soon as he saw me he turned his back and ran off. I am sure it was Weeks. I know him well." Weeks was fined £5 with 5/- court costs and 3/- police costs or in default two months' imprisonment with hard labour. Weeks had no money or goods and was committed to prison.

The early half of the century was characterised by a large increase in population. However, life in the 1840s and 1850s for the Hampshire agricultural labourer remained hard. While in the 1850s the agricultural wage, at 9/- a week, corresponded with the national average, by the 1870s and 1880s the Hampshire rate was said to be some 20% less than the national level. The "Andover Advertiser" regularly reported agitation by the workers, the rise of union membership and significant emigration to New Zealand and Canada, partly paid for by the governments of those countries. Small wonder that in a March 1875 report of a union meeting at Coombe, the Advertiser quoted a speaker: *"Wages must be raised to 18/- per week if a labourer is not to be driven from his native country. There are three empty cottages at Linkenholt, thirteen at Coombe and twenty-seven at Vernham."*

Tithes

The imposition of tithes (payable in kind to rectors and vicars from medieval times) was an important means by which the Church gathered income from farmed and other occupied land during the 18th and 19th centuries, although progressively the practice became unpopular, particularly as farm economies deteriorated steadily during the 19th century. In 1836 the Tithe Commutation Act allowed tithes in kind to be commuted to a tithe rent charge – hence all the Tithe Awards and maps after that date. The unpopularity of tithes was greatest from the 1870s, when the import of cheap American wheat resulted in an agricultural depression. Tithes were not abolished until 1936. The Hampshire Record Office yielded a tithe map for Vernhams Dean parish carrying the date 1839, with the Award dated 17th March 1841. Compared with the Winchester College map about 50 years earlier, the tithe map provides more detailed information and the map and Award are carefully linked. The most notable farms and their occupants are as follows:

Manor Farm – William Child – 623 acres (easily the largest holding).

Bowers – David Bevan – occupied by James Fermor.

Sargents Farm – David Bevan – occupied by James Fermor.

Bank Farm – Richard Lansley, (recorded in the church records as having died in 1866 aged 74, buried in St. Mary's churchyard.)

Box Farm – Suzanah Webb – in hand – 187 acres.

Littledown – George Hooper – 71 acres.

Beeches – Robert Alexander – occupied by William Clark.

Ankers Farm – William Hilliard – 80 acres. (He is recorded as having died in June 1848, aged 67.)

Poplars Farm – Harriet Margaret King – occupied by William Orchard but only the homestead and yard.

Upton – Corpus Christi College – occupied by Charles Church (70 acres).

Fowlers Farm – Jane Stevens, James Fermor – 26 acres.

Flowers Farm – John Mills, occupied by Henry Wheeler (homestead and 6 acres).

Halls Farm – John Martin, occupied by William Blake, Thomas Gibbs and Eliza Kingston (2 homesteads).

Herriott land – Thomas Herriott – 113 acres.

Neither was the farmer immune from the difficulties of making a living. The Advertiser of 31 August 1888 carried a report of tithe distraint. A tenth part of the produce of the land was paid in kind yearly to the rector of the parish. This frequently produced disputes, particularly at times of poor harvests. It was often the case that the church was well endowed and that clergymen had congregations who were "enormously rich" and capable of paying the stipends themselves. Distraints (compulsory assumption of ownership for the benefit of the Church) were raised in Vernham Dean on Mr. J.F. Child and Mr. Farmer, both of whom had failed to make their contributions. Three ricks of hay had been seized on behalf of the Ecclesiastical Commissioners, valued at about £100. Eight acres each of barley and wheat had been seized from Mr. Farmer. A man had been brought from London to take possession, no local having been found to take on the task. About 1,000 people had gathered *"who by groaning and hooting, gave unmistakeable expression to their feelings, taking care that this demonstration should be within hearing of Pulfer, the man in possession."* A speaker drew attention to the fact that Manor Farm, Mr. Child's living, comprising about 640 acres, was let for £50 while the tithe was £150. So heavy was the burden that several hundred acres in Vernham were not cultivated, the depression in agriculture being accentuated by the heavy burden of tithes.

Twentieth Century

An example of the relationship of the end of World War I with local activities concerns the occupation after WWI of Poplars Farm by Jimmy and Ted Hughes. They had acquired a war surplus mule, identified by the arrow mark on its hoof. When farmers spread dried blood on the land it was said that these old warhorses were very much disturbed. Eric Levell (Country Ways, Country Days) noted it was said of the Hughes they picked enough stones from the fields up Botes Lane, selling them to the Council, to enable them to buy themselves a tractor.

David Vining, a long-time resident of the village, has early recollections of Upper Horns Farm (OS ref. 336594):

"My parents came to Upper Horns from the West Country in September 1948. In those days it was a mixed farm, about half arable and the rest grassland that supported a dairy herd. The cows were milked in the fields using a portable 'Hosier Milking Bail' which was moved around the farm to the cows rather than the cows having to be driven into a yard to be milked in a fixed milking parlour."

(At this point attention must be drawn to two people, Arthur J. Hosier, who devised and developed many forms of agricultural machinery, and also Alfred Whatley, another pioneer in agricultural engineering. Alfred Whatley spent most of his working life designing and constructing agricultural machinery, sometimes in conjunction with A.J. Hosier, who was his uncle. It was in 1900 that Mr. Whatley made a three-wheeled front cut self-propelled mower of his own design and did all the machining himself but could not interest anyone in putting it into production. The following year he made for Mr. Hosier his side-rakes and a rotary milk strainer which took a medal at Smithfield Dairy Show in 1904. After a period in Australia Mr. Whatley responded to a request from Mr. Hosier, returning in 1928 to help him with the milking bail. In addition to remodelling this bail Mr. Whatley made his silver medal milking machine, steam sterilizing boiler and other implements. Several members of the Whatley and Hosier family still live in the district. Alfred Whatley's descendant, Jane Elliman, displayed at the Dorset Steam Fair in 2006 an exhibition of Alfred's life and work, including the 'Town Gas Engine' he made when he was 15, during his apprenticeship. At the time this engine was at the cutting edge of technology.)

To continue with David Vining: *"In those days the milk was transported in 10 gallon churns collected by a lorry based in Andover. Upper Horns was first pick up at about 7.15 a.m. so we had to make an early start at about 5.30 a.m. There were enough milk producers in the immediate area, about a dozen, to make up a full load. This was then taken some 40/50 miles to the receiving dairy at Petersfield where it was pasteurised, then taken by tanker to London for bottling and distribution. A dairy herd necessitated a daily routine which never changed seven days a week, year in, year out.*

Arable crop production was a little more relaxed, being more seasonal. We ran a rotational system, some of the arable land being re-seeded to grass and some of the grassland being ploughed up. Grassland was usually ploughed up in late summer, after a hay crop, and a seed bed prepared for autumn sowing of winter wheat or barley, the rest of the arable land being ploughed after harvest or during the winter and prepared for spring sowing of barley or oats.

Harvesting the cereal crops was usually a late summer operation which involved cutting by binder and the 'stooking' of the sheaves to dry out before being carted to the rickyard where they were stacked and usually thatched and left for threshing in the winter months. Threshing on most farms was usually carried out by contractors who took their threshing tackle from farm to farm. The wheat and barley grains were sold but most of the oats were used on the farm, being ground or rolled, and fed to the cows. This was all quite labour intensive and at one time up to six people worked at Upper Horns, but as the years went by machines gradually replaced manpower and, after giving up dairying in 1971 and changing to beef cattle, the labour force was reduced to one only with the use of specialist contractors at busy times and for jobs like hedge cutting and crop spraying.

Harvesting changed dramatically with the coming of the combine harvester. We acquired our first combine in 1952. In those days the grain was bagged and dropped off in the field to be picked up later. As time went by combines became bigger and much more sophisticated and fitted with bulk tanks, making them one man operated. The bulk tanks could be emptied into large tipping trailers 'on the move' and with continuous flow dryers and bulk storage bins the large grain sacks completely disappeared, as did the threshing contractors.

In the 1950s, Vernham Dean could be described as an agricultural community with most of the village menfolk working on the local farms. The few not employed on farm work worked on the roads or for the Water Board."

Another resident of long standing was Millie Seward:

"Farming as I remember – hard times in the 1920s and onwards at 'Fair View', Vernham Street. Long before the Second World War my father was what was termed a 'smallholder' – trying to raise a family on less than 30 acres. He probably started with one cow and gradually afforded a few more which enabled him to start a 'milk round'. This he did on a bicycle or walked carrying, maybe, a yoke on his shoulders, two buckets with lids and 1/2 pt. and 1 pt. measures hanging inside the bucket. Milk was put into customers' own jugs. In the spring when grass was lush there would be surplus milk and this would have been separated (cream from milk) which was also sold on the round apart from that being used by the family. The separated milk or skimmed was fed to pigs which were fattened for the household. As the cows' lactation progressed so a second round had to be done with the afternoon milk. As a schoolgirl I would be told to hurry home after school as it was our job to take this milk, as Father would be engaged in other farm activities. By now he had progressed and rented adjoining land, had two horses and would plough, sow, reap hay and later corn. He would be called a small farmer now.

At hay making and harvest everyone, Mother and us elder children, would be expected to help, turning the swathe of hay with a two-pronged fork, then when it was considered dry enough (not to overheat in a rick) it was put into heaps and the men would come along with horse and cart to carry it in for rick making. This was when neighbouring farmers and labourers would lend a hand and likewise Father would help them. No money would be transacted, they just helped one another. The younger children would lead the horse and cart from pook to pook – that is what the heaps of hay were called.

In 1938 Father had to leave Vernham Street and at the turn of the year was able to move to Vernham Dean and rent 'Beeches Farm', a small farm of about 100 acres, from Winchester College. Our farming days finished in the autumn of 1962 when the land was sold to the Whittinghams by Winchester College."

Michael Whittingham also has many other recollections:

"From very early times when humans were hunter gatherers, through early farming until today there has always been development, but it is the rapidly gathering speed of development which has been so great in my lifetime in farming.

My brief is farming and the village, but of course it was the advancement of outside aspects, such as the improvement and subsequent tarmacing of the roads, the provision of piped water and electricity, which cannot be ignored.

Older villagers told me that the centre of Vernham Dean used to become so muddy that faggots of wood were laid from the well (situated near the old pond and still marked today by a concrete slab) across the road to enable folk to cross without getting stuck.

Most of the soil around here is very flinty, the larger flints being known as 'Hampshire Diamonds'. These formed the basis of early roadmaking and the Hughes brothers were not the only ones said to have profited by the collection and breaking of flints for roadmaking.

I have heard many tales of the drought of 1922 when the well ran dry and carts from the village would fetch water from Knyght's Mere at the top of Ankers Lane, as the only source remaining. The installation of a mains water system (1934-5) with its own pumping station near the road into Shepherd's Rise and its reservoir at Littledown near the old Boot Inn was a remarkable early improvement, and the several water points dotted around the village saved much carrying of water by those who were not directly connected. The gathering of people at the well on a regular basis became a thing of the past.

With electricity and telephone wires already installed Vernham Dean was very well equipped in 1941 when I arrived here, much better than so many other remote places. As far as farming was concerned it had remained very much the same for centuries. The work was largely manual, progressing towards oxen, then horses for field work and transport. There were periods of great poverty and I was told by one old resident that he 'minded the time' when he was a child when he spent one Christmas in bed with his brothers and sisters and all they had to eat were turnips. That would have been about 1890. He lived then in a cottage opposite the school, the cottage has long since gone. However, the First World War gave farming a lift as food was scarce. There were few tractors in those days but steam engines were available for ploughing and other work which was really the beginning of mechanisation. The early use of steam engines for threshing brought about unrest and rioting at first because it caused unemployment for the workers who had had work all winter with a flail to thrash out the corn from the sheaves. For those who wonder how a steam engine could plough the explanation is that two engines were involved – one at each end of the field, and the plough, or cultivator, was connected to cables attached to winches on the engine. Each engine would pull in turn and move slowly across the field.

Mr. Coleman of Sargents Farm had steam threshing tackle which deserves a mention. The steam engine would arrive at each farm in turn, pulling the threshing machine, straw elevator and sometimes a strawturner or baler – quite a road train, in fact. Mr. Edgar Brook, the driver, was a well-known character and was most adept at manoeuvring these large items of equipment into small places between pairs of ricks. His mate was Mr. Fisher. The labour arrangements were usually that Edgar, having set up the tackle, would be in charge of sacking off the grain, weighing it on mobile scales and wheeling back to make room for each subsequent sack. Fisher would be on top of the machine, inches from the whirling drum, and he would cut the strings on the sheaves and feed them into the drum. The sheaves would have been passed to him by at least two people on the rick. They would have been removing the thatch whilst the setting up was being done. They then had the easy task of throwing down the top of the rick and eventually the much harder task of dealing with the bottom. The straw, having been threshed, would go up the elevator and it would need 2/3 people to make the straw rick. Meanwhile another person would be needed to take away the chaff and cavings from beneath the machine. This was usually the least popular job due to the dust involved and was often performed by someone a little simple! It therefore required eight people to run the operation efficiently.

Meanwhile the farmer had to ensure a supply of steam coal and water to feed the voracious appetite of the engine. He was also responsible for a supply of four bushel sacks, which were usually obtained from a hire firm such as Westlake Sacks Hire. The movement of these sacks from farmer to customer was carefully tracked and each charged on a timed basis.

The thresher would move from farm to farm often staying for only a few days at a time. Each farmer was anxious to get some of his wheat and barley onto the market as soon as possible and often needed some corn for feeding to livestock. Merchants would also keep an eye on the whereabouts of the thresher in order to bid for the corn, as often there would have been outstanding credits for the supply of feed and fertiliser.

Contrast this system with the modern combine driven by one man, and a tractor and trailer to take the corn in bulk to a farm with an 'on floor drying system' operated without constant attention. The 'other side of the coin' is that for the old system the farmer only needed to supply a number of pitchforks and for the modern system he has to invest very large sums of money in the combine harvester and barn. This means that he needs a farm exceeding 700 acres to justify the expense: this is one of the reasons for the disappearance of the small farm.

Having successfully weathered the 1914-18 war, farming continued profitably on a high labour system until the slump years. These slump years were very difficult and extended until about 1938 when there were signs of impending war again which brought some help for farmers and their men. The war that subsequently arrived in 1939 really changed farming out of all recognition and was the start of a massive mechanisation programme, helped by a 'Lend Lease' system from America whose government provided many tractors and early combines for willing drivers. From then on the speed of change accelerated and is still going on.

In the Vernham Dean area, in the 1940s, there were several separate farms, namely Box, Beeches, Poplars, Ankers, Manor Farm and Lower Conholt, three or four more at Vernham Street and Littledown, one at Vernham Row, two at Upton and the large estates of Linkenholt and Conholt. These had about 50 people employed full time. Today only the estates (Linkenholt and Conholt) and Box Farm, and two at Upton remain independent, the others having been amalgamated or absorbed into the estates. Minimal labour is employed, no farm workers live in the village as opposed to earlier times when there would have been over thirty workers in the village and many more on the estates.

The farm worker at the turn of the century largely walked to work (hence the large number of footpaths which go across fields to take short cuts). He also found his wife within walking distance. When bicycles became available he had increased scope, but largely settled down in his area of birth. Cottages were primitive but cheap. With the rapid improvement in his situation and the increased availability of cars he was able to find a job and wife wherever he chose. The result is that it is rare now to find several generations of the same family within the area (although there are exceptions to this statement: Ed.). *By the same increased prosperity the urban worker has been able to buy property within the villages. Thus there will no longer be a pool of skilled farmers or workers. They are going the way of miners and shipbuilders and other industries. The production of food is essential, however, so it is hoped that the lost country cultures and skills will not be needed in a hurry.*

The control of food production in World War II was undertaken by the War Agricultural Executive Committee (known as the WarAg), largely composed of the leading farmers with appointed officials. Each farm was ordered to grow the required amount of wheat, potatoes, etc. on pain of losing their farms as a final sanction if they did not. Happily this was a rarity, as most farmers were only too happy to find themselves in a position where their produce was required and their work again one of national importance. The WarAg also controlled the allocation of permits to buy many items, from tractors to barbed wire for fencing. Livestock food was rationed and only small quantities of pigs and poultry were allowed to be kept. The farming system now became largely arable, with a large number of small dairy herds.

In Vernham Dean one of the dairy herds was kept at Beeches Farm by Mr. Bulpit (Millie Seward's father) who delivered bottled milk to the villagers. It was common in those days for herds of cattle to move through the village, his herd being one which came in for milking twice per day. Woe betide the person who left his gate open.

During the war the farm workers were augmented by the Land Army: casual workers, even schoolchildren, were employed to help with unskilled jobs such as potato picking. For many years the number of regular farm workers countrywide averaged 600,000 employed by 300,000 farmers. There were also large numbers of ancillary workers in the feed mills and merchanting of supplies and machinery repair and sale. It is interesting to note that farming at that time and to some extent today was one of the few industries that bought its supplies in retail quantities and sold its products wholesale. The extent to which the productivity of farming increased at this time was evidenced by publication in the 'Farmers' Weekly' of 16 September 1960. Ministry of Agriculture forecast yields for 1959 were put at 28.8 cwt. per acre for wheat and 26.1 for barley. This compares with 16-18 for barley in 1946. By the end of the century, 40 cwt. per acre would have been regarded as a disaster."

The Twenty-first Century

Prominent Farming Families

Of the earliest recorded farmer/land owning families, two have continuous involvement in agriculture to the present day.

The Herriotts.

The deeds of Upper Row(e) Farm, on the north western edge of the parish, start from 1604. Family records show that the Herriotts hailed from Scotland and the dates suggest that this major transfer to Hampshire coincided with the assumption of the English throne by King James I. (A Herriott was jeweller to the king). The early English Herriotts were baptised in Vernham Dean church. The first Edward Herriott fathered 5 children, 2 daughters and 3 sons. The family has documents dated 1641, 1659 and 1661 which mention sale of land by Elizabeth, widow of Edward Herriott at 'Fernham Rowe'. The Elizabeth mentioned above was obviously the widow of Edward's second son (also called Edward) who was born in 1621.

Moving on a generation or two, John, William and Thomas Herriott (born respectively in 1776, 1779 and 1782) were all farmers. Mostly their farms were outside the parish, at Whitchurch, Buttermere and Ham, but William had Upper Row Farm. However, it appears that he did not undertake agriculture himself but lived and worked in London as a wine merchant. William, the wine merchant, married a local girl, rejoicing in the name of Basilissa, and there were two children, Thomas and William. They were born in London, but Thomas came to live at Upper Row Farm and bought his brother's share. Thomas died in 1864 having had 2 wives who were sisters. English law at the time forbade marriage to a sister-in-law, hence the ceremony took place in Scotland. It appears that there were no children of the first marriage. Jane Hedderly died only a year after marriage. Thomas married Hannah Hedderly in 1841 and there were 8 children, 6 daughters and 2 sons, John and Harry, born respectively in 1849 and 1854.

Thomas' son John inherited Upper Row Farm, but had to buy out his 7 brothers and sisters, incurring substantial debt. At the age of 53, John married Caroline Hedderly (Cara, his cousin) and had two sons, John Egerton and James. John bought Henley Farm in 1908 but in 1928 both Henley Farm and Upper Row Farm were put up for sale. It was fortunate that John Egerton was to be married at that time as his wife, Evelyn, was able to buy Henley Farm where they lived and prospered sufficiently to be able to buy back Upper Row Farm and move there.

John Egerton fathered 4 children, only one of whom was a son, John Cowan Herriott, but Graham Mark Herriott succeeded on John Cowan's early death in 1990. Graham now farms the land, Henley and Upper Row, together with his wife Patricia and, progressively, their 3 sons, James, Andrew and Iain, born between 1985 and 1989.

The Mills

It would appear that the Mills family were well established in the Bourne Valley as far back as at least 1725. The family has evidence of a Thomas Mills, born in January 1672, who died in August 1742. Records suggest that they were at that time shepherds, working on the Middleton Estate in Longparish. From that time, the family understands that sheep farming was the main skill, land being rented throughout the valley. Dates are difficult to come by but towards the end of the 19th century, it seems that the occupier of Ankers Farm was John Mills, the youngest child of his family of many girls. His son, also John, was probably the first of the Mills to occupy Vernham Manor Farm. He was born at Ankers Farm, as was his brother, Charles, and died in January 1941. His grave is in the Vernham Dean churchyard. The Manor was at this time rented from Winchester College by Abraham Quick. Among his offspring were a son, Edwin Harding Quick and a daughter, Kate.

On the death of Abraham Quick, the tenancy was taken over by Edwin and Kate (who was at this time a teenager). She subsequently married John Mills. The resulting arrangement was that John Mills and Edwin Quick held half shares in Vernham Manor Farm and the three of them lived at the Manor. Edwin never married. He died in July 1918, aged 63, and is buried in the churchyard.

Meanwhile Charles Mills had acquired the tenancy of Halls Farm, at Littledown, but later moved to The Malthouse, on the main road to Upton. He died in February 1942, aged 79.

We have now arrived at the 1930s and it is at this time that probably the best known of the Mills family emerges as tenant of Vernham Manor, still at this stage owned by the College. Vernham Mills, actually Edwin John Vernham Mills, was born to John and Kate Mills in December 1909 at Vernham Manor, hence his name. During the early stages of his tenure, Vernham tenanted the Manor Farm, producing mainly sheep. Apparently, in those days *"nothing else would do well"*. The advent of the Second World War changed all that. Feeding a besieged Britain was the national priority and the Manor became a mixed farm, remaining thus ever since. Vernham often spoke of the supply of horses and hay to the Southern Railway, delivered to the station at Hurstbourne Priors.

Vernham married Elizabeth (Betty) Dowse, a farmer's daughter from Upton. He is buried in the churchyard, having died in November 1991. Betty lives today at Manor Cottage. They had two sons, John and Richard. John, with his wife, Sarah, farms at Parsonage Farm, Upton. Some of their land is within the Vernham Dean parish. John inherited from his father the title of "Lord of the Manor of Vernham Dean." They have two children, Edwin and Bethany. Richard married Barbara and they have four children, Alex, Ben, Verity and Hannah. After his father's retirement, Richard continued to farm the Vernham Manor unit, establishing a milk and ice-cream supply business. On Vernham's death, the Manor was sold, the family moving first to Ankers Farm, then to Grafton.

SUMMARY

Of all the aspects of village life, it is probably the use of the land that has most changed in the past 75 years. What was once a series of mainly small farm units, employing a high proportion of the male and some female population, has now become a handful of large units, often owned by absentee landlords, with a small number of employment opportunities.

What has caused this rapid and significant change? There are a number of reasons but the two most important are recognised as the globalisation of food production and its transport along with the revolution in the capability of machinery to handle a multitude of tasks, quickly, efficiently and cheaply.

It would be hard to believe 75 years ago that all types of food could be delivered to the table in fresh and acceptable condition from thousands of miles away, as a matter of course. Equally, few would have foreseen the development of highly efficient machinery, capable of replacing the work of large numbers of men. Striking examples include the milking machine, the combine harvester, and seeding and cultivation methods.

That said, agriculture continues to thrive in the Bourne Valley, adapted to cope with the powerful retail buyers, the influences of European policies. Thus we see large units, concentrating on specialist crops, the growth of sporting estates for "corporate shoots" and the organic, premium price farm, with strong inclination towards the traditional. Side by side with this, we welcome the resurgence of wildlife, so much at risk and in decline since WW2, but which now returns to some strength after agriculture turned away from indiscriminate practices, particularly in the use of chemicals.

……………………………….

Overheard in the pub when the linseed was in full blue glory:
Visitor: "I just love your valley – your fields look like bright blue water".
Waggish villager: "We're a bit short of water here, that's how we store it."
Gullible visitor: "Really?"

…… …… …… …… …… …… …… …… …… …… …… …… …… …… …… …… ……

Vernham lies on the chalk downland, where the hills can form immense reservoirs of water which slowly percolates through the chalk and works its way into the valleys and the flint gravel waterways at the bottom of the chalk valleys. The water travels slowly through obstructed passages and usually the floors of the upper chalk valleys are dry with the flow at depth. It may be months before the effect of the rain in the hills is seen in the valleys. With sufficient rainfall the "bournes" flow in winter but a dry season means a dry watercourse, perhaps for many years. Complacent householders fill in the old watercourse, re-design their gardens, only to suffer inconvenient floods when nature reasserts herself, old wells fill with water again, springs come up under living room floors and streams meander over the roads in the accustomed fashion.

The old churchwardens tended to note weather conditions and *"Be it remembered that in the year of our Lord, 1774 March ye 15 the Springs was so high in Vernham's Dean that the Dean Well run over for a week and the Houses was so full of Spring Water for upwards of 40 poles above the George Inn that the inhabitants was forsed to open trenches to Draw it of Which caused a river all down ye Bottom and many quit the Houses and also the Springs at the same time rose in the Ditches, in Conholt Bottom near three furlongs as Witness our hands John Fowler J Mills Church Wardens. Robert Scullard Vestory Clerk"*

And again: *"The Springs were extremely high in the year 1828. Many Wells in the Dean run over which caused a large breadth of the Down call's Berry dean to be cover'd with water and made quite a River in the lane below Assam's fields which continued many weeks. The springs were up in Conholt Bottom same time. The winter of this year was remarkably mild. And the two summers but one prior to this even Remarkable for being excessively Hot and Dry. The two Dry summers here alluded to were in succession namely 1825 and 1826. Darius Bull – Church Warden Easter 1828."*

(As with the spelling of 'Vernham' the Bury/Berry/Dene/Dean/Deane appears in many guises. It has been left with the spelling of the archive from which it was taken. Ed.)

Mr. James Fermor added a variation: *"On Jan 22nd the Springs gained such a height that Vernham's Dean Well, opposite the George Inn began to run over and continued to do so for nine successive days and spring water rose in Hippenscombe bottom and ran as far as*

45

the gate at the bottom of Conholt Hill but did not join the Spring Water at Wheelers Farm. And Spring Water .... continued to run therefrom, that on the sixth day of the Wells running over it had washed away the foundation of a House, so that it fell, fortunately no lives were lost as it fell in the day time."

It was Criswick Child, of Vernham Manor, who unearthed the extract from the Parish Book relating to the 1774 experiences. Mr. Child remembered when he was 13 years old, in 1814, the well by the George Inn overflowed. He saw the cottage well above the parish school in Berry-dean run over, and the water ran down the Dean by Hen Barn through Upton to Hurstbourne. At the same time, he adds, a swift stream came from the Netherton valley (a neighbouring vale extending down from the watershed of Combe), the two becoming confluent in Hurstbourne village. This union has been called from early times "The meeting of the Cock and Hen".

Joseph Stevens' 'A Parochial History of St. Mary Bourne' contains further interesting information. *"Mr. J.H. Gilmour, of Hurstbourne Tarrant, furnishes 28 years' experience. He states that the watercourse crosses the road five times between Hurstbourne Tarrant and Upton, a distance of a mile and a half; and the course is complete to the Hen-pit, a quarter of a mile beyond Upton, where it becomes lost. It is most rare that water rises higher up the valley than this. He has known the water rise in all the hollows twice since 1857, and fill the low-lying grounds as far up as Vernham School, the pits in Bury Dean common being full. The highroad is then a watercourse for a mile and a half, till Hen-barn is reached. He has never heard of it coming down Hippenscombe and Fosbury valleys; but aged people say the well in the centre of Vernham village ran over about the time of the Crimean war, and at that time Conbolt Bottom was full, although there is no way of egress for it from there into the Hurstbourne valley. When the water rises in Hen-pit it is always found to do so in Cock-pit; but when the water overflows there it invariably rises in springs higher up both valleys. During the floods just alluded to the springs rose quite a mile up beyond the Cock-pit, which is as far up as Netherton barn, and nearly as high up as 'the Saxon landmark, Wodens or Wandsdyke' which here crosses the Netherton vale. The watercourse is distinctly traceable to the divisions between Faccombe and Hurstbourne parishes, where it is lost. When the water was so high at Vernham, Mr. Gilmour was told that it ran out of the farmyard at Netherton. He has seen the 'Cock and Hen' meet twice, in 1876-7 and in 1883. They have very nearly done so several times, but they receded just as the gravel-pits at the Dean at Hurstbourne got full. There are several springs in these pits; but in 1885 there was no water even in the main river-course, and the people were in great straits."*

Coming to the 20th century, the Andover Advertiser of the 29th January 1915 reports: *"High Water – the springs, which have risen so very rapidly of late, and reached the Berrydean, are now beginning to subside: the stream has not reached so high a point for eleven years."*

February 1940: *"FLOOD IN THE VILLAGE – On Sunday floods came to the village and several dwelling houses suffered by a rush of water from the surrounding hills. It was impossible to keep it out of the homes and in some cases it rose to three feet in the rooms. The worst case was that of the cottage occupied by Mr. and Mrs. Newport at the west end of the village where unfortunately, in consequence of Mrs. Newport's indisposition, she occupied a room on the ground floor as bedroom. The water reached to within about an inch of her bed. She was rescued and taken to a nearby neighbour's house on higher ground."*

In the wet summer of 2007, the stream was flowing in Hurstbourne in August, a feature not seen for 50 years.

Floods were not the only hazards:

Vernham Mills, who was born at Vernham Manor and lived there for most of his life, wrote: *"It was December, 1927, and had been freezing for days. I took a kettle of boiling water less than 100 yards to the kennels – the kettle was ice before I got there. Went back to the house to re-boil the water and wrapped a towel over the kettle for the trip over the yard and managed to thaw the water. There was frost till Christmas Eve – deeper and deeper it went into the ground. One night I went in just as it was getting dark and lit the sitting room fire, picking up 'The Scarlet Pimpernel' as I wanted to finish it that night. There was a bang at the door – I opened up, and all I could see was a snowman. In less than three seconds I was a snowman too, and the walls of the room were covered in snow. The man at the door had a wife and little child but in the road in an Austin 7, and they were fast disappearing in the snow in sore need of help. I started to walk down the path but suddenly felt I could not breathe. I turned round and put my handkerchief round my mouth but even so we both had to walk backwards to the car to be able to breathe in the fast-falling snow. The man got the little girl out and I helped his wife. We returned to the house and gave them a warm in the sitting room. I got on the 'phone to the baker in the village who ran an old T Ford taxi. Eventually he arrived and took them by Hurstbourne to where they lived at Netherton.*

One Christmas Day a path had to be dug from the Manor, where the organist lived, to the church; it was in the Reverend Iremonger's time (1928-35). The weather got worse and worse – the telegraph poles were little knobs and the treetops just stuck out of the top of the snow. The cottages opposite had snow up to the bedroom windows and all through January and February the hurdles kept the sheep penned and were held up with snow. Horses and carts brought food in – one day I was told to fetch a loaf of bread and saddled the seven year old mare. I tried for two hours to get to the village but never got there. The drifts were too high, the mare became exhausted. That week even the village ran short of flour and Freddie Hayes took a T Ford truck with a horse attached to the front to Hurstbourne and managed to get seven packs of flour.

47

Then came the thaw. Hippenscombe had been deep in snow and the ground was frozen hard. When the thaw came a river ran through the village wider than the road. The low houses behind the school, and all Berry Dean, suffered a flood of water which continued through Upton and tore up the road to Hurstbourne. There was no bridge then by the pumping station, so if a motor had a low exhaust, you pulled it out of the river. All the meadows below Hurstbourne were in flood, and around Netherton Bottom. The snow keeping the hurdles up and the sheep in melted, the sheep wandered happily all over the fields ......the deep winter was over."

The plight of Vernham Dean reached the national papers, and among the church documents the Vicar pasted a cutting from the 'Sunday Graphic', January 1st, 1928:

"SAVED BY A FORD – Rusty Vehicle Brings Food for Snowbound Villagers. Vernham Dean – Saturday. This tiny village in the north-west corner of Hampshire, four miles from a main road and ten miles from the railway, has been saved from starvation in the nick of time to-night by the almost heroic efforts of a firm of Stockbridge millers and the village carrier. As the last of the drifts had been cleared away in the afternoon snow again began to fall. The millers' steam wagon with flour for the Baker and meal for the cattle had struggled as far as Hurstbourne Tarrant, when the exhausted crew, who had been shovelling the wagon out of one drift after another for eight hours, could go no further. Then the Vernham Dean carrier in his rusty Ford ploughed through a foot of new snow, and though he had to be dug out three times on the return journey, he got home all right."

The vicar adds a footnote: *"The snow began on the evening of Christmas Day. By the evening of Boxing Day, the drifts were hedge-high and the roads were impassable. The fall was the heaviest remembered locally since 1882. J.A. Iremonger, Vicar."*

There were problems in 1963 as the Andover Advertiser and North Hants Gazette noted;

Andover, Friday 4th January, 1963: "Andover – or Antarctica. The worst snow blizzards for over 15 years brought chaos to Andover this week. All the week reports streamed in of appalling road conditions which resulted in many drivers abandoning their cars and lorries, of snow drifts up to 10 feet under which have been buried for days coaches and scores of cars, of people stranded in isolated houses, and of villages completely cut off for about 24 hours ......the Andover-Newbury road also suffered badly. The worst spots were at Enham Arch, Lillywhite's Hill, and, of course, the notorious Hurstbourne Tarrant hill .... ON THE FARM .... many farmers in the area were cut off and unable to get their milk through to the dairies, but Mr. F.H. Whittingham, of Vernham Dean, Chairman of the Andover branch of the National Farmers' Union, said he had no reports of animals being lost probably because farmers at this time of the year kept their 'delicate stock' under cover ...."

The following week, in the Andover Advertiser of Friday, 22nd January, the Editor's Post Bag relates: *"Praise for their sterling work in frightful conditions. We have received several letters this week praising the work of the Hampshire County Council and its employees, and of the many people who fought gallantly to get food and essential services to those cut off by the blizzard. One of the most dramatic stories comes from Mrs. M. Newman of Bernevall Cottage, Vernham Dean, who writes: 'I have been approached by several of the residents of the Vernham Dean/Linkenholt/Upton area who would like to mention the really fine efforts of rescue and snow clearance by the Council and especially by the farmers who contracted to clear snow for the Council. The lanes round here are narrow, extremely winding, exposed and in many cases very high up, besides being steeply banked. In spite of all these hazards, which added up to immense and recurrent drifts, the roads round this part were cleared in record time and at least one way through to each hamlet was made within 48 hours. Linkenholt Estate had all their workers and equipment on the job likewise Mr. W. Trott of Vernham Dean and Mr. A. Miller of Upton. The latter, working far into the night, managed to cut a way through to the experimental broiler houses at Upton Hills, where 50,000 chickens would have died without their rations – 32 tons a week are needed to keep them going. Combe village sent out an SOS since Berkshire seemed to have forgotten them, and Linkenholt Estate bulldozed a way up there in a blizzard, so that at least the baker was able to get round with his bread lashed to a tractor .... it is almost impossible to pick out individuals when so many were working for long hours without hot meals and under such appalling conditions, but Alan Smith, of Linkenholt Estate, seemed to keep doggedly on non-stop, on his bulldozer, with no cab, and looking frozen, his brother Ray Smith got through Combe Wood to Buttermere to rescue five marooned horses and take them hay."* (Mind you, on Page 7, col 4 in the Editor's Postbag there is a letter from Broiler Experiments which says Mrs. Newman's account exaggerates the predicament of 28,000, not 50,000 chickens).

Andover Advertiser, Friday, 1st May 1981 *"...................... at Vernham Dean residents awoke on Sunday morning to find three inches of snow covering everything and drifts were blocking roads. On Monday morning the regular bus service was disrupted for a while when its route between Linkenholt and Littledown was blocked by a drift. Many trees were damaged and the area was one of the longest without power. SEB engineers started work at Upton, Linkenholt and Vernham Dean mid-day Tuesday and by 5 pm power was restored."*

The editors are indebted to Mark Davison, Ian Currie and Bob Ogley for the following excerpts from 'The Hampshire and Isle of Wight Weather Book'.

"The winter of 1989-90 was again so mild that January and February's temperatures combined were the warmest generally in England in a record going back to 1659. It was also very wet, 12.4 inches (317mm) fell in this time at Vernham Dean. This had a dramatic

effect on rivers ……... in north west Hampshire there was a 48 foot rise in underground water levels. However, the price to pay for a wet winter was death and destruction caused by the storms which constantly lashed Britain during January and February. The worst was the tragic gale of 25th January, 1990 …….….." Residents in the Vernham area did not venture out without a chain saw in the back of the vehicle to tackle the many uprooted trees, and the then publican of 'The George', Mary Perry, had to try three routes into Vernham from shopping in Andover before she could get home.

Again from the Weather Book: *"1993. Another January devoid of snow. Many places had gone six successive mid-winter months without snow. After a dry February – the third driest this century - May brought some violent thunderstorms. On Wednesday 26th, 2.27 inches (58mm) of torrential rain fell in just two hours at Vernham Dean before dawn."*

One of the editors, with a mere 19 years' residence in the area, remembers well her first sight of the bournes running, in 1995, when Hen Barn (half a mile up the valley from Upton) was flooded, and water ran intermittently down the valley from the Bury Dean playing fields to Hen Barn. There was chaos in the valley, and no wonder, scoffed a long-term resident. The conduits had not been cleared for years, and the Council, for the most part, did not know where they were so long was it since the job had been done. The 'old-timer' had to tell them himself. Where wells had been filled in the water started to flow with such force that the bottoms of the wells were flushed out, the water rose up and several gardens in Upton were flooded, including a much-loved vegetable patch where duckboards had to be laid for the resident to get to his door. Those who said 'the streams will never flow again' were deeply confounded. It may happen only once every 30 years or so, but happen it will. Builders refuse to create cellars in the Upton area as they are all too well aware of the dangers from the water, even if prospective tenants and owners are not. In the Andover Advertiser of Tuesday, 6th June 1995 Mr. Terry Gilmore, Assistant Director of Legal and Technical Services, told councillors that the severe flooding in the area is only expected to happen once every 60 years: *"As we have had flooding for two years running it should be another 120 years before it happens again ……..."* It would appear that this gentleman may have had to eat his words, in view of later flooding, when the newly-built school appeared to be surrounded by a moat ….. he can always blame climate change.

In the past, the above horror stories notwithstanding, it has usually been the lack of water rather than its abundance which has caused more trouble. Prior to mains water the villagers relied on wells, which had a distressing tendency to go dry in summer.

From the prologue to 'Church Accounts, Vernham Dean, Vestry Book' copied by H. Pooley, Hon. Treasurer, Vernham Dean PCC: *"1929. A very dry Season. The Vicarage well quite out, also the Manor one, and the Meadow one. The Manor Well lowered by Duke & Ockendens to 275 feet, so never without again, cost £250. Water had to be fetched from Fosbury and Linkenholt."* The records are peppered with the hardships of dry summers and even when water was 'on tap' the stories continued.

Andover Advertiser, Friday, 19th August 1949.

"VERNHAM GOES DRY – WATER RUSHED TO THIRSTY VILLAGE – R.D.C.OFFICIALS' EMERGENCY SUNDAY MEASURES.

Vernham Dean (population about 600) was without water on Sunday and Monday, due to a breakdown of the borehole pump. The pump actually stopped working on Saturday night, but it was not until early on Sunday morning that the 20,000 gallons reservoir at Vernham Street went dry. it was then that trouble started for Andover Rural District councillor, G.E. Evans, who owns a family grocery and bakery business, as well as running the local Post Office for Vernham Dean. He was inundated with messages from irritated villagers asking what had happened to their water, and telephone calls from angry farmers wanting water for their cattle. For a few hours chaos reigned in the village. Being unable personally to contact any of the R.D.C. officials (the Surveyor being on holiday) Mr. Evans rang up the Police and the Hurstbourne Tarrant constable, P.C. Brodie, soon got busy. The Assistant Surveyor, Mr. K. Burnett, was fetched from his pew at the Stockbridge Parish Church, and he quickly collected members of the staff and proceeded to devise 'Operation Water'.

PUB AS H.Q. – Miss Smith and Mr. T. Redman (Assistant Clerk) and Mr. Burnett set up an enquiry office at 'The George' to explain to the villagers what had happened. Owing to the fact that the Fire Service had to stand by for calls, Mr. Burnett was unable to obtain the services of a water tender, so he had to set about finding alternative measures. The R.D.C. foreman, Mr. Alexander, was contacted just as he was about to board a bus for a day's trip to the sea. He rounded up two other members of the staff, and with two 500-galls. tankers (which Mr. Burnett had managed to borrow) proceeded with a lorry to Ibthorpe. Water was taken on from the Council's supply there, and a shuttle service was commenced to Vernham Dean. The people received their first supplies by 4 p.m. on Sunday, and in the words of Mrs. M. Board, the daughter of Mr. Evans 'the Council workmen were most courteous and they stopped at every door in the village and shouted to ask if the occupants wanted water'. Every person was told that the water must be boiled, and notices to that effect were posted all over the village.

SOME SKIPPED LAUNDERING: Monday was a rare holiday for the housewives, for many of them did not have enough to do the weekly wash but, as Mrs. Ripley, of 3 Upton Street, said: 'some of us used soft water, but the people in the new houses were not so lucky, and most of them did not have any water at all other than what was delivered'.

Most of the villagers agreed that the Council responded very promptly to their S.O.S. and that the men had worked extremely well and hard, for it was after 11 p.m. on Sunday before they had finished supplying the village and local farmers with water. Farmers suffered hardships, for besides the worry of supplying cattle they had to have water for the cowsheds. Mrs. Higginbotham, wife of Commander P.H. Higginbotham, of Fairview Farm, said that as they were unable to cool their milk it had to be rejected 'but', she added, 'the R.D.C. were most helpful and supplied us with the water we needed until it came back again on Tuesday.'

TAILPIECE: Bouquets to the grand old lady who refused to have more than a bucketful of water so that others would not go without: to the Council employees who put down water for the dozen or so dogs that greeted the water lorry when it arrived in the village (they must have lapped up nearly three gallons, said one official) and to the inhabitants themselves who are setting the wheels in motion to suitably acknowledge the work of the Council employees."

The Andover Advertiser, Friday, 9th September 1949: *"EXPRESSION OF THANKS – Recently Mr. G.E. Evans, a well-known local resident, of Vernham Dean, took £3 to the Rural District Council offices, Andover, as a gift to be divided between the Council employees who brought water to the parish when the pumping station failed some time ago. This amount had been collected by Mrs. M.G. Broad (Vernham Dean) and Mrs. P.H. Higginbotham (Vernham Street) and was a token of appreciation by the local ratepayers."*

Before mains water, the villagers were dependent upon wells, and those who did not have wells in their own houses had to draw from the village well. George Brickell, writing in *'End of era for village well'* quotes from a village correspondent who wrote: *"It is by no means the oldest well in the district, that distinction probably belongs to the well at the George Inn, reputed to be at least 400 years old. Compared with that, the village well covered in yesterday is a modern upstart, possibly less than 100 years old: for there were those who can remember being told that a century ago the village well was at a spot now in the middle of the main road. The site is indicated after a light snowfall by a circular patch which stands out from the surrounding surface."* George Brickell continues: *"The village well was a little too close to the pond for the peace of mind of the Medical Officer of Health, and although it was about 120 feet deep, its powers were failing. In view of the general drying up of wells in the district the A.R.D.C. had four or five years previously decided not to rely on such shallow sources and bored more than 700 feet through solid chalk to the greensand to supply good water to Vernham Dean, Vernham Street and Littledown. At the time there were some village die-hards who swore they would never take water from the Council's standpipes; the old well was good enough for them: but the march of progress (or perhaps the back-breaking toil of winding the buckets up and down) soon converted them".*

Enid Brooks, writing in the Parish Magazine in 1968, recalled: *"you could scarcely ever go through the village without seeing somebody drawing water from the well, and this was a meeting place in the evenings .... many a yarn has been told there ....."*

Mains water was also treated with mixed views. Eric Levell in 'Country Days, Country Ways' in The Andover Advertiser for the 20th September, 1991, writes: *"When the news got around that the water was to be 'laid on' at Vernham and the old well by the pond sealed, some of the villagers were very upset. My grandfather was furious. It was rather like the reaction in later years when it was decreed that milk was to be pasteurised. 'What do "they" want to go messing about with the milk for?' In the case of the well it was resented that "they" should "mess about with the water". "What's wrong with the well? Tis good water and don't cost nothing. 'Pend apon't they'll want to charge us money for the stuff that comes out of the pipes! That there piped water'll be full of chemical tackle". Grandfather came round quite quickly – he talked endlessly about the wonders of the project and you could be forgiven for thinking that he had never opposed it! Some of the standpipes for the supply are still in place: one opposite The George, outside Pond Cottage, and another up at the church which is in regular use around the churchyard and for the flowers inside."*

Water, wells and the pond have featured regularly in the business of the Parish Council from its inception:

13th April 1896: *"It was proposed to write to various owners of property calling attention to the dilapidated condition of the village well and ask them to assist in pulling (sic) the well in repair."* No doubt things dragged on for the next 25 years for.

9th January 1922: *"Proposed that the Council take over the Parish Well from this date. One day's work to be done at the well by way of cleaning and sinking, and if no water is reached the work shall be continued for one more day but no longer and the price per day to be 45/- for three men."*

And again:

4th January 1923: *"It was agreed that the Village Well be taken over by the Council and kept in repair. Mr. Shergold to supply and fit at once a new wire rope and the Clerk was instructed to ask all the owners of property whose tenants used the well to contribute towards its maintenance."*

15th February: *"Owners of all the cottages to be asked to contribute at a rate of 1/6d per each cottage towards expense of fitting a new wire rope to the well for those who use the well....."*

14th December 1925: *"Complaints were laid about the water in the Parish Well – a report to be made to the R.D.C."* On the 11th January 1926 a letter from the Surveyor and County MO said the water in the parish well was satisfactory for all domestic purposes, including drinking ………. BUT………… On the 22nd February 1926: *"The Councillors to meet the Surveyor at the Parish Well."* 19th April: *"Mr. W. Scull to do the necessary repairs to the Parish Well ……."*

By the 27th September the Parish Well had been repaired at a cost of £3.12s.0d. + 12/- for the extra slab over the top of the well.

And so it went on: 1st November 1929: *"Wallis paid 13/- for repairing the well ……."*

Eventually the Council agreed unanimously that the Chairman should make enquiries into the possibility of supplying the village with water, and on the 30th July the Minutes read: *"Water Supply: the Chairman to put it to the RDC …………."* but the grinding of the mills of God were nothing compared with the slow motion of procuring a water supply.

29th March 1932: *"The Council considers the supply inadequate: the Chairman to report."*

27th April: *"The Chairman had reported the situation regarding the water supply in the parish, and would see Mr. Johnson, the Sanitary Inspector, again, at the next RDC meeting."*

19th May 1932: *"Decision to make an application to the RDC for a water supply. Mr. Hamsley against it as an unnecessary expense – no support for him. The Chairman would lay the reasons before the RDC."*

12th December – the sample of Parish Well water was noted as satisfactory.

The big guns are now brought into play:

27th September 1933: *"A well-attended parish meeting TO CONSIDER THE SHORTAGE OF WATER IN THE VILLAGE. Mrs. Gibson, the headmistress of the school, said every drop of water had to be boiled as the only supply was rain water, and by courtesy water of uncertain purity from a well of a neighbouring cottage. Mr. Giles of Littledown reported that they were very badly hit. Mr. Sherwood had helped them out, but in this water shortage, similar to 1921, all cottagers were unanimous in the opinion that a new water supply was necessary."*

"This Parish meeting strongly condemns the present water supply as inadequate, and urges the RDC to enquire into the matter immediately as the question is one of pressing urgency."

In September it was reported that Mr. Wallis had repaired the Parish Well: Mr. MacKilligan of the RDC was at the meeting and said he knew how badly a water supply was needed, but the Parish must place a sound scheme before the District Council before the Ministry of Health would come and investigate. In the December the RDC was waiting to see what grant could be extracted from the government towards a water supply in the parish.

5th March 1934: *"Water supply – nothing to report – would call a village meeting as and when **BUT the Council would emphasize the resolution and urgently call the attention of the RDC to the desperate shortage of water supply in Vernham Dean, Vernham Street and Littledown and ask whether the RDC can give any definite proposals for overcoming the shortage.**"*

A parish meeting was called for the 19th April, and by the 25th a special committee had been appointed to enquire into the request of the Vernhams Dean Parish Council for a more adequate and wholesome water supply. This had been presented to the District Council on the 13th October 1933. The details of the scheme were as follows:-

Area of Parish: 3,919 acres: Rateable Value £1,437: A Penny Rate produces £5.6s.2d. Proposals: the 130 ft Vernham Dean well to be bored to 270 feet with an 8 inch bore, making a total depth of 400'. Estimated costs:

Bore hole 270'	£136.00
Power Plant	£300.00
Power house/gate	£75.00
Reservoir 3,100 gl	£130.00
Total:	£641.00

Vernham Street and Littledown were to purchase a site for boring from the South Berks Brewery Company at the highest point about 650' OD

Bore hole 650'	£375.00
Power House	£75.00
Reservoir 3,100 gl	£150.00
Purchase of site	£30.00
Total:	£930.00

The total estimated cost for the two was £1,271.00

The Parish Council were happy with the presentation and thanked the RDC but made the following suggestions:

1. That a pipe line be run from a site near The Boot to Vernham Dean and so do away with the power plant there.

2. That the route for such pipe be from The Boot to the church, from the church to the school, via the footpaths, which may provide a shorter route.

3. That Slack Pipes be used at intervals and also a pipe running to Littledown.

4. That a pipe be carried down to Upton and the other to Vernham Dean

5. Smallholders want provision for their cattle – Vernham Street in particular. They said they would be prepared to pay a reasonable charge.

(In short – the outline of the scheme was to bore the parish well, the water to be pumped from there to the site near The Boot. Slack pipes to be erected every 200' with a branch to Littledown. Cost (£4,500): 3 grants of £750 were obtainable from the Ministry of Health, County and District Councils. The remaining £2,250 to be met by the inhabitants by means of rates.)

THOSE WHO WISH TO HAVE IT ON THEIR HABITATIONS COULD DO SO AT AN EXTRA CHARGE – Colonel Footmer to attend the Parish Council meeting and expound further).

Before the scheme was passed there would be a public enquiry in the village hall, but meanwhile a temporary supply was laid on from the Fosbury estate for inhabitants of Vernham Dean. Water was urgently needed for Littledown as all the wells were dry and a temporary supply was being carted from Linkenholt. The Public Enquiry was held in the Village Hall on Wednesday, 3rd October 1934 .... but on the 26th November the Chairman thought a letter should be sent to see if anything was being done about the water question as the well at the bottom of Vernham Street had given out.

Mains water, after many changes in the proposed scheme, first came to the parish during 1934-35. Trenches were dug by hand from Vernham Dean up to Vernham Street. Improvements in supply must have progressed, for at the parish meeting on the 18th March, 1935, at which only 8 parishioners were present, it was decided to ask the RDC what rates would be placed on the parish for the water supply .... the matter rumbles on ...... 24th March a discussion on water charges .... and by 18th June 1937: *"The Village Well should be made more safe THE LID SHOULD BE NAILED DOWN"* At long last the complete switch had been made to 'mains' supply.

However: 15th April 1940: The Council were still not happy about the Water Rate and the RDC were to be asked for a list of all expenses incurred on the Vernham Dean Water Scheme for the year ending 31.03.1940. The Parish Well had to be re-opened during an emergency and a brake was to be fixed as the bucket was too heavy to be let down by hand. Repairs required.

24th March 1941: Reply re Water Scheme expenses: detailed statement received. Increased water consumption which necessitates many more hours of pumping. This increased consumption to be investigated. A padlock was to be put on the Parish Well door and the brake repaired.

THE VILLAGE POND

Vernham Dean has had a pond since its earliest days, a vital resource for cattle on a twice-daily basis, and a never-ending source of amusement for generations of children. Eric Levell writes: *"Most of our ponds, some of which have been around since prehistoric times, have died of neglect but Vernham Dean has at least escaped the indignity of the Aldbourne pond, which has been encased in concrete and is now merely a concrete saucer. The grassed-over basin has a pleasant appearance but someone has pulled the plug out. I remember with pleasure this pond in the twenties when it was in the centre of events in the village together with the old village well crouching in its wooden tent at the very edge of the water. Surely in times of excessive rain before the concrete top was set on the well, pond water must have poured down the shaft and the two become intermingled. Chuffy traction engines and the big brassy Stoke's fairground engines paused to top up their water tanks and here the cows came twice a day to drink, together with horses which, being more particular, waded well out into undisturbed water before taking their fill ….. I remember an old mule joining in, a big sturdy sort of mule, a survivor no doubt of the horrors of Flanders ……….. and the villagers with buckets trying to douse a thatched cottage conflagration and to hold the flames a bit until with luck a fire engine came from afar. Children pursued frogs around its margins in summer and slid over its frozen surface in winter, the ice pinging and singing as they sped across. It was never a pond with much weed as I remember, and the variety of its wild life was not great."*

It will be no surprise to learn that the pond also featured regularly in the business of the Parish Council:

10th June 1921: *"It was resolved that the Clerk write to those who use the pond for subscriptions to assist in the expense"* (of clearing and cleaning the pond).

8th August 1929: *"Mr. Mills had had the pond cleaned out at a cost of £4.4s.0d. Notice to be erected and affixed to the Well 'No rubbish may be shot in the village pond – by order of the PC'.*

Although cattle had always used the pond for watering, by 1938 people's attitudes were changing:

"Village pond ought to be fenced as cattle taint the water and cause it to smell".

In the Minutes of the 15th March 1939 is found the first reference to a matter which still concerns the Parish Council today: *"Pond when full caused overflow of five yards wide over the road. The RDC to be informed, and enquiries made about the proposed increase in the water rate."*

25th April: *"The Surveyor proposed digging a gutter in Mr. Bulpit's meadow near Boat Lane to prevent water running down from there into the pond, which should relieve the pond considerably."*

30th October: *"The pond was considered dangerous and should be made safe during the blackout: agreed to erect white painted posts."*

18th March 1940: *"Had spoken to the Surveyor about the erection of black and white posts around the pond, but owing to shortage of labour they would have to remain over for the time being. The increase in the water rate necessitated because of the attendants' increased wages and the depreciation of machinery ...."*

31st July 1944: *"It was resolved to have the pond cleaned out when it was dry again."*

13th December: Flood water from the pond: letter was sent to the Surveyor asking to have a pipe line laid from the pond to the meadow close to the pumping station as that would prevent water covering the road, at times 2-3 yards wide. (The pumping station was at the bottom of the now Shepherd's Rise).

Friday, 23rd March 1945: The Surveyor had suggested deepening the pond and trench dug in Mr. Bulpit's meadow to divert water from Boats Lane – the RDC might give help with digging.

15th May: More pond trouble – asked if mud, when the pond cleared, could be dumped in the ditches on the Bury Dean.

16th October: a letter sent to the County Medical Officer: *"a pond considered detrimental to the health of the village."* This motion was carried unanimously.

12th February 1946: The County Medical Officer's letter to go to the Sanitary Inspector.

28th October 1949: Urgency of cleaning out the Village Pond. The RDC must give a definite undertaking that they are prepared to do the work but not to tip the pond material on land adjacent to the pond. Trees and shrubs should be planted around the kiosk.

29th November: *"Trees have been planted by Miss Lennard by the pond."*

14th July 1950: Surface water: Surveyor said: *"very little could be done about it"* as provision could not be made for abnormal weather conditions.

1st September: resolved to write to the County Surveyor re water as something must be done to prevent this trouble happening every time there is heavy rain. Failing this, application to be made to the Ministry of Health.

6th October: the pond half full of mud and unhealthy.

11th December: County Council estimate for surface water and cleaning out of pond: £80. The County Council offered 75%. Approved – apply to the Hampshire Rivers Board to undertake the work.

12th January 1951: the Hampshire Rivers Board would do the work, the Parish Council to ask the RDC for a substantial contribution to the proportion of the expense of cleaning out the pond and also to ask the RDC to allow it to be put on the rates.

9th February: The Hampshire Rivers Board decided to postpone the operation to allow the water to recede so as to get to the mud in the centre (operation cleaning out and soakaway). £15 grant from the RDC towards the cost of cleaning out the pond.

8th June: the Hampshire Rivers Board would undertake the pond work in the summer.

19th October: query over the work to the pond – had it been done properly? The County Surveyor to get a competent engineer to check the work before the account is paid.

9th November: *"not at all satisfied with the state of the pond."*

14th December: *"soakaway – leave for 12 months and see what happens".*

4th June 1952: letter to Hampshire Rivers Board on unsatisfactory soakaway to pond not being properly sealed, thereby allowing water to filter through so quickly that the pond is always empty. They are to be asked to seal over the soakaway.

11th July: the Parish Council wants the soakaway sealed and the centre overflow tube left as it is, without extra cost to the Parish Council. The Rivers Board is agitating for the account to be paid.

27th May 1953: the pond area is full of grass and weeds. *"Neglected appearance spoiled the village. Mr. Stacey said he thought he could arrange for it to be cut and it was left in his hands to attend to it".*

1961: shrubs and trees removed somewhat ruthlessly from pond area.

7th January 1963: fence around pond to be removed because the number of cattle is reduced.

AND SO THE SAGA CONTINUES IN SIMILAR VEIN TODAY

5th May 1958: "What could be done to prevent children riding through the mud on bicycles?"

Decided Council could not take effective action. This was a game much enjoyed through the ages since the bicycle was introduced. Mrs Bulstrode, whose father Edward Piper rented Poplars Farm for a period prior to 1913, said she and her brothers usually did this the day before the end of the holidays, as the punishment was always having the bicycles taken away.

At the present time the pond area is a pleasant green oasis in the middle of the village, with the listed red telephone box next to the roadside. The large concrete slab still marks the old village well, and the pond area itself soaks away the excess when rainwash rushes down Bulpits Hill and sweeps across the road. Newcomers to the village yearn for the pond to be restored but with the lowering of the water table the only supply is rainfall and the oil-tainted storm rush. There is no reasonable way of supplying good water to the pond, and many grandiose plans fail. The Council has the grass cut once a fortnight along with the recreation field, the pathway up to the church and some of the churchyard, maintaining a pleasant, not over-manicured verdure.

The Kenward Stone
(Unknown provenance)

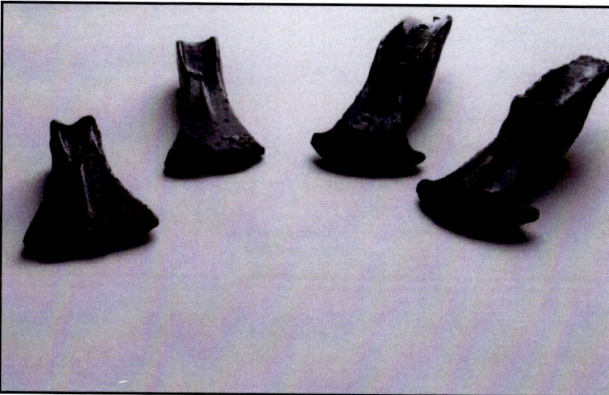

The Vernham Dean palstaves (handaxes)
(picture taken with the kind permission of Andover Museum)

Vernham Manor early 20thC
(Unknown provenance)

**Vernham Manor
interior early 20thC**
(Unknown provenance)

**Manor Farm
Cottages**
(John Marchment)

**Cows being watered
at the Village Pond**
(John Marchment)

**Herding the sheep
through the village**
(John Marchment)

**St Mary the Virgin
- early view**
(Unknown provenance)

**St Mary the Virgin
- today**
(G.L. Palmer)

**St Mary the Virgin
- west doorway**
(Unknown provenance)

**St Mary the Virgin
festival of flowers
19thC**
(Unknown provenance)

Jon Fairbrother's map of the village in 1776

The Village in 1776

Note:

In 1776 the area between what is now Back Lane and the valley road was still an open area, perhaps the village green. It was not built on until the early 19th Century.

Once Wheeler's Farm now Sargent's Farm

The George with what is thought to have been a barn by the road

The Parsonage

Key

C	Copyhold
F	Freehold
L	Leasehold

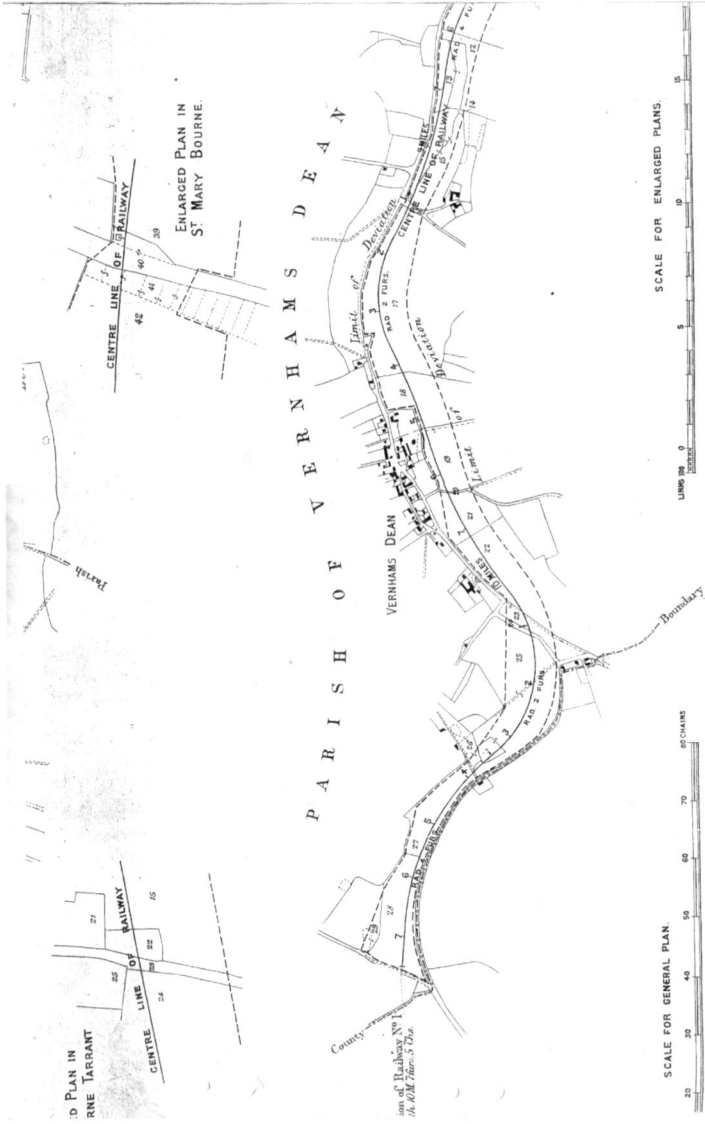

The Railway *Reproduced by permission of the Hampshire Record Office. Reference No: DPO B40.*

Chapter 6

THE PARISH CHURCH OF VERNHAMS DEAN

ST. MARY THE VIRGIN

Situation

Set in a steeply banked churchyard beside a small wood, this Grade II listed Hampshire church serves a scattered parish of isolated hamlets close to the Wiltshire border. The Saxons brought Christianity to the valley in the 6th century, although no evidence of a pre-Norman foundation has been discovered.

The building sits between Vernham Street and the Jacobean Vernham Manor, and might mark the original nucleus of a medieval village, although opinion is divided as to whether there was ever a village near the church. A trench dug in 1995 by the late C.K. Currie (CKC Archaeology) prior to the extension of the churchyard produced no evidence to support the contention that major medieval settlement shift, from the church down into the valley below, had occurred. There is, however, a tradition of a 'Plague Village' lost in the Black Death of the 1340s but it could be that Vernham Dean, in common with a large number of other Hampshire villages, may have always been an area of dispersed settlement. A former name for the area partly studied by Mr. Currie is the 'Old Orchard' which suggests possible smaller scale settlement – perhaps an isolated dwelling or small group of dwellings – existing near the church at some time.

The Church

From earliest recorded times St. Mary the Virgin was a chapelry of St. Peter's at Hurstbourne Tarrant, but in 1871 Vernhams Dean became an independent parish and a new vicarage (now a private residence) was endowed, adjacent to the churchyard. Vernhams Dean was joined with Linkenholt in 1914 but on the 11th June 1979 a United Benefice was approved, consisting of Hurstbourne Tarrant and Faccombe, Vernhams Dean and Linkenholt.

Records begin in 1598, but are not continuous, one notable exception being the Parochial Church Council Minutes from 1927-1945. Church records are housed in the Hampshire Record Office in Winchester, as is a Tithe Map, dated 1843, found under the eaves of the church. This unwieldy archive requires two archivists to handle it and is a source of fascinating information. A list of the clergy since 1887 includes the Reverend Frederick Athewold Iremonger (1928-1935) who was subsequently appointed New Religious Director of the B.B.C. It was during his time that a Village Hall, Men's Club and a Women's Institute were founded, but a former curate, Sidney George Gillum (b. 1835) must not be forgotten as being instrumental in the building of the village school, still known as Vernham Dean Gillum's Church of England Primary School.

The church is said to have been burnt down in the 19th century, but the relevant records have not yet been researched. *The Religious Census of Hampshire 1851* (1993) p 203 (770) (Hampshire Record Series Vol 12) noted: *it is known that the population of the village in 1801 was 459, and in 1851 it was 744. No date is given for the consecration of the church* (dates were only given when a consecration took place after 1799). *The total of morning worshippers was 97, the afternoon 152, with an average of between 100 – 150.* This seems somewhat miraculous in view of the remarks *"a portion of this church is at present under repair. The sittings in the part now used are so dilapidated that it is impossible to give account of the accommodation"*.

When builders holed through to a crypt in 2005, ample evidence of a fire was seen in the sooty deposits on the walls. Coffins were found in this crypt, two adults and two children, obviously interred subsequent to the fire as the coffins bore no evidence of any conflagration. There were no names on the coffins, and researchers are still seeking enlightenment.

The church re-opened in November 1851. A sketch of the old church in the vestry shows it to have had a similar plan form to the present building but with a weather-boarded belfry and a south porch.

The re-built church was re-roofed, the south and north porches were removed and the doors blocked off: evidence of the porches can be seen on the south and north walls today. The effect of a fire would have been to alter the chemical properties of the materials in the walls, and it is likely that additional buttresses were provided as a precaution.

It was thought the chancel arch was damaged during the fire and reconstructed, and the chancel itself was closed for three years prior to the 1851 re-opening of the reconstructed church. The rubble walls are faced with flint, having stone dressings, top openings, and the pitched roof is clad with clay tiles. Until the church was re-built, services were held in 'Macey's Cottage' just up the road towards Vernham Street. This is a rendered flint structure whose Gothic-style windows give it a chapel-like appearance, and it was lived in by the verger when services resumed in the church.

The earliest part of the church – now the chancel – is Norman, probably built for the benefit of the inhabitants of the Manor, and the first section of the current nave was added in the 12th century, with a further extension sometime after 1420. There is evidence of 'Churchwarden' repairs probably in the 17th or 18th century.

The edifice was necessarily much rebuilt in the mid 19th century under Arthur Aspittle (architect) possibly from plans by the curate, the Revd J.H. Rawlins. All the windows, including the large cast window of five narrow graduated Early English-style lancets, date from the rebuilding. The west wall at one time extended further, and was topped by a 'Hampshire Tower'. Dates found during the rebuilding of the west wall in 2005 signify that the previously most recent building work was carried out between 1890 and 1920, but details of this have yet to be researched. The Hampshire Record Office holds the Diocesan records, but details of faculties relating to this period appear to be missing.

The church has a very fine western doorway from circa 1220. This 'Norman' doorway has two inner rows of chevron, two inset columns at each side with simple foliage caps. Proof of a late Norman, almost Early English date is seen in the dog-tooth enrichment of the hood mould. It is a very good example of the often splendid late Norman and Early English work in Hampshire, and a fine feature of a rather humble building with its excellent detail in Binstead stone from the Isle of Wight. It is likely that this doorway came from Andover Parish Church when it suffered its redevelopment in the mid 19th century, as an identical doorway can be seen in the Upper High Street in Andover.

The church now consists of nave, chancel and north vestry with a small stone gabled west bell turret, with one bell, inscribed SK 1681, exposed in the single pointed arch. 'SK' stands for Samuel Knight, the Reading bellfounder.

Interior

Inside the church the atmosphere is Victorian, and there is a gallery at the west end. A new altar, made by 'Mr. Knight the builder at Hurstbourne Tarrant' was dedicated in 1922 and the early model – possibly 16th/17th century, was re-housed in the vestry, from whence it was stolen in the 1990s. The brass cross on the altar was given in memory of the members of the Leeper family. The oak lectern also was given in memory of Frederick James Leeper, 'Priest of this Parish 1886-1906' and is inscribed: 'Thy Word is a Lantern unto my Feet and a Light unto my Path'.

Revd Leeper must have found the church somewhat draughty, as he presented a baize curtain for the west door in 1901 at a cost of £1. 7s. 9d. He also gave two brass flower vases to the church at Easter 1903. His curtain has been replaced by heavy dark blue velvet drapes, again effective draught excluders, but a significant drain on cleaning costs. (£90 during the 2005 repair programme).

The floor of the nave displays the usual 17th and 18th century sepulchral slabs which bear the names of Mary and Timothy-Merriman Geater: William Geater: Daniel and Margaret North: Daniel, Elizabeth and John North. The one nearest the chancel steps is mostly indecipherable.

Working round the church in a clockwise direction, the north wall of the nave displays a plaque detailing the Geater family, and near to it is the Memorial to the 1939-45 World War, with a separate plaque for Edward Talford Salter. The Memorial was dedicated on Armistice Day, 1956.

The pulpit was given by the late Mrs. Kate Mills (wife of John Mills) in 1920 in memory of her brother, Edwin Quick, who leased the Manor House in the late 19th century and which stayed in the Mills family until 1987, having been purchased from Winchester College in September, 1977.

Round the base of the pulpit are plaques to some of those who have served as churchwarden and are interred in the churchyard: Edwin Quick, John Mills, Gordon Leslie Arthur Elmer, Herbert George Maber and Robert Smith. Above the chancel steps is the Royal Arms dated 1838 (VIC 1 REG 1838) actually a Hanoverian Royal Coat of Arms, probably a repainted version of the one hanging prior to the 1851 rebuilding, as in the account 1768-1861 (HRO 110M70.PW1) there is an entry for 1775: 'payment for painting the King's Arms' (£4.4s.0d.) Royal Arms appeared in churches from the time of Edward VI onwards, to indicate the monarch was the head of the Church of England.

In the chancel the most engaging feature of the church is the colourful stained glass, which has been described by Pevsner as 'naïve, very lovable'. The 1850s were not the most exalted of periods for the production of stained glass, indeed 1800-1850 has been described as a period of dull colours, with limited palette. There were few sources of stained glass in England, which gave rise to the tale that Vernham's glass was procured by 'mail order' from Germany. Be that as it may, the designs are purported to be those of the curate, the Revd J.M. Rawlins, and are well drawn, nicely-proportioned and appropriate to a small country church.

The north side of the chancel has one window: *"Those that sow in tears shall reap in joy"*, whilst the east has five lancet windows arranged with a medallion and inscription on each – the first the promise to Abraham: *"In his seed shall all nations of the earth be glad"*. Second: the Virgin and her child and the birth of our Saviour: *"Unto us a child is born"*. Third: the Crucifixion of our Saviour: "It is finished", and fourth: the Angel declares the resurrection to the women at the doors of the Sepulchre: *"He is not here but risen"*. The fifth shows the Ascension: *"Thou has led captivity captive"*.

The south wall of the chancel holds two commemorative windows, the first in memory of Thomas Hooper, who died on the 12th June, 1846, aged 50 years: *"Oh Lord and Oh God"*. (The two chamber tombs in the churchyard are listed monuments which relate to the Hooper family).

The second window is in memory of Samuel Gerrish who died on the 31st October, 1848, aged 79 years: *"The Lord killeth and maketh alive, he bringeth down to the grave and bringeth up"*. The two windows nearest the chancel on the north and south walls of the nave have a certain curiosity value, as they are composed of cheap industrial glass, yet emblazoned with very carefully painted emblems.

On the north wall of the chancel is a small mural tablet of 1703 to Thomas King and a memorial to Cyril Roland Eyre Miller of Upton Manor, who died on the 23rd November 1914, from wounds received at Ypres. The south wall of the nave has the Memorial Tablet to those men of the parish who fell in the Great War (1914-18). It contains 17 names, and was dedicated on the 19th October 1921. To the right of the Memorial Tablet is a plaque for the Bull family who leased the Manor for some years in the 19th century: John and Sarah Bull, their sons Abia, Darius and Hiram Bull, daughters Arabella Andrews and Thirza Bull. It was Thirza Bull who was responsible for 'Miss Thirza Bull's Charity' mentioned in another chapter, a bequest established in 1864 for the poor of Vernham Dean. The interest on £112.16s.8d. from Consolidated £3 per cent annuities was to be given away to the aged poor, in bread or clothing, before Christmas annually at the discretion of the Trustees "they having regard to the recommendation of the Minister and churchwardens". The Bull charity was amalgamated with the Upton School House Charity and is now used for "religious and educational purposes for the benefit of the parishes of Hurstbourne Tarrant and Vernhams Dean".

Church Plate

It is unfortunate, that for security's sake, no item of the church plate can be displayed in the church. All is removed after each service. The Paten which is in current use is inscribed *"Thanks be to Thee, O Lord"* and was given to the church by the Curate in Charge 1906-7, Alan Williams and his wife Annie: the hallmark is indecipherable.

Queen Elizabeth I issued an edict that all parishes should have a chalice, and the circa 1590 chalice is displayed in Winchester Cathedral. This silver chalice is inscribed: *'This is Ye Communion Cuppe of Wernum'*. It is considered not to be the work of a silversmith but perhaps that of a good metal worker, possibly local. Probably in order to avoid paying duty the chalice was not sent to London for hallmarking, and is therefore unmarked, but is typical of a late 16th century lyrical style. Braithwaite, in "Church Plate of Hampshire 1909" describes it as: "Chalice – Silver. The bowl is tapered and is engraved with a band in the usual Elizabethan style, the knop is close to the bowl and the domed foot has an engraved band of similar style to the bowl. The height is 7 1/2", the weight 8 oz.".

The chalice which is now in use was given in memory of Mr. William Charles Doswell in 1978. A silver paten, kept in the bank, is described thus: "Paten – silver. Plain with a deeply sunk centre and a plain wire edge to the rim. Diameter 9", weight 12 oz. Marks: London Assay for 1774".

A flagon was given to the church in 1794, and was originally a silver domestic hot water jug, dated 1780, with a basketwork handle. Braithwaite writes: *"Flagon – silver – (A secular Jug) is described as jug-shaped (!) plain, with a beaded edge to spout and foot with a wickered handle: it has no cover. Height 10", weight 22 oz, 5 dwts. Marks – London Assay for 1780, probably made by Gabriel Sleeth".* A lid and new handle were added in 1917 by Mr. J. Mills and Mr. E. Quick of Vernham Manor. A copper baptismal ewer, inscribed "The Baptismal Jug of Vernham" stands 16" high next to the octagonal 19th century perpendicular font and is on its own oak stand, which was the gift of Mr. J. Marshall of Vernhams in memory of Noel Marshall (1923).

In 1948 the Vicar complained *"the altar cruets were usable but odd and not worthy of their use"* and the late Colonel Whittingham, of 'Masons', Vernham Dean, said he would defray the cost of new ones to be ready in time for the Christmas Communion. These were unfortunately stolen, and in 1977 cruets were given by Mr. and Mrs. Maurice Bryant in memory of the late Mrs. Bryant, who lived at Church Farm, Fosbury. Again, these have to be kept in safe keeping and modern glass ones are in general use, being removed after each service.

Music

In the PCC Minutes of 1908 there is an entry: *"Mr. Wallis did not wish to serve as churchwarden because he did not like the singing at evening service ...."*. One would wish for more comments like this to lighten a church history. Mr. Wallis would no doubt have been pleased with the new organ installed in 1995. When this organ was serviced in 2006 for the re-opening of the church it was found that mice had had a fine time during the closure, using the circuit diagrams for their nests. The previous single manual organ was purchased in 1967, assisted by a legacy left by Mr. Downing *"a quiet gentleman who lived in Upton"* and this has now been installed in Linkenholt church.

Funds for the new Allen organ were raised by the Friends of the Church (estab. 1982) who with innumerable efforts have raised since their formation magnificent funds towards the needs of the church. The Friends of the Church are a very active group who hold a Christmas Sale each year, have Garage Sales, run series of lectures, organize concerts, quizzes, and have also been responsible for two large-scale 'Village Weekends', the most recent being held in 1995. Their efforts towards raising funds for the 2005 repairs were particularly praiseworthy.

FURNISHINGS – various

There exists in the Hampshire Record Office, dated 1753, a plan of the pews and the people entitled to sit in them, but there is no such formality nowadays. In 1199 chests were ordered to be made and placed in all churches to collect alms for the Crusades, but the current reproduction chest, at the back of the church, was bought with insurance money obtained after the theft of a previous antique chest given by Olive and David Marjoram on leaving the village, as their marriage had been blessed in the church. Many of the kneelers, including those at the altar rail, were the work of Colonel Palmer (d. 1987) who lived at Street Farm House, aided by his step-daughter Ann Broadwood and several other ladies of the parish.

Until quite recently all the candle holders in the nave were at a lower level. However, a photograph (produced by Mrs. E.M. Mills) showing the interior before electricity was available indicated that early in the 20th century the holders were at a much higher level. This being so, they have now been raised, and this has the advantage that they are clear of children's hair, women's hats and bridal veils – a churchwarden relates that he once watched in horror as a bride's veil swept through a flame *"but she was moving so fast it did not catch alight"*. The movable gate at the altar rail (blessed in 1991) was the gift of Robert and Renée Smith (late of this parish) and carved by Peter Middleton in 1990.

The chair behind the altar was a gift from the late Nancy Higginbotham of Vernham Street in the 1980s *"because she liked it"*. It is inscribed "Oak from Trinity Hall, Cambridge, 1872" and has a tapestry cushion. The wrought iron flower stands at each side of the altar were bought with the remainder of Mr. Downing's legacy to the church. The churchwardens' staves were given by Mrs. J. Mills, of Vernham Manor (d.1947) at Easter 1925. The oak Litany desk was the gift of Mrs. Gamble of Rowe House in 1927. (Rowe House was later dismantled.) Her husband, Admiral Gamble (d.1926) gave a lamp post (now lost) and lamp in 1902 and a flag pole for the churchyard in 1921. The offertory plate was donated in memory of Mrs. Helen Pooley, late of "Woodside", Vernham Dean, by Mr. Henry Pooley in 1983. A new stove was installed in 1903 (Tasker's bill was £9.13s.3d., subscriptions £9.7s.6d, the deficit being made up by the then Captain – later Admiral as above – Gamble R.N.) A further but now redundant "Chase" pipeless heater was installed in 1945 at a cost of £187.10s.0d. and electric radiant heaters appeared in 1959 (£76), electricity having arrived in 1946: 10 electric lights were installed at a cost of £25.0s.0d. 2006 saw the appearance of new wall mounted quartz halogen heaters required to conform with health and safety regulations.

The loss of the 1927-45 PCC Minutes means that the ancestry of some artefacts may have been incorrectly recorded, but acknowledgement must be made to the countless people who have contributed church linen over the years, suffice perhaps to mention the green altar frontal and pulpit falls, almsbags and two book markers, the gift of Henry Pooley in memory of his wife, Helen, in 1983.

Recent years

The first months of 1996 saw a campaign to involve all the people of Vernhams Dean in the future of their church. In response, over a third of parishioners offered help in many different ways, this in addition to the teams who already cared for the church and took responsibility for all the activities. Promises of finance quadrupled and the Church Electoral Roll expanded to a number far in excess of the record for many years. A second campaign "Caring about the Future", with a particular emphasis on support to all members of the community, again involved a vast number of parishioners who offered help in varying ways.

Serious cracks were observed in the fabric of the church in November 1995 but after essential shoring the church was re-opened for Christmas 1995. Ten years of fund-raising followed, and with the aid of many generous personal donations and grants from English Heritage and other charitable bodies the monies became available.

In 2005 the church was closed and repairs commenced. The main concern was with the west wall which was no longer vertical, and the consequent racking of the roof. It had been hoped to bring the west wall down to the level of the doorway, grout the remaining wall and underpin with concrete, in stages, to produce the necessary verticality. The wall proved to be far too weak to accept this remedy. It was taken down to the base, then built up again on concrete foundations. The roof work went well, but the extra work required to the wall gave further concern to all involved in fund-raising. The ten years had seen great efforts from the Friends of the Church, the PCC officers concerned with finding grants, and parishioners generally.

The closure of the church and removal of services to the Millennium Hall and Linkenholt has delayed the carrying out of many plans, but the re-opening on Sunday, 29th January, 2006, was the fulfilment of a vision for the future in Vernham Dean.

Acknowledgements

Pevsner & Lloyd "The Buildings of England, Hampshire and the Isle of Wight".

Braithwaite: "Church Plate of Hampshire, 1909".

Mr. Hardacre, Curator, Winchester Cathedral

Mr. Jon Callan (glass)

Hampshire Record Office

Local Studies Section, Winchester Library

Archives of the "Hampshire Chronicle" and the "Andover Advertiser".

Andover Library

The Reverend Michael Harley

The Churchwardens and the inhabitants of Vernhams Dean for help, stories and pictures.

The Women's Institute in the Vernham area was originally inaugurated in April 1933, and catered for women in the Linkenholt, Littledown, Henley, Upton, Oxenwood and Fosbury areas. Being so near the county boundary it inevitably drew in people from both Hampshire and Wiltshire, and the situation is the same today. At the first meeting, 47 members were enrolled, and at each meeting the focus was on business, a talk, a demonstration, entertainment and a competition. By the 18th October membership had increased to 73. There are excellent pictorial records of the WI and the villages generally, dating from 1965, 1977/78 and the 90s. These have proved their usefulness: in 1967, when the case against Eastwood Poultry establishing in the neighbourhood was being prepared, the solicitor asked to borrow the 1965 scrapbook as evidence of the present way of village life and the effect the concern would have on it. The scheme did not come into being.

The first committee was convened on the 4th May 1933, and the scene was set for a considerable number of years. Mrs. Dudley (of Linkenholt Manor) became President and her largesse was advantageous to the Institute, if perhaps the aura of 'Lady of the Manor' may have made membership uncomfortable for some women in the community. She insisted that all her female staff become members. She enabled a Christening mug to be given to each child born to a WI member, ordering the mugs from London. However, a Minute of 14th August 1935 states clearly that members who had not paid their subscriptions would not be eligible for Christening mugs ...... five were presented in 1935. 19th May 1937; ....
Mrs. Dudley promises to pay half all members' fares on the Southsea outing ......

Competition at the June 1933 meeting: .... The best darn in wool 1" square or more.

In true WI style the members quickly began to make their presence felt in the village, and suggested that a woman should be appointed to the Board of Management at the Village School. On the 2nd October Mrs. Dudley was appointed. The WI quickly found itself appointing representatives to several other village organisations, in particular the Village Entertainments committee. Cookery classes were inaugurated, and there was a firm movement to stop the rise of membership cost of the WI from 2/- to 2/6d. By 2007 the cost of yearly membership had risen to £26 for, usually, eleven monthly events.

A Dancing Class must have been held as the Minutes state that only 1/- could be afforded for the use of the piano, not 2/6d. which would mean that the class would have to be discontinued: .... *more than 1/- would be paid when and as it could be afforded* .... and the Men's Club were to be invited to the Christmas Party. These events seem to have been one of the highlights of the winter in the village. They often took the form of a Whist Drive and Dance, with the Vicar as MC for whist and Mr. Hiscock for dancing: ....

Mr. Kingsland's band played and 50 balloons were purchased ...... There was an allowance of 1/- each on two prizes for the Spot Waltz Competition and the Balloon Dance. Events became a little rowdy on occasion and a complaint was minuted in 1938: *.......... the intoxication of some of the guests was dreadful, and the bad language was the worst they (the members) had heard for years ....*

The piano seems to have been a bone of contention for several years and also a source of concern: *......... Miss Gunner very kindly offered to lend two blankets with which to wrap up the piano, which was suffering from cold and damp .....*

From the start the WI mixed education and enjoyment. 1934 sees a competition for the largest number of potatoes from one seed potato and Mrs. Dudley's gardener was to judge. Glove making classes were popular, a demonstration was given on skincuring, cookery classes continued and rug making was demonstrated. A proud comment in 1957: *...... July 15th ......Mrs. Bryant's chemise has been shown at the Royal Show and much admired by the Princess Royal.*

WI March 1940: *First prize for a handsome hearthrug made from an old cloak, the second with sports stockings made from an old pullover. An ankle competition was judged by Dr. Filder and Mr. George Hall who awarded the first prize to Mrs. Matson.*

Transport was minimal in the early days, but meetings were arranged so that members could use what there was, and there were sufficient people from each location for the tasks to be divided between them. The 'Upton' members would do teas one month, the 'Fosbury' section offering the entertainment, with other sections taking over in rotation. As rural transport faded, members were not able to come from such a large area until the car was in general use, but today members again come from a wide catchment area of Hatherden, Tangley, Wildhern, Hurstbourne Tarrant, Stoke and St. Mary Bourne.

It was amusing to note the register of the Institute: members were placed in alphabetical order, but the married women were ranged first, and the spinsters second. Indeed, it was not until the 1990s that an unorthodox secretary instigated the use of 'Jane Smith' rather than 'Mrs. Smith'.

The war disrupted regular meetings of the Institute, but in 1942 Minutes begin to record the activities of Nancy Higginbotham whose influence in the WI must have matched that of Mrs. Dudley. Nancy took over as Treasurer in 1942. The war made it impossible to arrange programmes in advance, although Mrs. Dudley had carried on with her glove-making classes by which she hoped to create a village industry. However, on 31st December 1943 in spite of good advice from an official from WI Head Office, it was decided to suspend meetings until April .... and in 1944 Mrs. Dudley decided she could not carry on because of the difficulties generated by the war, and in any case could not combine the duties of President and Secretary. Unless a Secretary were found, the Institute must be closed or suspended. It was decided to suspend until a Secretary could be found, and the Books and Funds were sent to County Office for safe keeping.

The phoenix rose again on the 20th November 1946, with Nancy Higginbotham as Treasurer, Miss James as Secretary, and Mrs. Dudley still in place as President. Transport was a problem, a charabanc had been arranged for outlying members. The cost was £2.10s.0d. per night, with only 16/6d. collected from the users. Transport had always been a concern for rural women and in 1947 representations were made to the Dorset and Wilts company to send the Newbury bus every Thursday through Linkenholt, Vernham Dean and Oxenwood. Success – nil.

At the end of 1947 membership stood at 70. In the 1940s it was customary for members to bring cakes for the tea interval. Some members omitted this duty, and a member of the committee was delegated to stand at the door and charge 3d. to all members who did not bring cakes. This move was extremely unpopular and in 1949 it was decided to charge 4d. and the cakes and buns would be bought. The Secretary was to apply for a licence to obtain tea, milk and sugar, and to ask Mr. Evans and Mr. Edgington (local shops and bakery) for four dozen cakes and buns. A licence was eventually obtained for tea, sugar, butter and milk. Members had to pay 2d. for each cake and 1d. for a cup of tea. By 1951 the price of cakes had risen again and Mr. Edgington was asked for the price of buns and a few biscuits which were to take the place of some of the pastries. Membership money was again in contention as the committee wished to raise the membership charge from 2/6d. to 3/- per annum, which was more than the normal fee, in order to ease the burden of the cost of the bus to bring members to meetings. It was ruled out of order for all members to pay the extra, only bus-users were to pay the extra shilling, the deficit to be made up out of Institute funds.

The Institute had always been very active in fund-raising and apart from Whist Drives and Dances had regular sales of work and allied efforts. Money-conscious as always, the cost of the hire of the school for committee meetings was more than the 3/6d. the Institute was willing to pay, and in 1951 it was decided to meet in members' houses, a practice which continues to the present day. The bus which brought members to meetings was proving a heavy drain on finances and members had to content themselves with the service bus, taxi and private cars. By 1953 ……. the buses were no longer helpful …… but individual initiative must have had great success. A Minute of the 13th November states: ….. *Mrs. Hill congratulated Mrs. Mason on her hard work in getting 30 people to come from Oxenwood ………* almost the entire population, one would have thought. Petrol rationing in 1957 threw another spanner in the works – it proved impossible to arrange transport to and from Linkenholt and Oxenwood, but when the situation eased representatives would again be co-opted from Linkenholt and Oxenwood. By 1958 a dormobile was being used for Linkenholt and Vernham Street members.

A few snippets picked up from here and there:

27th August 1948: *RE-DECORATING THE VILLAGE HALL*

The Village Hall is now being re-decorated at an estimated cost of £90. This is the first time any such work has been carried out since the hall was built. The inside will be painted in an attractive colour scheme of cream and chocolate. In order to meet the cost an appeal for donations has been made, and a contribution has been promised from the Hampshire Education Authorities who, during the war, used the hall as a school and now in connection with the school dinners. The Sports Club and Women's Institute have each given £10 towards the cost. The work is expected to be finished early in September. The Trustees are also hoping to renew all the curtains, as it is felt the present ones would look out of place when everything else is so spick and span.

8th October 1948: *BRING AND BUY SALE*

Organised by the Vernham Dean and Linkenholt WI in aid of the grant which they have made towards the cost of redecorating the Village Hall, a bring and buy stall was held on Wednesday week in the Village Hall. Tea, which was very welcome to those who had travelled from a distance, was served almost immediately after the opening of the sale. Mrs. R. Dudley was present, and Mr. R.P. Smith (Headmaster of Chute Forest School) gave a very interesting talk on Approved Schools and exhibited several articles which had been made by boys of his school. He made a contrast between Approved Schools past and present, pointing out the many improvements which were now prevalent in such schools. Mr. Smith also said that Chute Forest School was open to visitors and invited his hearers to inspect it whenever they wished. A vote of thanks was passed to Mr. Smith for his talk. Members of the Dramatic Section of Bedwyn WI provided a play, entitled 'For Amusement Only' and Mrs. Stokes (hon. sec. of the Dramatic Section of Bedwyn WI) and members gave recitations and songs, all of which were well received. Thanks were later expressed to the Bedwyn WI members for the entertainment they gave. Altogether about £13 was taken during the evening.

1949 saw Mrs. Dudley's final resignation and on the 21st December Nancy Higginbotham was elected President and remained an influential character during her whole time in Vernham Dean. Sadly, Nancy died in 1994 and has been much missed by her wide circle of friends. Her parting comment to some friends: *'If I'm still alive next week for goodness' sake shoot me ……'* was typical of her humorous attitude to life.

In the 1950s there was considerable concern about sanitation at the school and there was correspondence with the Ministry of Health. It would seem that all was not sweetness and light in the Institute either because:

10th April 1953: …… *it was suggested that members be asked to stop talking after the Speaker had finished at the monthly meeting while the Vote of Thanks is proposed….*

12th May: ……….. *it was requested that members should again be asked to keep silence during demonstrations or talks except for addressing the Chair ……….*

(15th February 1965: …. *A suggestion has been received that members should refrain from talking during a talk or demonstration.* 12th September 1966: …….. *members should be asked to keep quiet and pay more attention to what is going on at meetings …..)*

A regional competition of particular importance to Vernham Dean is the Silver Bell Trophy. A Miss Darling presented the local group of institutes with a Silver Bell as a prize. In 1950 the Institute won the trophy with their cakes, and has had notable success in many years since.

Research in both the Parish Council Minutes and the WI records produces an amusingly different outlook on a happening in 1951. A letter from the Andover Rural District Council asks whether the WI could undertake the manning of a Welfare Centre in Vernham Dean. This was in respect of a provisional arrangement for evacuees in case of necessity and involved a survey of available accommodation in the area. The Institute decided it could not be responsible for canvassing, but two volunteers would join the Reception Committee which was in process of formation. They begged to point out to the RDC that although the WI had 40 members they came from four different parishes, and the numbers from Vernham Dean itself were relatively small and therefore it was difficult to arrange for sufficient support. A blistering Parish Council Minute records: ….. *that as certain members of the Institute are willing to serve on the Reception Committee they should also be willing to take their share in the necessary canvassing of the available accommodation in the Parish, and that failing this they would scarcely be eligible or in possession of the necessary knowledge vital to the Reception Committee ……*

Age-old disputes raise their ugly heads. 17th February 1954: ….. *the Press Correspondent raised the question as to whether another member was doing press reports besides herself, as the reports in the Press were entirely different to those she sent in …….* The Village Correspondent in the 1990s, a WI member, found herself asking the Andover Advertiser just how it was possible to mis-spell all three names which had been submitted in typed format. (pre E-mail days).

In 1995 the WI resurrected their Flower and Vegetable Show which had lapsed after a successful run of several years. The Playing Field Association's Fete tended to dominate summer events and although the WI played a considerable part in the early years this gradually diminished and the Institute concentrated on other affairs. When the playing fields were being created on the Bury Dene, members contributed to no small extent with the necessary work, and it looks as if the Institute was somewhat 'miffed' at no mention of the WI's contributions being made in the Press. It is, however, thanks to their share of Fete proceeds that the WI were able to buy some good WI china for their own use at a price of £74.95. In the late 90s the WI again provided the refreshments for the Fete, glorying in the kitchen accommodation in the resplendent new Pavilion.

The Drama Group seems to have been an integral part of the WI until, perhaps, the village Theatre Group was established and developed into today's first class organisation with productions each year and success in regional drama competitions. The WI entered a float in the Andover Carnival in 1971 but decided against it in 1972. Their own Drama Group was still effective in 1973 when a team won the Silver Bell for their production. The Jubilee celebrations of 1978 were an event of terrific moment in the village. A Jubilee committee was formed, with two representatives from each village organisation and a Jubilee scrapbook was made. One of the aims of the celebrations was to provide a hard core play area on the playing fields, and movement towards a tennis court. Notes during this year reveal that there was a Parents' Association and also a Youth Club in the village at this time, and during the year there was glory for the Institute when they again won the Silver Bell trophy, this time with savoury dishes.

1983 was a landmark in the history of the Institute as it held its 50th birthday party. This was the year of the creation of the current tablecloth, a magnificent piece of work designed by Elizabeth Holmes and worked on by a number of members whose names are embroidered around the hem. It was finished for the Christmas Party in December. The previous tablecloth, mooted in October 1954, had been made by Mrs. Napthine and embroidered by Mrs. Strange.

1985 offered another opportunity for community sewing: the 'Test Valley Tapestry' and again Elizabeth Holmes, together with Renée Smith went to see Councillor Porter to set the scheme in motion. Laurie Porter did not live to see the end of this ambitious idea, but in 1995, ten years after its inauguration, the tapestry was completed and displayed proudly in the Council Offices. These 19 panels are a testimony to the complex history, beautiful landscape and domestic life of the Test Valley. People from the United Benefice of Vernham Dean and Linkenholt, Hurstbourne Tarrant and Faccombe with Upton all worked on the panel which is displayed in large photographic format both in the Millennium Hall and in The George.

Today the Institute in Vernham Dean still performs a very valuable service for a mixed group of women from the surrounding area. An Exhibition in 1989 as part of a 'Village Weekend' showed an amazing variety of craft work, much contributed by members, and although craft demonstrations at meetings do not play as prominent a part as in previous years, there is an important Sewing Group in the area. WI members can also take full advantage of a variety of classes offered at county level and at the WI's own college, Denman, near Oxford. In 1995 a Book Circle was started, with members meeting on an irregular basis to share suggestions for reading with help, twice a year, from Jim Douglas of Waterstones' bookshop in Andover, who brings along a vast selection of the latest books to whet members' appetites, and also hosts an evening in the shop from time to time when members can browse – and purchase – to their hearts' content. Also in 1995 ten members took advantage of computer classes at IBM headquarters, a far cry from the glove-making of 1933 but as relevant to today's women as glove making was then. Computer classes were later established in the Millennium Hall and proved extremely popular with the village in general. In 1999 members heard the experiences of their home-grown Mayor and Mayoress, Tony and Andrea Jackson: they also learned Line Dancing, studied Hampshire Pub Signs with Greg Gregory, were cajoled into more recycling, were initiated into Feng Shui, relaxed with Mr. Atkinson on 'Fashion and the House of Dior' and changed course with a Tasting, Touching and Looking Quiz with the Revd J. Bentall; went on outings, entered competitions, had numerous raffles and coffee mornings, culminating in a Christmas Party. The 2006 programme welcomed Brendan and Frankie Rose for their talk on their world trip and the work done by Brendan's son during the Boxing Day 2004 tsunami. Members heard about rallying for women, the Fair Trade movement, Eating and Feeling Well, went to Salisbury and explored the Close and the town, had a wonderful presentation from Andover MIND, visited the Poppy Factory, listened to a talk about Naomi House and celebrated Harvest with Mr. Jordan, who insisted on audience participation in all his songs. And yes, members do still sing 'Jerusalem' – sometimes, if there is anyone who can play the piano - and they make jam, but jam and pickles sell well for funds to enable members to enlarge their horizons, attend courses, fulfil ambitions and enable them to be:

TODAY'S WOMEN WORKING FOR TOMORROW'S WORLD.

It was on the 5th July 1899 that the Parish Council Minutes first mention the railway. There was unanimous decision that the proposed Light Railway 'is the great need of the District.' The Council considered a bridge should be erected over Road 24 on the plan (Fosbury Road) and they were to ask the Company to give them a station near the centre of the village, by Botes Lane (No: 21 on plan) and ask the Authorities at Winchester College to support the wishes of the Council. This station would have been in the field alongside Botes Lane, going up the side of 'Underwood' which has narrowly escaped being named 'Railway Cottages'.

From work done at the Hampshire Record Office on (then) uncatalogued papers from Winchester College letters have been unearthed from Vernham Dean residents to Mr. Thomas F. Kirby, onetime bursar at the College.

7th December 1882: letter from Criswick Child to Mr. Kirby: *"The enclosed requisition has been sent to me to forward on to you asking for the College supported signature. Should it succeed it will wonderfully enhance and improve the College property. I am not waiting for the College support before signing it myself and passing it on for the signature of the other more local landowners who I know are not only ready but wanting to help us all they can and offer their land free, where the proposed line runs over."*

10th March 1883: Mr. Child again to Mr. Kirby: *"Now again forward you our railway requisition, thinking as you will now see all the other College bodies in our neighbourhood are willing and pleased to sign it – and aid the project all they can – and from the chat we had about it when you were here I thought from what I explained you would then be willing to do so. Broad Acres in such a case gives weight so I'll forward it asking if you will now attach the College seal or your name on behalf of the College and so to add your approval to our scheme. If carried out it must greatly improve all property in the neighbourhood of the line and give a great convenience to this now isolated part of railway accommodation."*

Light Railway Commissioners – Session 1899. Light Railways Act, 1896. Bourne Valley Light Railway: Notice is hereby given that application is intended to be made in the present month of May 1899 to the Light Railway Commissioners … … to authorise the Promoters to make and maintain a railway in the County of Southampton, to be worked and maintained as a light railway, with all necessary and proper stations, approaches, works, buildings, sidings, and conveniences connected therewith respectively, that is to say:-

Railway No: 1, commencing in the parish of Whitchurch, in the County of Southampton, by a junction with the Didcot, Newbury and Southampton Railway, at a point thereon about 60 yards north of the centre of the bridge, carrying the London and South Western Railway over the said Didcot, Newbury, and Southampton Railway at or near the Whitchurch Station of the London and South Western Railway Company, and passing thence through and along or near to the towns, villages and places of Whitchurch, St. Mary Bourne, Stoke, Hurstbourne Tarrant, Ibthorpe, Upton and Vernhams Dean, and terminating in the parish of Vernhams Dean at a point about 110 yards eastward of the junction of the public road leading from Vernhams Row to Fosbury, with the main public road leading from Vernhams Dean to Fosbury, close to the northern corner of Oakhill Wood .... it is intended to construct the before-mentioned railways on a gauge of 4 feet 8 1/2 inches, and the motive power to be used will be steam, electrical, or any mechanical power .... the quantity of land proposed to be taken for the purposes of the before-mentioned railways and works will be 76 acres, or thereabouts, chiefly consisting of pasture, arable, or other land used principally for agricultural purposes. It is also intended to take in connection with the before-mentioned railways certain common or commonable land of about one acre in extent, known as Upton Common or waste land situate near the village of Upton.

Andover Advertiser, 23rd June 1899:

Report on Andover RDC: The Bourne Valley Light Railway ..... the crossing at Vernham Dean, plan 24 cross section No: 17: the company will undertake to carry the railway over the road or reduce the road gradient to 1 in 40. Major Turtle moved an amendment that the road to Vernham Dean be bridged .... and on a later page a mention is made of a bridge to be built at Fosbury Road in connection with the Bourne Valley Light Railway.

17th November 1899: *An application has been made to construct a Light Railway – 12 miles in length from the Didcot, Newbury and Southampton Railway: near Whitchurch, up the Bourne Valley to the County Boundary near Vernham Dean.*

But .... although a Light Railway Order was received, authorising construction, nothing happened as no money could be raised. In 1906 it was resolved to write to the Great Western Railway to consider the question of instituting a motor service through the Bourne Valley, and the Parish Council asked Hurstbourne to support this. On the 12th March the council reported that as soon as the G.W.R. had cars available they would endeavour to extend services to this district. But on the 9th June 1908 a letter is recorded from the Hurstbourne Tarrant Parish Council that the G.W.R. Co. could not see their way clear to institute a motor service through the Bourne Valley ... ...

Some years later Messrs. Pullen & Sayers explained the proposed HIPPENSCOMBE CONSUMPTIVE SANATORIUM and the necessity of a light railway to improve the communications to it:

Parish Council Meeting held 7th December 1910: *"There was a very good attendance including several ladies and the Chairman explained to the meeting that its object was to support the application for a light railway up the Bourne Valley. He explained the advantage which would be gained by it and stated that a petition would be laid on the table and those in favour would be requested to sign it. It was also proposed that a consumptive sanatorium be constructed at Hippenscombe and the necessity of a light railway to improve communications to it. A lively discussion then took place".*

Vernham Mills related: *"Two gents in frocktail coats and top hats came down from London with the idea of farm property at Hippenscombe and turning it into a Sanatorium for very rich people to bring their children with tuberculosis. The country air and sunshine would change their white faces into rosy-looking children and cure the tuberculosis. The meeting was held in Vernham School. The two Londoners told a very full meeting what a splendid thing it would be for the local inhabitants. They said that the local people could be shareholders if they would send them some money to buy the farm and start the proposition going. Members of the audience asked how the parents of the children would get from Hurstbourne Priors Station to visit their children. Their reply was it would be difficult at first, but as soon as they could get about a dozen children they were sure the parents, seeing how well their sons and daughters had improved in health, would be pleased to invest large sums of money to build a railway from Hurstbourne Station to the Sanatorium. This would encourage more people to send their children, also the railway would be a great asset to Vernham Dean as it could also be used to bring many amenities to the village and also take back farmers' corn, hay, straw, instead of as now having to send it down with horse-drawn wagons. Some of the farmers said they would lend two or three hundred pounds as they thought it was such a good idea. The meeting closed with the Londoners returning in a week's time, hoping many more would lend enough money for them to start. There was great discussion in the village in the next week. Mr. John Mills* (Vernham's father) *thought the two Londoners were sharpers, and at the next week's meeting he intended to ask them how much money they were putting into the scheme. He went and saw his friends who had promised to put money into it. He told them not to part with any money until they had more time to find out about the Londoners. At the next meeting the two came with great hopes that a lot of money would be forthcoming. Mr. Mills asked them how much money they were putting into the scheme. They replied that as they were ...."* Vernham never finished this story, but it would seem that John Mills' fears were well-founded, as the scheme for the sanatorium went no further, and neither did the railway.

Further entries from the PC Minutes:

1914: *"Mr. Quick to wait on Sir W. Portal with a view to securing better services at Hurstbourne Station. As soon as the memorial is received from Rev. Arrowsmith re approaching the railway authorities a meeting to be called. This was considered excellent, and Rev. Arrowsmith to be thanked." ………….. And in 1919: "It was agreed to mention the light railway question at the next meeting."*

7th May: *"It was agreed that Hurstbourne Tarrant, Shalbourne and St. Mary Bourne Parish Councils be asked to support Vernham Dean Parish Council in asking the Ministry of Transport to install a light railway running from Hurstbourne Station to Grafton."*

BUT NOTHING HAPPENED.

Let's start by coming along the Upton Road to Vernham, at Ankers Lane, opposite the Bury Dean. Just after the junction there used to be a cottage, long gone: the well was used to supply the school before mains water arrived. Next is a modern bungalow, divided by a field from a more substantial building – Poplars, possibly late 18th century, two storeys, flint with brick dressings, colour-washed white, a ridge thatched roof brought down as pentice to the right; there is a modern extension to the rear. Poplars used to be a small farm (previously called Parsonage Farm according to the Tithe Map) and a contributor, Mrs. Broadhead, tells: *"my father* (Edward Piper) *rented it in 1900 and left in 1915. I remember horses used for transporting the vans in London went down to Poplars for a rest. They travelled in horse boxes on the railway from London and could be taken off at Andover, Hungerford or Newbury and then driven to Vernham. My father had three nurseries round London and always exhibited at the Chelsea Flower Show and won lots of gold and silver cups. Father had shooting parties at Poplars."* She also remembers that there used to be a long whitewashed thatched wall along the frontage. Much is still intact, capped with tile, instead of thatched, and continuing in front of the next modern bungalow, built on land previously part of Poplars Farm. Mrs. Broadhead recalled with glee riding bicycles with her brothers through the pond – a delight reserved for the last day of the holidays because the punishment for a muddy riot was confiscation of the bicycles.

The Hughes family later farmed at Poplars and possessed an ex-Army mule, who used to react in horrendous fashion when dried blood fertiliser was used. He obviously remembered all too well the horrors of WW1. Kept in a field at the back of "Deer's Leap" a bone protruded from his neck and local children used to take hold of it, much to his distress.

After the modern bungalow is a row of cottages, formerly three, now converted into two. Originally early 19th century, Sheila and Ivor Thomas's bed and breakfast 'Upton Cottage' along with 'Ann's Cottage' to the right suffered a disastrous fire on the 14th February1995, but was rebuilt in modernised but appropriate fashion. There is a modern 'granny annexe' to the rear of Upton Cottage. Eric Levell (now sadly deceased), was horrified to hear about the fire at his ancestors' house. He explained that at the latter end of the 19th century his great grandfather, Samuel Smith, owned the rank of cottages – there were three dwellings at that time. He lived in the middle cottage. Around 1890, his son (Eric Levell's grandfather), George Smith, moved into the cottage furthest from the pond with his bride, Hester. They set up in business as baker and shopkeeper. There was a big bread oven at the back of the house in a 'lean to' extension. The bavins for the ovens came from woods at the back of Poplars. George Smith also baked pies for the Slate Club which functioned in The George – kept prior to the 1914-18 war by Eric's great-uncle and aunt, Mr. and Mrs. W. Farmer. On Bank Holidays George would provide all the bread, cakes and hot cross buns for Good Friday and cook the food for the Club Dinner: roast beef and fruit pies. This important village occasion took place in the big barn which used to stand in front and to the left side of the current pub car park. (Taken down c.1929). This barn also served as a carpenter's shop, for Mr. Farmer was a wheelwright. Enid Brooks, writing in the parish magazine in 1968, remembers many a coffin being made in the old barn. Mr. Farmer left to run a carpenter's shop in Marten, but came back to live in the middle cottage, setting up a workshop behind Eric's grandfather's house. His further claim to fame was that he was a wart-charmer. A famous tale relates how he attempted to charm away the warts of a somewhat highborn lady, assuming she had told him where all her warts were. Later she complained he had not done the job: *"Well, did you tell me where all your warts were?"* She had to admit to one in a rather delicate place, after which the charm worked.

In the early years of the 20th century smallpox came to the cottage. Friends George and Hester had met in London came to stay with their young baby, who developed smallpox. Gran caught it and became seriously ill, although grandfather only produced one spot in the centre of his forehead. As usual at that time, Gran was taken and left to fend for herself in a tent out on Andover Down. 'Uncle Will' was a babe in arms and went with her. It was winter time. There was no contact. Food was left at the gate and Gran collected it. She recovered, but was sadly disfigured. Back at home all their possessions were burned in case of infection and although flour and one guinea were offered, Grandfather would not start up the bakery again. He died in 1942, and all his life had a fear of fire, particularly during a thunderstorm.

Eric Levell mentioned that after the death of great-grandfather, Georgey Goodman had the middle cottage, a gentleman somewhat taken to drink which further increased Grandfather's fear of fire, imagining careless goings-on. Eric's aunt and uncle were the Staceys, who lived in the cottage on the right with their numerous offspring. They kept a small shop in the 1930s, continuing into the 40s and 50s. The Americans from Tidworth liked it because 'Auntie' gave them cups of tea. The name 'Ann's Cottage' was apparently named after Ann Hewat, by her husband, Tim. The Hewats moved in after the Staceys.

Pond Cottage comes next – much altered and restored, a rear extension appearing in 2005. Initially it was a two storied, colour-washed brick and timber-framed structure, thatched roof, probably 16th century. The non-matching extension with weatherboard facing was added in 1978, planning permission being granted because there had been another semi-detached cottage to the right, destroyed long ago by fire. There is a tale that originally this line of cottages between the pond and the modern bungalow were called 'The Six Cottages' but living memory cannot substantiate this. Five, at least, but there was always a lane between 'Ann's Cottage' and 'Pond Cottage'.

Behind Pond Cottage is a modern bungalow built on land formerly belonging to Beeches Farm. Beeches itself has a prominent position at the back of the pond and was previously somewhat larger, now a one family dwelling. It is apparently 18th century, two storeys plastered facades masking earlier timber-framed structure – thatched roof to the front, slate to the rear, wood casements. It has (or had) a large brick oven in the kitchen, and was once a doctor's surgery with the kitchen table serving as an operating table. In the 1920s Mr. J. Bulpit farmed at Beeches, doing a milk round either on foot or with a bicycle with two large cans, and 1/2 pt and 1 pt measures to dip out. He also supplied butter and cream to order.

The 'pond' is a pond no longer. Nowadays the only source of water is a storm rush down Bulpits Hill or a direct rainstorm. It would have been fed with water off the fields, but the increasing use of chemicals turned it into a species of morass. Originally a dew pond, it was of considerable value for watering livestock.

Mr. Tony Vincent, a resident of the village, relates that apparently a soakaway pipe was placed in the centre of the pond to keep the water level from rising too high and flooding nearby houses, but the project misfired and the pond drained away, never to recover again. The remaining grassy meadow is a welcome venue for communal picnics and theatrical performances by the village Theatre Group.

The village pump had a prominent position close to the pond, now covered by a concrete slab, surplus to requirements with the introduction of mains water and the sealing of the village wells. The village well was a favourite gathering place for villagers and the one time hut over the pump was a useful depositary for bicycles owned by people coming to Vernham from the surrounding villages such as Fosbury.

A drinking fountain can be seen just outside Pond Cottage, similar to the one outside the church which is used regularly by the church flower ladies. Both are examples of the Victorian foundryman's art, water being discharged from the mouth of the lion's head. They have fluted iron operating knobs. The pump at Pond Cottage is in need of repair; its pillar is embossed 'Glenfield & Kennedy Ltd, Kilmarnock'.

To the right of the pond lies Vernham House, previously 'The Firs' There is a picture which shows it earlier facing the pond, but nowadays a hedge hides the façade from prying eyes and access is gained from the rear side.

On land formerly belonging to Vernham House is the chapel whose history is amply covered elsewhere, the original building being replaced in the 1960s, and now used regularly during the week by 'Little Fingers', a pre-school group.

The last group of bungalows is the modern 'Botisdone Close' the name a remarkable attempt to commemorate Botes Down, the area up the hill from the Close. There will be more on modern developments in the village later.

The final house on the left towards Conholt Hill is Underwood House, originally built by a Mr. Evans (of the shop and Post Office in the early years of the 20th century) now much extended to form a substantial dwelling in keeping with the original structure.

To the right of the house Botes Lane leads up to the down, with Botes Copse on the right and Thornycombe (or Dardycombe) to the left, previously offering the site for the village refuse dump before collection was introduced.

The main road goes past Sargents Farm to a junction where the road to Conholt meets the parish and county boundary at Woodside – old name Goudyses Gate – an ancient boundary point where the roads to Conholt and Hippenscombe enter Wiltshire. Mentioned in a perambulation of AD 1410 the site used to hold the 'New Inn' and the original doorway can still be made out on the frontage of the two semi-detached dwellings, with a path up to the right leading up the hill to Knollys Down, popularly called the fort. Another pair of cottages to the right of the previous New Inn have been amalgamated to form one house and a smaller cottage to the right has long gone, although it used to house Italian prisoners towards the end of WWII.

Returning now towards Vernham Dean, Sargents Farm (early 19th century) has always been a substantial edifice with a considerable amount of land. Originally two storeys, flint rubble with bands of red brick dressings, low pitched slate roof and wide spreading eaves with plain wood casements, the front door to the road, which had a flat projecting roof on cut brackets was replaced by a window and access is now round the back through a utility area and the kitchen. Through the original back door a grey lady was seen coming into the house, and indeed before the door was replaced by a window the door had a mysterious habit of opening itself. Sargents Farm figures in the years of the 'Swing Riots' and the tale is told in another chapter.

Farmland, some of it sown with a superb display of wild flowers, separates Sargents Farm from West Dene to the east: two storeys, colour washed flint and brick, much altered and extended but with original features retained. In February 1940 there was a rapid thaw, and old Mrs. Newport had to be carried to Edgington House as West Dene flooded.

Ashton Cottage in Back Lane follows (previously two cottages), two storeyed, thatched, an extended dwelling. Next door is a series of three cottages – now two dwellings: 'Yew Cottage' and 'The Cottage'. Previously thatched, these cottages were the site of yet another serious fire in the village, and another house where the kitchen table was used for the doctor's operations. Appropriately enough the cottages also housed undertakers. It was additionally used as a slaughterhouse. One can only hope the various activities were not concurrent.

'Allways' was, according to one source, a barn. It has been much altered with varying degrees of sympathy. At one time the village carter, Mr. Hounslow, lived here, and carried out errands to Andover. It is constructed of brick, with some hanging tiles to the frontage.

'Meadow Cottage' offers a much more comfortable 'village' feel. It consists of two storeys, of flint and brick structure, thatched at the front and slated to the rear, the core of the building is timber-framed with an internal supporting post, an old ship's timber, dated 1686. It is unusual to find such a timber, especially so far inland. Often they are just re-used timbers, but it is particularly interesting that this one is dated. The cottage has wood casements with square panes under segmental brick lintels. It was once three cottages, and has two inglenook fireplaces.

Next to Meadow Cottage is the first modern development in the village: 'The Dell' dating from 1968, with the 'New Dell' leading off at right angles half way up. For many years this land was used for fetes, camp meetings and fairs, but was eventually sold by Mr. Lance Brooks for development.

Great was the controversy about development in the village: the population had sunk to just over 300 and there was a move afoot to introduce new housing, initially substantial houses such as The Dell, and later smaller houses which appear in Shepherd's Rise. In 1979 there was a particularly strong protest against the twelve houses which now form the New Dell – there was a large attendance at a parish meeting objecting to the density of 6.4 houses per acre, compared with the 4.1 of the 'old' Dell. There were fears that the village would turn into a red brick suburb of Andover. It would seem local fears were overridden. Although The Dell and Haydown Leas were later pronounced satisfactory, many considered that the houses in Shepherd's Rise were not in keeping. It was admitted that the school needed an influx to keep it viable, but nevertheless there was much anxiety in the village. Botisdone Close was also criticised but all in all the new developments brought the population up to c. 555 and a viable community was maintained.

Next to No: 1 The Dell, on the old 'Back Lane' is Cheyney Cottage, sometimes called 'Chapel Cottage', a two storeyed thatched dwelling of flint and brick on whose forecourt sits the whitewashed previous Primitive Methodist Chapel, rendered brick with grey slate roof. 'Hidden Hampshire' (1959) says: *A less happy instance of ecclesiastical neighbourliness concerns the Primitive Methodist Chapel of 1869 which was built right in front of and within a few feet of the 17th century (?) Cheyney Cottage, almost completely obscuring the view.* Incidentally, the land was given by the then Cheyney Cottage owner who must have had other than purely practical thoughts on his mind. The perambulant minister apparently used to doss down in a shed to the left of the cottage.

'Long Thatch' is, as may be expected, a lengthy thatched building, previously called 'Thatchways' which glories in a small door at the right hand side which was for the use of the sheep. Stories abound about Thatchways: the carriers did a good trade in the winter months conveying the rabbits from the catches of poachers, of whom there were plenty. There was an ever open window at Thatchways where they used to dump their hordes at all hours of the night. Incidentally, a newspaper article of 1966 written by Tim Hewat notes: *"Vernham Dean had enjoyed for years the reputation with officialdom for bad character. It was not for nothing that 50, 60 and 70 years ago the country's toughest policemen were posted here. In those days, the village produced the valley's champion wrestlers, and wrestling was a rough old sport, as the local curate reported at the time: they fought bare-headed, with the left arm fastened to the waist so they might not use it to ward off blows. To hit an opponent on the face was against the rules, but to hit him on the top of the head was the grand point, and the grandest of all to hit him so as to produce blood"*.

'Vine Cottage' lies to the right of Long Thatch, and was previously a small farm. In contrast to Vernham House, the original entrance was to the rear but a front entrance was subsequently made to face the road. Brick and flint, two storeyed. Many years ago Fred Sims mended shoes here, in a small shed adjoining.

'Masons' was another of the village pubs, and figures frequently in the annals of the village. As with many village inns, the beer was made on the premises and it still retains the original malt kiln, now incorporated in a living room. Constructed of brick, tiled, two storeys, it has been much enlarged and modernised.

'Apple Thatch', facing the pond, was formerly three cottages, now one, the core of the building timber-framed. Two storeyed, thatched, of brick and flint construction. Annie Hayes used to have a shop in the right hand cottage with the entrance up the lane. The photograph shows her standing in the doorway. The inscription read 'Frank Hayes Grocer, Provisions, Licensed to Sell Tobacco'. The poster in the window depicts Fry's Breakfast Cocoa and a plaque on the wall 'Remember the Good Tea – Brooke Bond '. A later resident, Joan Linnell Burton, is pictured at a much later date in similar stance. Annie Hayes's husband Frank was a carrier, first with horses and carts, then a bus with rails around the top. Frank had a reputation for taking a drop too much, but the horse always brought him home. Bruce Seward, former villager, remembered one occasion when he saw the bus coming up the Bury Dean with the engine red hot. Frank's sons were Bert and Fred. Bruce related the story of Bert jumping up to get the luggage from the top of the bus and losing a finger with his signet ring.

At one time Apple Thatch was a hostel for boys working at Horns Farm under the auspices of Dr. Fagan's Charity, a concern which cared for orphaned or destitute boys, with links to Canada.

Up the side of Apple Thatch is 'Dean Cottage' (House), a two storeyed timber framed building with brick and plaster infilling, part brick and flint. A timber framed weatherboarded barn has been converted for office use, and recent years have seen much general renovation. The large garden was in former times the site of yet another two dwellings.

The preceding 'tour' has omitted the section between Back Lane and the current main road. On Jon Fairbrother's map dated 1776 (qv) there were no buildings in this area, probably due to the fact that the bourne, or intermittent stream, used to flow in ancient times through Vernham, crossing the fields from Woodside to the double bend of Vernham Row, through the back gardens of the now existing houses and thence into the pond, down the road, across the Bury Dene and on to Upton. The area is now fully built up with houses of considerable interest and it would be appropriate to start with 'The Nook' to be seen at the left as you approach the village from Conholt. Currently occupied by an architect, it is not surprising to find its history has been meticulously detailed by David Holmes, to whom thanks are due:

'This cottage is for the most part built of puddled chalk and straw, which has been generally rendered (although there is an unrendered section of wall on the west elevation) and painted. The south wall is modern unpainted brickwork and in all probability dates from the re-roofing (see below). There is one original brickwork crosswall that incorporates two flues. It is one of only two remaining houses in the village that are built of chalk. The other is David's Cottage. In the 1930s chalk houses of this type were commonly thought to harbour diseases and there were grants available for their demolition. It is difficult to date the building, but it is probably in the order of three or four hundred years old.

'The roof is of interlocking concrete tiles on a replacement timber framing that dates back approximately 50 years, when the original thatched roof was replaced.

'As late as 1978 the building was divided in half with a two storey barn at the south end and a pair of cottages (one up, one down) that had been amalgamated to form one dwelling at the north end. In 1978 an extensive refurbishment took place in which all of the building was made into a single dwelling, with five windows added as necessary to suit the new plan and modern facilities provided. The porch on the west side dates from those works. The form of the original building was preserved in the 1978 remodelling and the position of the original animal and cart entry to the barn can be seen at the long west facing window, with its gently arched head.

'Until 1977 the house was occupied by the baker employed in the adjacent bakery (now Edgington House) and The Nook had been in the ownership of the owners of the bakery building for at least two hundred years previously, when the road now called Back Lane was the main road through the village and was known as Lower Dell road. What is now the main road was Upper Dell Road.

'The name 'Nook' derives from the Saxon 'n'oeik' meaning 'house on the corner or bend' which is the case here. The building is listed Grade 2'.

As with Vernham House, the main entrance is to the back, and the front one unused – the story goes that a piece of land between The Nook and West Dene was more or less shared between the owners – when one had money he bought it from the other and vice versa. This arrangement must have broken down at one stage for now some of The Nook's original garden belongs to Edgington House and the main garden is to the former rear.

To the right of The Nook is the afore-mentioned Edgington House, whose deeds are known to go back to 1740; this former shop and bakery even boasted a petrol pump. Pictures show the Edgington family who ran the shop – Bert Edgington is to the left. The façade, now the living room, shows the shop area.

Next comes 'The Lodge' at one time used as a Post Office which closed in 1920. This house has been variously extended.

'Myrtle Cottage' – 1926, a much extended dwelling. One claim to fame has been unearthed, it used to house petrol pumps before more modern facilities were established at 'Edgingtons'.

'David's Cottage' is, as mentioned above, one of the two chalk built cottages in the village. Two storeyed, pink washed flint and brick structure, with thatched roof. Square cut around two upper windows, four modern casements and a modern light timber porch.

'The Old Forge' – working until at least 1940. (Entrance from Back Lane) Enid Brooks remembered three people employed there – two storeys, a whitewashed flint and brick structure, partly thatched brought down as a pentice forming a porch entrance, modern additions with a tiled roof. Some of the original chalk wall has been retained, requiring great care to avoid it being dried out.

A small lane divides The Old Forge from a set of buildings which now comprise three dwellings and a small PO/shop. For many years a substantial shop housing another of the village bakeries, it has been well described by Harry Waldren, who was employed there from 1903-5 and also by Wilfred Dawkes who sent his memories of the shop in the 1930s. Their memoirs are included elsewhere. Bruce Seward gave his memories of working here until the bakery finished, and afterwards as roundsman. He remembered the original faggot ovens which were replaced by the steam varieties. 3-4 faggots (cut locally by a few older men from nearby woods) were put into the brick ovens which were heated for one to one and a half hours, then the ashes were scraped out into a big bath and a scuffle was used to collect the dust and bits. The scuffle was a bag tied on the end of a stick in the style of a mop, dipped in water and then whipped round the oven. Millie Seward, Bruce's wife, somewhat wryly commented that it was not a very efficient method: *the bottoms of the loaves were always pretty black*. 280 lbs flour, 4 lbs salt, 16 gallons of water and 1-1 1/2 lbs yeast made 240 x 2 lb loaves – often taking a 12 hour day. A peel (a long handed wooden shovel) was used for putting in and taking out the loaves and at Edgington's bakery there was also a branding iron with the initials HE (for Henry Edgington). The millers' wagons came from Bridge Street, Andover, and hoisted the flour up to the warehouse window in the passage – now dignified with a balcony. Bruce told of Charlie Siney, who could carry 112 lbs on his back. And what is the meaning of the teapot spout high up on the opposite wall of The Old Forge?

Millie pointed out that before the motor car people had to be more or less self-supporting, so local shops carried as much variety as possible. Edgingtons kept buckets, nails, tacks, boot protectors, wicks for oil lamps, and glass chimneys, boot laces in the 1930s and even up to the 1950s 'Imps' for cleaning chimneys, as well as all the grocery lines and poultry corn and meal. One of the most hated jobs was measuring off paraffin. Groceries were bought in bulk and weighed out in the shop – cheese, sugar, flour, dried fruit etc. Sweets came in large bottles and had to be weighed out into screws of paper. Deliveries came from the surrounding area; over the years suppliers altered, but Millie gave several examples: hardware came from Woodrows of Salisbury once every three months, Hardy's Grocery and Provisions of Salisbury every two weeks, with Kingdoms of Reading providing on alternate weeks. Edwards & Barnard of Andover, followed by Wills & Sons have also been mentioned, with orders being fulfilled in two days. The principal biscuit companies came about once a month, and D.C.L. yeast each week from Basingstoke. Another supplier came with writing materials and birthday cards. Mr. A.R. Norgate supplied paraffin, batteries and accumulators from Andover, as did Mr. Spreadbury of Burbage. Mr. Razey, from Hungerford, did the same, electrical goods also. Another paraffin supplier was Mr. Davies, who came over from Wiltshire with paraffin in his pony and trap. Before 1930 coke and coal was delivered by Watsons, in 1930 by Hope & Sons and now, in the 21st century, by Mundys. Mr. Cope, of Parsons & Harts, Andover, collected orders for furniture, outfitting and haberdashery, to be delivered. Mr. Kemp of Buckland & Sons, Andover, also delivered clothing to order. The butchers were Webb & Wilson, Andover, W. Smith of Stoke, and Cuttings of Hurstbourne, delivering probably twice a week. A Mr. Alfred Cook rode a bicycle from St. Mary Bourne with patent medicines which were far cheaper than ones bought in town – this was, of course, before the days of the NHS. Fish came once a week from Newbury, the supplier sold vegetables also. Betty Banbury, formerly of Fosbury, considered that the villages were well served before the age of the car but inevitably much produce was grown at home, with amicable sharing and bartering of surplus produce.

The two main shops supplied much the same things, and used the same suppliers, though Mr. Filmore, who at one time owned what we have to call the 'Post Office Stores' gave an additional service for clothes – he would supply clothes on receipt of an order. He owned a pony and trap, but also obtained the first motor car in the village. The public telephone box was inside the shop. Mrs. Filmore sold to Mr. Evans c. 1927 – Mr. Filmore having died of cancer and been buried in a lead-lined coffin. Mr. Evans continued in much the same way, additionally supplying refreshments for village whist drives and dances – Mrs. Evans's speciality was cream horns, but jam puffs, rock cakes, sponges, lardy cakes and dough cakes were also popular. Christmas cakes were baked on Sundays when the ovens were cooler, but taken elsewhere for icing.

Finally in this central area 'Gardia' of two storeys, colourwashed, flint and brick structure. Formerly two cottages. A previous resident 'Budgie' Austin, used to enjoy drinking her morning tea in bed and watching the comings and goings along the village street.

Continuing now along the road to Hurstbourne past Bulpits Hill, the centre of the village is dominated by the George Inn – possibly dating from 1633. This is a restored timber framed structure, long ridge tiled roof with eaves swept back over upper windows and half-hipped at either end – four plain wood casements. The front has a superimposed façade of exposed timberwork and infilling of thin bands of flint and brick. There is a rustic timber porch and an old well at the extreme right – now sealed, with access only afforded to the Environment Agency who measure the depth at regular intervals. During the fire at Upton Cottage in 1995, access for a hose would have been much appreciated. As it was, hoses snaked up to a private swimming pool up Bulpits Hill. The old well is covered by an open tiled pentice. Originally thatched, The George was tiled around 1920. Mr. Elmer took over in 1922 from the afore-mentioned William (Bill) Farmer, followed by Mr. and Mrs. Hall, formerly of Masons.

The next house after the old Wilts and Dorset bus garage in the corner of The George forecourt is Denver Cottage, previously called Ivy Cottage (until 1965). One story from Denver Cottage is of an unfortunate child who was named 'Mons' in memory of her father who was killed at the battle of Mons. The cottage is mid 19th century flint with red brick dressings and bands, thatched, with two storeys, two wood casements, recessed brick panel over the porch. In 1936/37 Dr. Margaret B. Savory had her surgery here before moving it to Beeches. The dining room in which she held her surgery still appears more or less original, with the addition of wooden panelling on the lower halves of the walls. This came from the original Wesleyan Chapel when it was dismantled – next to Denver Cottage, now the site of the school kitchen. The sitting room of the cottage has been extended but retains an interesting fireplace. This 1969 extension included a bedroom utility, whereas the garden room, leading off from the kitchen, is dated 1972. The original kitchen would have been a 'lean to' but is now quite a substantial affair. Formerly divided into the kitchen and a larder and store in 1964, later occupants decided it was too dark, opened up the larder and store into the kitchen itself, and enlarged the window. 'Mons' visiting some years ago, confirmed that there was only an outside privy in her time, now a modern cloakroom. The effluent flowed through an open drain and was of great benefit to the rhubarb and the runner beans which grew up complete with shreds of newspaper. Strangely enough there is a cellar to the house, at one time thought to be used as a crèche run by a former occupant. As the bourne, when active, runs more or less through the lowest parts of the village cellars are rare in Vernham, but this particular cellar has fascinating features including an obviously original beam. Of special architectural and historic interest, this small two up/two down is thought to have contained two families at one time. John Freer-Smith, verger and current occupant, explained that his bedroom door contains a 'spyhole' which would seem to indicate that this door would have been the entrance to the second family's apartments. One suspects the accommodation would have been severely restricted.

The village hall – the 'Millennium Hall' - was rebuilt and opened in February 2000 by courtesy of public subscription, grant aid and much hard work to replace a one-roomed hall with small kitchen and offices, plus stage, dating from 1934, and now houses very superior accommodation for all occasions. To the left is the school kitchen, still functioning as such, on the site of the old Wesleyan Chapel which was entirely chalk walled. Many years defunct, but remembered as being used by the football teams for changing prior to games on the somewhat sloping field to the right of Botes Lane and Underwood House. (Bullocks Close). If the team lost the referee was firmly dunked in the pond ….. the Bury Dean at the end of the village was only reclaimed for modern games use in the 1970s.

To the right of the hall is 'Apple Tree Cottage', timber-framed with flint and brick infilling. Originally single story with gable attic window and thatched roof, much altered. The drive between the hall and Apple Tree Cottage leads up to a large, recently built house which replaced the smaller 'Long Meadow'.

'Lilac Cottage' (the birthplace of the afore-mentioned Tony Vincent) comes next, two storeys, with whitewashed flint and brick structure, thatched roof with wood casements, formerly two cottages.

Deers Leap' (formerly 'The Homestead') originally 17th century, is of two storeys, with a flint and brick structure with a modern extension to the rear, and thatched roof. Casement windows, those on the ground floor under arched brick lintels. This is another house where a 'grey lady' is said to walk – not, however, reported by the current inhabitants.

Before Shepherd's Rise are two small modern houses, 'The Hayrick' and 'The Beeches',

Shepherd's Rise itself being a response to a need for smaller modern housing and named in honour of Michael Shepherd, who served on the Parish Council for many years.

Dean Terrace was Council housing, now mainly privately owned, six dwellings, of semi-detached nature, set back from the road. 'Mulberry Cottage' is a modern two storeyed house squeezed into a triangle between Dean Terrace and the main road, sharing a driveway with 'Sunnyside' which, with 'School Cottage', are sizeable older semis next to School Close, comprising three detached modern dwellings, near to the school.

Vernham Dean Gillum's School has a chapter to itself, but originally it had walls of undressed flints with brick dressings, slate roof, typical of many of its period (1860s-70s). In olden times the building had a bell tower, the head-teacher's house standing behind the original main building and now a private house. A massive rebuilding programme did not disguise the original structure and it is now the core of a popular village school of considerable numbers.

The Bury Dene with car park also houses a modern sports pavilion and tennis court.

This tour of the core of Vernham Dean does not include many interesting houses in Vernham Row, Dean and Street, but this must suffice for now although there is much of interest at Anchor – or Ankers – Farmhouse, dated 1719 over the porch. There is exposed timber framing on the upper floor with corner bracing, the limewashed flint rubble below possibly conceals original overhang. Two lattice Victorian canopied porches, two lattice casements above with small square window at half level doorway, the ridged thatched roof has an attic dormer, a later brick addition projects at the side. Details of modern alterations are not to hand. 'Macey's Cottage' and 'Berneval Cottage' up Vernham Street deserve further research, Berneval Cottage is supposed to be of venerable antiquity.

The central area of Vernham Dean is a conservation area, and jealously guarded as such.

Source : Hampshire Treasures.

Harry Waldren's memories of the Shop and Bakery, 1903-5
(now Post Office Cottages, Baker's House, and PO)

Harry Waldren was born at Westley, near Sparsholt, in 1888. In 1900 he was living with his family at Freefolk near Whitchurch where, after leaving school in that year, he worked on a farm until the autumn of 1903. The following are excerpts from his manuscript account, written some time after 1935 and now housed in the Hampshire Record Office, of his young days at Vernham Dean.

…… …… …… …… …… …… …… …… …….

One day whilst in the town (Whitchurch) my mother met the traveller for Long's jam factory, Mr. Hibberd, who told her that there was a grocer at a village called Vernham Dean who wanted a boy to learn the trade ….. the first thing, however, was to write for an interview which I did and then came the time of waiting for a reply. I had not long to wait for a reply to my letter to Vernham Dean. It came by return of post. It was written by the manager, Mr. Beck (Shop was called Bells) and it said that the following Friday would be a suitable day for the interview. My mother then told me that she would go with me and sent me to Whitchurch to hire a pony and trap for the journey ……. I soon spotted the shop …… …… …. we were met by the manager, Mr. Beck ……… …… it was arranged that I should live with them and occupy a small bedroom at the end of the house. In passing I would add that at some time the house had been two and to get to my bedroom I had to go out and along to another door which had at one time been the entrance to the second house.

I was to receive to start with 1/6d. per week plus of course my board, laundry, etc. At the end of a month, which was to be probation, I would be required to sign an agreement to remain there two years and there were also certain conditions relating to doing business within the area of the shop ……. mother agreed. She made one condition only. She explained that the family were Methodists and she wanted me to attend Chapel at least once on each Sunday. Mr. Beck then said that they too were Methodists and that he was a local preacher. He said that there was a Methodist Chapel in the village and just opposite the shop there was also a Mission Hall and this place was the most popular with the younger people …… …… ..

He then took me back to the shop which I found to be quite a good roomy place. There were three counters – Grocery and Provisions one side and on the other the Drapery Counter. In addition to these three items the shop carried a stock of boots chiefly for men and boys It also catered for such things as oil lamps, lanterns, etc. There was also a Bread trade. The baker was married, Mr. Knight, and there was also a boy named Bert Gibbs. His job was to tidy up the shop in the morning, assist in the Bake House, deliver bread round the village and any other odd jobs …… he was local and lived with his widowed mother who was a semi-invalid.

The whole premises were formed like an inverted "L". At the top was the shop, next a covered space where wood for the bakehouse was stacked and other things, then the bakehouse, through a short passage to the house kitchen. The room forming the corner of the "L" was the store. The house took up the remainder, first the living-cum-dining room, then the sitting room, with a small room adjoining used by Mr. Beck as an office, then the room which I had to enter to reach my bedroom overhead.

There were two ponies and it would be my job to look after them, except every other Sunday, when the baker would care for them. We went to the stable, which was a well-constructed wooden building, with two stalls and a horse box. Space for hay and straw and next to it space for two carts to stand side by side. The whole building had a good brick and cement floor and was very easy to keep clean. One pony was brown and the other white and the latter was in the stable at the time. The baker had the other out on his round. Mr. Beck told me that the baker looked after his own harness and I should be responsible for the other set. I would start work at 7 a.m. by cleaning out the stable, groom the ponies and feed and water them. Breakfast would be at 8 a.m. after which I would be in the shop, except on days that I had a 'round' to do. This would all be explained later, however.

We returned to the house, had lunch, I had previously fed our pony by nose bag and we were then ready to return home. Before leaving it was arranged that I should go by train from Whitchurch to Andover the following Tuesday morning and that I should wait on the station platform until Mr. Beck arrived and then drive out to Vernham Dean with him. The return journey was uneventful. My mother was very pleased with the arrangement and I too was quite happy about it. I remember I had one little worry. I was left-handed and had always used a knife and fork left-handed. I had been compelled to write right-handed at school, everything else, however, I did left-handed. I told my mother this and she suggested that I should try and use a knife and fork right-handed. This I eventually did after much fumbling trying to use the fork as a knife and vice versa. I succeeded however in time but except for writing and using a knife and fork I am still completely left-handed. A left-handed person is not considered an oddity these days as in my young days.

On the way home my mother told me of the various articles she would buy me and told me that she expected me to replace some things from my wages, but more expensive things would be supplied by her. She also said that she would buy me a tin trunk to pack my clothes in. This was the usual thing in those far off days. Suitcases had not come into general use. This tin trunk was fastened by a small brass padlock and key – both of which I have to this day.

Tuesday came, my box packed and locked, my brother Bill helped me to carry it to the station on his way to school. I then waited at the station for the train to arrive. I had a second hand bicycle and we arranged that my mother should send it to Bells' shop at Hurstbourne Tarrant and I would have to arrange to get it the last four miles.

This morning was in effect my real departure from home except for the odd day or two I never lived at home again …………… soon I found myself at Andover Junction ………… I saw Mr. Beck driving up to the station. With my box placed in the back I climbed up beside him and soon we were well on our way to Vernham which was to be my home for two years and in spite of the fact that I seemed always to be at work they were two very happy years.

On the journey Mr. Beck told me that the shop was open from 8.30 a.m. to 8 p.m. on Monday, Tuesday and Thursday, Wednesday till 4 p.m., Friday till 9 p.m. and Saturday 10 p.m. I would, as soon as I had learned the way about, have two bread rounds. Wednesdays to Buttermere, about four miles away, and intervening hamlets etc. Thursday to Coombe, about 6 miles away. The baker had two rounds each of which he did twice a week, on Saturdays he did the second Buttermere round. The Coombe round was also done on Mondays but Mr. Beck did this himself always, with me in attendance. Coombe was a sleepy little village situated right on the Hampshire-Berkshire border and some time previously he had worked up more or less a complete grocery and bread trade throughout the village.

Before reaching Coombe we passed through Vernham Street, Littledown and Linkenholt, and at all these places he had some customers. On Mondays on arrival at Coombe Mr. Beck took orders for groceries and received payment for the previous week's supplies. He also told me that every other Sunday would be a free day as the baker took care of the horses on that day. I would have to feed them and see them safely fixed each night after the shop had shut. During meal times he, Mrs. Beck and I would go to the shop to attend to any customers, there was a bell which told us when the shop door opened ……… he also told me that they had supper at 9.30 p.m. each evening and I would have to be in by that time. This I thought would be no great hardship.

On arrival at Vernham we took my box off then went round to the stable. He showed me how to put the cart away, the pony found her own way to her stall, we unharnessed her, gave her a good rub down and placed her rug on. Then instruction as to the composition of oats and chaff for each feed. He also told me that at night I should fill each of their hay racks with hay and water them.

This all done we returned to the house, had a meal and I carried my box to my room. After this for the remainder of the time the shop was open I just stood around watching the shop activities and also memorising where certain things were kept. The next morning,

Wednesday, we loaded the cart with a certain amount of bread and off we started on the Buttermere round. This I had to learn as I was to do it alone as soon as possible. That day I realised that it was not at all difficult. The pony knew the way and pulled up at the house of each customer. The bread book helped as the names were in strict order of calling so that it was impossible to miss a house. I told him this and he replied: "Do you think you can manage next Wednesday alone?" and I said I was sure I could. The next week I went alone and everything worked out according to plan. The next day, Thursday, he accompanied me on the Coombe round, here again I found it quite easy. As he always went with me on Mondays I was quite ready to go alone the following Thursday. I soon settled down and people had ceased to say: "You are the new boy at the shop" and I became known by my first name "Harry".

I went to the Mission that first Sunday and afterwards soon found myself in company with boys and girls of my age. There was absolutely nothing to do in the village and as it was winter it was very dark. Life in the shop was interesting, especially Fridays and Saturdays when the bulk of the shopping was done. Mr. and Mrs. Beck, Bert Gibbs and myself were all kept very busy. During the daytime the fixtures were more or less my responsibility: sugar to be weighed and packed in various weights, soda likewise, the caddies to be kept filled. Dried fruit to be cleaned, etc., a hundred and one jobs. In addition of course there was harness to be cleaned and the cart washed.

As one approached the centre of the village from Hurstbourne the road forked and became two roads through the village, one called the top road, the other the bottom ……….. our shop opened on the top road and the house position backed on the bottom road.

I have never been certain whether it was the summer of 1904 or 1905 but I think the former, Mr. Watson, who was in charge of the Mission Hall announced one Sunday that provided a party could be raised he had thoughts of arranging an outing to Southsea. He outlined the plan, that was to travel to Andover by farm wagons, thence to Southampton by train, boat to Southsea calling at Ryde. I forget what the cost was to be, but it was announced at the time and anyone wishing to go was requested to give the name during a limited time.

At that time Mr. Watson was also running a Christian Endeavour Group to which most boys and girls of my age belonged and it was really under the auspices of this society that the outing was to be run. It soon became the topic of conversation and quite a number said they would go, provided they could get the day off from work. I approached Mr. Beck and he agreed that I could go. The girl in the house also obtained permission, as did her fiancé Herbert Blundy who was employed as a coachman/gardener by a retired Admiral living near the village. Others whose names I forget also made the necessary arrangements and amongst them was a boy named Stockley and when the great day came he and I spent the day together.

I had been in the habit on occasion of getting up early and watching the baker 'break the sponge' and make the dough for the bread. Also I sometimes watched him 'set the sponge' at night .... during the spring of the second year there my knowledge came in useful. The baker was taken ill. Mr. Beck also had some knowledge of breadmaking, but if anything I knew more about it than he did and I told him that if he was agreeable I would have a go at it. I did, and according to my numerous customers my first few efforts were not up to the usual standard, but practice makes perfect and soon they were telling me that my way was as good, if not better than the baker's. This of course changed my routine completely. I still had two ponies to look after. This work I did while the dough was rising. Mr. Beck and Bert Gibbs made the actual loaves from the dough. I took on the baker's rounds and Mr. Beck did mine. The only time I was in the shop during this period was Saturday nights as there was no sponge to be set that night and of course the shop was very busy. The baker returned in due course and I reverted to my normal duties.

My time was nearly up and the question of future employment had already been talked over by Mr. Beck and myself. I had, however, already decided in my own mind that I was going in the Army if possible. I was due to leave on the 30th November (1905). The two years I spent at Vernham were very happy. I worked hard, perhaps the hours were too long for a boy of my age but I don't think I noticed it at the time.

I visited Vernham once, about the middle 1930s. At that time there seemed outwardly to be little change. The shop was still there. I went inside and noticed that the drapery side had ceased to exist and was now taken up by the village post office. The people I knew had either died or left the village.

I would like to visit it once more and would also like to see Coombe again. I wonder if 'Coombe Gallows' still stands on the top of the hill behind the village? I believe it was one of the very few gallows still standing in the country ....

....

On 6th December 1905 Harry Waldren became No: 1342 Private F.H. Waldren, The Hampshire Militia. His manuscript ends with his account of his Army unit arriving in Bermuda in September, 1907.

....

Wilfred Dawkes

The Editor had the good fortune to extract the following from Wilfred Dawkes, who unfortunately died on the 6th September, 2006, but whose account is an interesting follow up to Harry Waldren's experience.

"I have received a letter from my brother to say you may be interested in my short time in the Vernham shop. As I have to think back 72 years and more, my recollections may be a bit hazy. Firstly, though, when I was a schooboy, very few people in Vernham had a radio, or the wireless as it was known then, but the shopkeeper had one. It could have been Mr. Evans. Every year, when it was the football Cup Final day, he would bring his wireless to the front of the shop and we boys would stand outside, by the post box, and listen to the commentary. Looking back, I think it was a very nice gesture.

I left school in January 1934, when I was 14, and started work in the Vernham store, and left a year later, when I went as a boy soldier to the Army Technical School, at Chepstow, Monmouthshire. On our epaulettes we had the brass figures A.T.S. so I can always say I was in the A.T.S. but the name must have changed during WWII (or people would think we were a lot of females).

The owner of the shop was Mr. Evans, a Welshman, who had a wife and daughter, Marion, who worked in the shop, and in the enclosed Post Office. (Previous owners were, I believe, a Mr. De'Ath, after Mr. Filmore). Mr. Evans was a good man, and a hard worker e.g. on Sunday mornings he would go to Chapel (to keep in with the Chapel people), and in the evenings he would go to Church (to keep in with the Church people). Then after church would make the dough (all by hand) for the Monday mornings' bread. Every Good Friday morning he would make Hot Cross Buns, and at Xmas, if required, would cook peoples' Xmas birds in his bread oven. Every Friday he would make dough, and delicious lardy cakes.

Each regular customer had a grocery notebook, in which the details of the week's shopping, with the prices, would be entered. I think he had to be patient and trusting, as sometimes it was several weeks before a bill, or bills, could be paid.

When I started work my pay was five shillings for a six day week, later increased to six shillings, and the job was to keep the shop clean, deliver bread to the customers every morning, and also telegrams. To assist in the bread and grocery round I had the use of a heavy bicycle, with a framework on the handlebars to carry a breadbasket, etc. After a time I was allowed to serve in the shop, which had everything required for country living: groceries, tobacco, sweets, biscuits, galvanised buckets and, in the summer, a box of tomatoes would arrive for sale.

If I remember rightly, sugar came in 1 cwt. sacks, and cheese in a large circular lump about 1 ft. to 1 1/2 ft. high, covered in cheesecloth. (the proper name eludes me). It was kept in the cool storeroom abutting the back lane. Mr. Evans, using cheese wire, would cut a section out, to be taken to the main shop, awaiting orders. Butter also came in a large slab and had to be similarly reduced (by a knife) for orders. In the shop was a bacon slicer, but that was out of bounds for me.

On a Wednesday and Saturday I had to take bread, on the bike, to the Warren (the house on the hill below Fosbury Camp, known to us as Haydown Hill).

Mr. Evans had a small van for delivering bread and groceries to outlying areas, which sometimes gave me a small diversion, as occasionally he would leave without taking an order with him. Once he went to Conholt to deliver to regular customers, when in the shop it was found he had left the grocery order behind. So it was Wilfy on his bike, up to Conholt, where luckily I found him. All in the day's work.

Being a village, Mr. Evans knew all his customers: one, a lady customer (whom I will not mention by name as her daughter probably still lives in Vernham) was very poor but had some weak looking children and used to come into the shop asking for goods like Bovril, etc., which were rather expensive. He knew she could not afford those 'luxuries' so I had to say the items were already ordered for someone else or if I saw her coming I had to take them off the shelves and hide them. Mr. Evans would usually correctly estimate the number of loaves required for the next day's customers, but sometimes there was one left over, and then I was instructed to sell it to a person. So I would try, but housewives are pretty canny, and with a bit of luck, I could usually drop it at an old person's house (shame). But the next time I called, I would get a telling off, but I would be all innocence, and say sorry for the mistake. After the war, when I was demobbed, Mr. Evans asked me to work for him again, but as I had other ideas, I had to refuse, which turned out to be the right decision, as I eventually found pensionable employment.

Hope this does not seem too humdrum. It was a quiet time, and the days passed peaceably, or seemed to, but with happy memories of a village shop, a centre of activity, which will never be seen again."

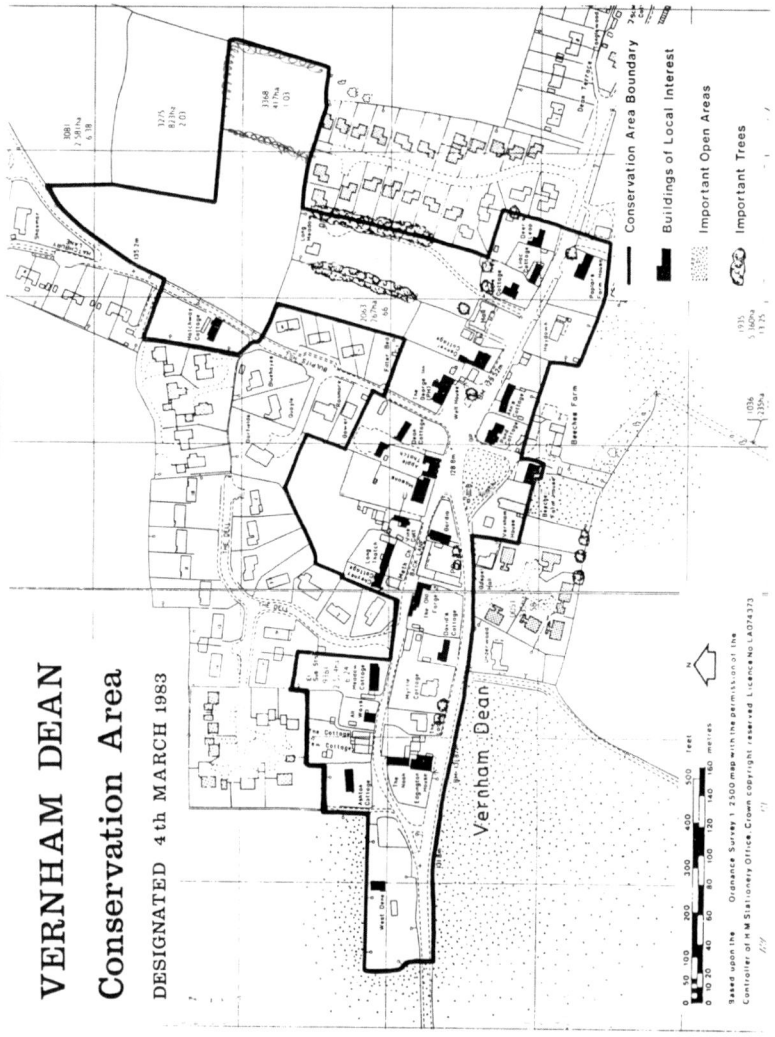

VERNHAM DEAN
Conservation Area

DESIGNATED 4th MARCH 1983

Conservation Area Boundary

Buildings of Local Interest

Important Open Areas

Important Trees

Based upon the Ordnance Survey 1 2500 map with the permission of the Controller of H.M Stationery Office Crown copyright reserved Licence No LA074373

Vernham Dean

Conservation area of Vernham Dean, reproduced by kind permission of Test Valley Borough Council.

**Poplars - then
early 20th C**
(Mrs Bulstrode)

Poplars - now
(David Post)

**Looking west along
the village street**
(John Marchment)

Looking east along the village street
(John Marchment)

The George Inn and the wheelwright's barn
(John Marchment)

The original Pond Cottages
(John Marchment)

Beeches Farm
(John Marchment)

**The Firs
(now Vernham House)**
(Postcard)

Vernham Pond.

S. J. Bell's Series.

**Woodside -
(formerly
the New Inn)**
(David Post)

Back Lane - then
(Postcard)

Back Lane - now
(David Post)

**The Chapel
in Back Lane**
(Peter Dawkes)

**Masons and
Apple Thatch - then**
(Postcard)

**Masons and
Apple Thatch - now**
(David Post)

Mrs. Millie Seward was responsible for much of the research on the Methodists in Vernham Dean, and she was able to get permission to have records, closed under the 30 year rule, opened for her inspection. Millie (Bulpit, later Watts) Seward was born in the village and for many years lived at Beeches Farm which is behind the pond. Her father, John Bulpit, was for 37 years Treasurer of the chapel in Back Lane. Regrettably Millie is one of the several researchers who passed on before the history was completed.

The original chapel was built on land where the school kitchen now stands, to the left of the Millennium Hall, and was entirely chalk walled. An Indenture was dated 16th September 1817 between William Alexander (yeoman), Mary his wife and George Piper (yeoman) and the Trustees: Harry Noyes of Thruxton, John Sweetapple, and George Cotton. There was a right of way to and from the chapel four feet wide bounded on the west by a tenement and garden in the possession of Seymour Stratton (labourer). On the North it was bounded by the said garden, and on the East by land belonging to Richard Coleman (labourer). It was bounded on the south by a yard in the occupation of the said Seymour Stratton. The Lease was for 99 years from the 29th September 1817 on a Peppercorn Rent on the Feast of St. Michael. The Religious Census of Hampshire informs us that the chapel was consecrated in 1816, and had free places for 108 persons (others 12, total 120). The afternoon attendance would appear to be ca 69, the evening 49. George Piper was the steward.

20th June 1854:

To: The Registrar General of Births, Deaths and Marriages:

I, the Undersigned, Peter Parsons of Winchester Street, Andover in the County of Southampton, Minister, do hereby, under and by virtue of an Act passed in the 16th year in the reign of H.M. Queen Victoria entitled "An Act to amend the law relating to Cert. & Reg. of places of Religious Worship of Protestant Dissenters" certify that a certain building situated at Vernham Dean in the County aforesaid, within the Supt. Reg. District of Andover is herewith intended to be used and will be forthwith used as a place of religious worship by a congregation of Protestant Dissenters from the Church of England to be called Wesleyan Methodists ......

Trouble arose about the £5. which was charged for the rent of the chapel land. Although it was officially just a peppercorn rent, a later landowner thought the Methodists should not have their religion for nothing, and extracted £5. yearly although there was no legal foundation for this. Yet another person queries: "Was that all their religion was worth?" The Chapel was built on farm land belonging to the Pipers, and was indeed rent free until the land was sold to Mr. and Mrs. John Purver, and it was these people who charged the £5. a year rent for the Chapel.

A letter from John May, Manor Farm, Collingbourne, dated 16th April 1902 to the Revd F. Traves talks about closing the Chapel *"as Wesleyan Methodism seems to have died after Primitive Methodist Chapel, C. of E. Church and, newly opened that year, the 'Plymouth Brethren Hall'....* (Mr. May was obviously not aware of the true nature of Mrs. Watson's prized Mission Hall)........ *so it was closed there having been no congregation for four consecutive weeks"*.

Even after the demise of the chapel, the Pipers were still an interested party. B. Piper wrote from Forest Gate, Essex, on the 26th December 1902 to the Circuit Minister, complaining that panelling behind the pulpit and two lamps fitted in memory of his mother had been sold without permission from the family. The Circuit would not acknowledge liability. The panelling, incidentally, found its way into Denver Cottage, where it was installed in the dining room.

Eventually the deeds of the property were returned to the Revd H. Hopkinson in Andover on the 6th November 1911 by the Revd John Hornabrook in Manchester, the Board having considered they had no hold on the property.

Eric Levell, writing in the Andover Advertiser in 1998 relates: *My maternal grandfather, who lived at Vernham, was quite a character. He sometimes amused us children by telling us about the old chapel preachers who came to Upton and Vernham when he was a boy in the 1870s or 80s. A favourite tale was about one old chap who always chose the hymn 'We'll roll the chariot along'. To urge the congregation to greater vocal activity the preacher rotated his right arm in time with the singing and this effort sometimes brought on an attack of the hiccups. I can seem to see Grandfather singing 'If the Devil's in the way we'll roll it over him – if the Devil's in the way we'll roll it over him – and we won't drag on behind' – the meanwhile whirling his own around and 'hiccuping' away in between breaths as he demonstrated to amuse us.*

If research on the old Wesleyan chapel, whose demise prompted Mrs. Watson to create the Mission Hall, is somewhat meagre, there is more detail about the Vernham Dean Primitive Methodist Chapel, situated in Back Lane. Consecrated in 1845, there were 'free' places for 80, 'others' 28 – total 108. There was standing room for 12. The afternoon attendance was c. 70, the evening 80. The stewards were Charles Hunt and Robert Dawkes.

From the Minute Book of 1887 researchers culled that the chapel was built on land donated by the then owner of the cottage to the rear of the chapel in 1869. Until 1898 candles were used and cost 6d. per pound: in 1892 the coke for the stove cost 1/10d. per cwt and carriage. Oil for lamps in 1892 cost 1/- per gallon – a scrubbing brush 6d. In comparison, coke in 1979 was £16.50 for 5 cwt. This was the last bill for fuel as the chapel installed electric heaters.

The usual efforts were made to raise money and Harvest Festival/Thanksgiving Services were held at the end of September. After the Monday evening service an auction would take place, proceeds going towards the upkeep of the chapel: in 1890 the sale realised £1.0s.6d.: 1921: £4.1s.8d.: 1982 £35.40.

The Account Book dated 1887 makes interesting reading

INCOME		£	s	d
Balance in hand 1887		4	1	0
May 30th	Profit from Whitsun Tea		16	1
	Collection Whit Monday		15	0
	Given by friend		5	0
	Allowed from Club		10	0
Oct 30th	Golden System	2	16	6
	Sunday Collection		18	0 1/4
Nov 1st	Collection		9	0
	Profits of Tea		7	6
Dec 8th	Seat Rents	1	7	0
Mr. Dawkes House Rent per annum		3	0	0
Feb	Thatching cottage		12	0
	Books for Chapel		2	0
	2 galls Oil 1 lb Candles		2	6
Mar	Poor Rates		7	8
	3 lbs Candles		1	6
Aug	Poor Rates		6	4
	Insurance		4	6
	Quato New Stove		3	0
	3 galls Oil		3	0
	2 lbs Candles		1	0
Sep	Mrs. Dawkes for coal		4	0

		£	s	d
Nov	3 lbs Candles		1	6
	Stove for Chapel	1	4	0
	Coke & carriage		2	6
	Mrs. Dawkes Interest on loan	2	10	0
	Mrs. Hunt Interest on loan		15	0
	Cleaning Chapel 1 year		15	0
Dec	Paid to Mr. Dawkes	5	0	0

Andover Advertiser 31st March 1899: *A Dastardly Trick – "someone took away the pedals of the Wesleyan church organ to prevent the old organist from playing ….…"*

28th July 1899: …………… *James Hughes and James Newport summoned for assault on Francis Augustus Clark, the society steward at Vernham Wesleyan Chapel who was attacked after attempting to stop a relief organist (Miss Mills) from playing the organ, as he was the rightful organist, and Walter Strange, one of the congregation, gave witness in his defense (sic).*

(Ed: although this passage refers to the 'Wesleyan' chapel it is thought it refers to the chapel in Back Lane).

Letter from the Malthouse, Upton, dated 6th April 1893 to George Piper from Allan Hedderley …..*requests G. Piper to give up the key to the Chapel*. Signed by Allan Hedderley's brother John, no reason is given for this request.

A sighting of the Vernham Dean Sunday School Account Book for 1906 shows that teas and anniversary celebrations took place in January most years, with an outing or sports in the autumn. The Anniversary Tea bill on the 16th April 1906 amounted to £1.6s.4d. plus 12 reading books, apparently for the scholars, 2/-. The collections on the Anniversary Sunday and Monday, and the takings from tea on the Monday, amounted to £3.5s.6d. so even then there was a profit. In July 1916 the Sunday School were taken to Savernake Forest by 'Mr. White's Motor' for £2. Hot water and milk for the picnic cost another 4/6d. Friends went with them on this day and contributed 15/0d. towards the 'motor'. Cakes sold for 1/3d., Mrs. Piper took a collection of 2/1d. - not an expensive day out for the Sunday School.

There was an appeal for funds in 1919 and it is recorded that Admiral Gamble, of Rowe House, gave 10/6d., Mr. Knight £1.1s.0d., Mr. Prosser of Windmill Hill, Hurstbourne Tarrant, gave 5/-, and Mr. Bull (probably Andover), 2/6d.

Recorded in July 1920: Car & Wreath 16/4d., recorded at the same time: *collected for wreath 3/-,* unfortunately there is no record of the deceased involved.

The last account to hand was for 1922, when £32.13s.0d. was paid for the charabanc and £34.0s.5d. was received for the outing fund. At the close the balance in hand was £2.13s.4 1/4d. Sunday School books were bought most years, tea parties continued, subscriptions were sent to the Sunday School Union and the meticulous book keeping was always audited. The last page to hand was by the Revd. J.T. Smith on the 25th January, 1923.

To mark the Primitive Methodist Church Centenary 1807-1907 a fund of £250,000 was set up, the local Sunday Schools took part and a Roll of Honour bears many familiar names.

A certain amount of income came from letting Chapel (sometimes Cheyney) Cottage which lies behind the chapel. In 1887 it was £3. per year, continuing in like vein with slight increases until in January 1923 it was let quarterly at £1.16s.0d. There was always a tenant, and often this person acted as caretaker for the chapel.

There was a Sewing Class connected with the chapel and an Account Book dated June 1911 reads as follows:

INCOME			EXPENDITURE		
2 iron holders		3d	Thread		1d
2 little holders		2d	5 yds Braid		2 1/2d.
1 pair stays		4 1/2d.	1 yard Calico		3 3/4d
Another ditto		5d	Pins & Needles		2d
1912					
Tea Cosy	(1)	6d	1 yard ribbon		0 3/4d.
Cushion	(2)	6d.	3 yds Sateen	(1)	8 1/4d
Little dress	(1)	3d	1 yd Wadding		2 3/4d.
1 Toilet Tidys	(1)	6d.			

10/- was sent to the SE London Mission.

The sewing went on with small amounts received from many ladies, but only Christian names were used. Later, a few men's names appear. The book closes in 1933 still recording money sent to Missions abroad:-

To Russian Saints in need	2/ 6d.
Egypt Mission	1/ 6d
To Waifs 1/- To Leper Mission	2/ 0d.
To Jews in Russia	2/ 0d.
To Armenians	5/ 0d.
To Leper Mission	2/ 0d.

Millie Seward wrote:

I was born at Vernham Street, therefore from a baby I went to Chapel, as my parents were good Methodists and helped with whatever would be going on there. Chapel was three times each Sunday: school in the morning and preaching services afternoon and evening, and often a Prayer Meeting would be held after Evening Service and this would sometimes go on a long time. We children got very bored. There were the Hughes, Colemans, Ryders, Russ, Jennings, Chandlers to name but a few. At Easter we would celebrate Sunday School Anniversary when we children would learn probably two recitations, one for each service, as well as new music. We nearly always had a new dress and hat for this occasion. Then on Monday a tea would be provided, using the copper that was in the caretaker's washhouse to provide water. Very soapy tasting tea, as the caretaker's family washing was boiled in it. I can taste it now. Tea would be quickly cleared away and we would give another performance. People would come from some of the other valley chapels for this.

On Whit Monday there would be a Rally, one of the valley chapels more or less taking it in turns to put it on. A guest preacher would be invited and he would most likely be a very keen evangelist. Another weekend there would be a Camp Meeting when the pews were carried outside into the field that is now housing in The Dell. On this occasion there would be as many as three preachers, long sessions in those days for little children.

Another memory was Sunday School prize giving when books were presented for attendance. I think every child got a book, some bigger than others. Mrs. Sydney Watson, who lived in the Mission Hall Bungalow, would often give and present these books, usually one she had written herself. I possess two of these books. 'A Village Maiden's Career' and 'Village Maiden's Eventide'.

Harvest Festival was celebrated at the end of September. Chapel was decorated on Saturday and there was the usual Sunday Service and a short service on Monday evening, when the vegetables, fruit and flowers were auctioned: the local Chapel was allowed to keep these proceeds for maintenance, fuel and lighting. The week by week collections were forwarded to the head church, as contribution for the minister's salary. At the beginning we 'belonged' to the Hurstbourne Tarrant circuit, later East Street, Andover, and after amalgamation in 1933 to Andover. This was when the Primitive Methodists united with the Wesleyan Methodists who were a stronger force and were more wealthy.

During the summer an outing to the seaside was arranged. We would fill about a 40-seater coach and set off at 8 a.m. for Bournemouth, Southsea, Bognor Regis or Weymouth, a vote having been taken as to where they would go. Children travelled free and it was always exciting to be the first to see the sea. We took all our own food and enjoyed sandwiches with sand in them. We would reluctantly leave the seaside at about 5 p.m. and usually came home via Salisbury where a stop was made to buy fish and chips. Arriving home at Vernham Dean about 9 p.m. or later we (the Bulpits) had to walk home to 'Fair View' at Vernham Street, tired and sometimes a little cross.

The Primitive Methodist Chapel was built in 1869 on land donated by the occupier of Cheyney/Chapel Cottage (sometimes known by one name, sometimes the other). For very many years the tenant acted as caretaker. In 1969, the Centenary Year, the cottage was sold to Mr. and Mrs. D. Golder for £600 and the proceeds used to renovate and refurnish the chapel. The outside porch was added and a part partitioned off at the back. A sink and drain were fitted, also an electric point so that we were able to make our own tea. The membership over the years grew less and less, and in 1985 it was closed and the building sold to Mrs. Campbell-Harding, the then occupant of 'Long Thatch' for use as an embroidery workshop.

Chapel Cottage gave the Chapel Trustees a few headaches. At a special meeting in May 1960, after the then caretakers, the Carpenters, had left on the 30th April, a decision was made to pull the cottage down as it would cost too much to repair, even with a Council grant. By the 10th October 1961 it had been decided to put an Elsan behind the chapel but to leave the cottage as it was. Then it was decided to sell the cottage, but not the land at the side, only the cottage and the garden. On the 19th May 1962 Mr. May valued the cottage at £500. By the 27th November 1962 they had received an offer of £200. But no-one would move *"until Mr. Brooks is offered his land back"*. Mr. Brooks is to be asked if he would agree that the piece of land at the side of the chapel be kept for a car park and he be given new ground out of the garden at the back of the cottage. 10th November 1964: the land at the side handed back to Lancelot Charles Brooks. The Trustees wanted more than the £200 offered for the cottage, and received another offer for £500. Out of the proceeds of the eventual sale for £600 to the Golders, mentioned above, the Trustees repaired the chapel for £490. *"The field at the side"* was sold to Gibbs of Hungerford for £12. This is the beginning of another story, for it was in this field that the first new housing developments in Vernham Dean took place.

The list of the Trustees in various years makes interesting reading as regards residence and occupation:

7th June 1916: Trustees

William Coleman	Lower Chute, Farmer
Richard James Coleman	Farmer
George Wiltshire	Baker
Edward Hounslow	Carrier
Albert Dudman	Baker
Thomas Chandler	Labourer
Frederick Knight	Baker
Charles Culley	Hungerford Postman
Herbert Filmore	Grocer
Philip Hughes	Farmer
David West	Hurstbourne Tarrant Butcher
Colson Holloway	Stoke Farmer

And on the 22nd May 1945

George Wiltshire	(now retired)
Philip Hughes	Poplars Vernham Dean
Thomas Chandler	(now retired)

New Trustees chosen:

Howard Rich	Andover, Civil Servant
John Bulpit	Beeches, Farmer
Margaret Eliza Mary Bulpit	Beeches, Married Woman
Lilian Margaret Harding	Woodside, Married Woman
Annie Jennings	Woodside, Married Woman
Edgar John Brooks	Box Farm, Agricultural Worker
George Henry Briant	Hurstbournt Tarrant Agricultural Worker

106

Daisy Mary Briant	Hurstbournt Tarrant, Married Woman
Arthur Bulpit (Millie Seward's father's brother)	Andover, Farmer

By the 8th December 1970:

Walter Edward Ponting	Wildhern, SEB Meter Reader
Dorothy Annie Ponting	Wildhern, Married Woman
Dora Joyce Knight	Ibthorpe, Married Woman
Alfred George Knight	Ibthorpe, Forestry Foreman
Jennifer Ann Scull	Horseshoe Lane, Ibthorpe, Head Clerk in Supermarket
Lawrence Christopher Strange	Winterside, Littledown, Farmer
Christine Kathleen Giles	Chapel Lane, Littledown, Spinster
Enid Effie Brooks	Bethelea, Vernham Street, Married Woman
Anthony Izzard	31 Oxenwood, Head Gardener on the Fosbury Estate
Dorothy Izzard	Married Woman
Dorothy May Wyld (Millie Seward's sister)	
Eric Francis Wyld	HCC Charge Hand
Millicent Winifred Watts (Millie Seward)	Beeches, Widow.

At an Extraordinary Meeting on the 8th May, 1985, attended by the Revd Jenkins, it was agreed to close the chapel.

(formerly the MISSION HALL)

At the beginning of the 20th century the closure of a Wesleyan Chapel near the site of the present school kitchen inspired Mrs. Lily Watson to give a plot of land, part of the garden at 'The Firs' (now Vernham House) for the building of a Mission Hall.

Elizabeth (Lily) was the eldest of the eleven children of Enos and Harriett Smith. At the time of her birth, on the 16th September 1855, the family were living at Chilmark, near Salisbury. She died on the 28th June 1934 and is buried in the churchyard of St. Mary the Virgin, Vernham Dean. The entire Smith family is commemorated on a particularly ornate family tombstone surrounded by wrought iron rails on the south west side of the church, adjacent to the footpath linking Church Path and the Old Vicarage drive. At the time £100 was invested in Consols 2 1/2% stock – nowadays yielding about 61p per annum – to keep the edifice in order. The current custodian of the family stone in this 'Upton Corner' area of the churchyard is Andrew Smith, the great-nephew of Olive Smith, whose father, Alfred, was the youngest surviving brother of Lily Watson, with 20 years between them. A visit by Olive Smith and her great-nephew in 1995 gave some welcome first hand memories of Lily Watson: 'Aunt Lizzie' was very big physically, and was addicted to three-tiered hats, certainly a figure who would command attention. To her family she did not seem overpowering, but her flamboyant personality carried considerable weight in this village. Olive Smith (who herself died in 1998) remembered seeing both Lily and Sydney Watson when visiting her grandparents. Grandmother Harriett's leg was amputated when father Alfred was a baby – she was in a wheelchair prior to her death in 1907. Other memories of Lily Watson came from Dora Knight, May Nutley, Enid Brooks and Jim Hughes, former residents of the village. They all remember her as a tall person, who wore brightly-coloured flowing clothes, never seen without a hat. Her preaching was also flamboyant and she was known as a forthright lady who stood no nonsense. Dora Knight recalled being given a hat by Lily, and May Nutley remembered posting Lily's mail on her walk home from school to West Dene, and getting paid a penny ha'penny each time. During the visit of Olive and Andrew Smith the editors called on Enid Brooks and her sister Chrissie Giles at Littledown. The family had been friends of the Watsons, and Edward Smith, Lily's brother, made the pews in Littledown Methodist Chapel with Harry Davis, who was uncle to Enid and Chrissie. Edward 'Uncle Ted' came every year to the Sunday School celebrations which were held on the second Sunday in May at Littledown Methodist Chapel.

"In later years my husband, fancying a pet name for his own use, discarded the 'Lizzie', choosing 'Lily' in its place" relates Mrs. Watson in her book *'A Village Maiden's Career'* and tells how she heard an evangelist on her 19th birthday and became a born again Christian on 30th September 1874. She trained as a milliner and worked in Salisbury and London before

going on to the Isle of Wight, where she met her future husband, Sydney Watson, a sailor. She remarks in her book that a Christian sailor in those days was almost a living wonder. They were married in Chilmark, her birthplace. Lily's parents, Enos and Harriett, moved to Vernham Dean in about 1882 and Lily and Sydney joined them in an adjacent cottage. Eventually Lily and Sydney moved to 'The Firs' and it was from there that their evangelical work prospered and expanded to the whole country.

It is thanks to Olive Smith that Sydney Watson's background has emerged. Prior to her visit Sydney was believed to have been a London city urchin with no schooling who ran away to sea where he was taught by an officer and eventually converted, but it now transpires his father was Scottish, an artist, and his mother English. They lived in London, and Mr. Watson Senior took commissions to paint families of children in their houses. He took to drink, and eventually committed suicide. This must have resulted in straightened circumstances, because Sydney's first job was a crossing sweeper in the days when crossings had to be kept clear of horse droppings. He was one of four sons, two having died in infancy and two, himself being the elder, living at the time of his father's suicide or, as is otherwise expressed 'died under the influence of drink'. After a period of apprenticeship in London and 'after a variety of strange adventures' he joined the Navy as a second class boy. This he loathed, as he was prey to continual sea-sickness and disliked foreign service. Olive Smith said he habitually deserted and on being recaptured had to start his eleven years all over again. Once he deserted in India, and made his way home via Australia. He became a waiter in Fleet Street, but after three years was caught and made to start once more. When he met Elizabeth Smith at a mission in the Isle of Wight he was serving on Queen Victoria's guardship 'Zealous' and had been converted a few months earlier. He was not allowed to purchase his discharge because of his desertions before his conversion. Bible readings to his men on the 'Zealous' resulted in his banishment to the revenue cutter 'Francis' where he was asked by the captain to conduct a service on board every morning – not quite the result expected from his banishment – but he was still sea-sick. Eventually his release after a total of 14 1/2 years was 'wangled' by a lady who visited Lily's millinery establishment, heard the story, and facilitated his discharge.

Sydney Watson was later known as a writer of books on religious topics, and as an evangelist of considerable drawing power. He was one of the first writers for Horners' Gospel Stories, a cheap form of literature that came out successfully in the 1890s as an antidote to the 'streams of pernicious horribles' that were being issued by nearly all the London publishers at nominal prices. (Andover Advertiser, Friday 28th December 1917). In later years he wrote several works bearing on the second coming of Christ, which had large sales. Lily was also a prolific writer of religious books, some of which were reprinted in the 1990s. In 'A Village Maiden's Career' Lily paints a vivid picture of her childhood, adolescence, and her early married years. In 'Eighteen Years After' her evangelical life in Vernham Dean, including the building of the Mission Hall, is recorded.

Andover Advertiser, Friday, May 25th 1900:

OPENING OF A MISSION HALL – Saturday, Sunday and Monday in Vernham Dean saw the opening of one of the prettiest and most comfortable mission halls to be found in the South of England. The building, which seats 120, but which with the help of extra seating was made to hold 157, was erected by Mrs. Sidney Watson, authoress of 'A Village Maiden's Career' and innumerable other popular books. The services began with a dedication service on Saturday night, conducted by Pastor Pitt, of Bramblebury Hall, London. On Sunday at 10.30 a.m. and 6.30 p.m. Mr. Pitt preached to interested and delighted congregations taxing the utmost limits of the building even when the partitions were removed. On Monday afternoon there was a bible reading, and in the evening the crowning service of the whole series was held, taking the form of a lecture on 'The Tabernacle in the Wilderness', illustrated by a magnificent model (said to be the largest of its kind in the world) "Usually," said Pastor Pitt, "I require at least a dozen nights to give a lecture on 'The Tabernacle in the Wilderness' and how I am to pack the salient truths and leading points into one brief evening is a little difficult to conceive. However ...." Here he plunged into his subject, and after showing that God's idea had always been to dwell with man, and to meet with him on his own ground, he went on to show that when Israel dwelt in tents He, too, desired to have a tent in which He could commune with His people through His chosen priesthoods. For an hour and a quarter the lecturer, by aid of the model, with its 10 ft square of 'five twined linen walls of righteousness', the brazen altar of sacrifice, the laver, the modelled beasts (sheep, goats, heifer etc.) the holy place with its seven-branched candlestick, its altar of incense, its table of shewbread, the Holy of Holies with its wondrous veil, its ark with winged and bowed cherubim on the mercy seat, the high priest in his robes, his breastplate etc. with these things in full view of the congregation Mr. Pitt made all plain to the dullest mind. The beauty of the model was highly appreciated, and at the close of the lecture a large proportion of the audience moved slowly forward to more closely examine its varied parts, Mr. Pitt answering many questions, the people, as they were satisfied, passing out of the side door of the hall to make room for the stress of other eager visitors."

The congregation was large from the outset and continued to grow so that Lily Watson was able to write in her book 'Eighteen Years After': *"This morning, 8th July 1913, as these lines are being penned, we can say that the congregation has remained good the whole time."* There is plenty of documentary evidence to prove the popularity of the Watsons' efforts as the Andover Advertiser, for Friday 27th July 1900 declaims:

CHRISTIAN ENDEAVOURS IN THE MISSION HALL – That wonderful international Convention of Christian Endeavourers, just concluded at the Alexandra Palace, London has, in a specially interesting fashion, touched this quaint old-time village. It was a happy idea of Mrs. Sidney Watson to secure two of the delegates to this convention to take the services last Sunday in the New Mission Hall. Mrs. John Chadwick, of Barrow-in-Furness, a well-known evangelist in the South of England 17 or 18 years ago, had been an old friend of Mrs. Watson's and had married that remarkable all-round Barrow gentleman John Chadwick, Esq. Husband and wife are alike attractive speakers and singers, and the limits of the Vernham Hall were taxed to their utmost last Sunday to accommodate the people who came to the three services. In the evening it became an absolute impossibility even to stand another person in the building, which was packed even to the lobby doors, there being over 200 present. (modern fire regulations are obviously far in the future).

Three months after the main hall was erected a smaller addition was built alongside as the need was felt for an additional room that could be used for prayer meetings and young people's meetings. A strip of ground to the far side of the hall, the same length but slightly narrower was constructed with similar colourings and fittings to the original hall, with the side adjoining the hall moveable to enable the halls to be made into one for large gatherings. In the first year of the mission more than 100 total abstinence pledges were taken, and a Christian Endeavour Society established of over 60 active members, with a branch at Buttermere.

Time took its toll on the original Mission Hall with its timber framing and corrugated iron roof, and in 1961 the Trustees minuted that it would need £500-£600 to start on work which the hall needed. The Trustees thought it would be much better to wait on the Lord and have a new building, and in 1963 it was decided to go ahead and apply for planning permission. 26.09.64 *"It was agreed that with regard to the new hall and on the advice of Mr. Fairhead it would be much the best to replace with a brick building ...."* 24.09.66: *"It was left that Mr. Fairhead's advice should be taken with regard to the Hall Building and all thought it best to build in brick ...."* Mr. Fairhead, with the assistance of Messrs. R.A. Cummings, Adams & Day, Warwick Bros, the SEB and Southampton Corporation Water Works constructed the new hall for the sum of £2,511.17s.6d. However, a Minute dated 24.09.66 of a meeting held in the Village Hall, as the Gospel Hall had been demolished by then, reads: *"Mr. Piper thought that thanks should be recorded to the brothers and sisters of the assembly for the hard work which they had done, getting the site ready, and footings out ready for the builders to start work".* The new Gospel Hall was opened on Saturday, April 22nd, 1967.

The old timber four-bedroomed bungalow with a private entrance into the Mission Hall was not touched at that time as it was necessary to re-house the tenant prior to demolition. It was in 1967 that the Gospel Hall car park was constructed on the site of the bungalow, still remembered by many people living in the village, and in which Lily Watson lived until her death in 1935. 'The Firs' had passed from the Watsons and after 1920 the bungalow was her home. She left the bungalow to the Trust, together with £500. Sydney pre-deceased her on the 19th December, 1917, while on a visit to the Fegan orphanage at Stony Stratford.

The Mission Hall is administered by a Trust which meets once a year, the original members being Sir George Pigot, Messrs. Bryant, Cameron, Dibben and Shawyer. Formerly held by The South Western Counties Evangelization Trust, the Hall became independent as The Vernham Dean Gospel Hall Trust and eventually Mr. David Chandler and Mr. David Sullivan became two of six trustees to carry on the tradition set down at the inception of the Mission Hall of teaching the gospel to everyone without recourse to any particular creed or sect. They succeeded Mr. Jim Hughes, formerly of Vernham Dean, and Mr. Bert Edgington, well known to many present villagers as the baker and shopkeeper at 'Edgingtons' (now Edgington House) before he retired to Pamber Heath.

The Hall saw its first wedding in 1902, when James Newport was married to Emily Mills, later the parents of Mrs. May Nutley who for many years lived a few yards away from the hall in Botisdone Close. The Andover Advertiser reports: *"The first wedding celebrated in this hall took place on Saturday last at 2.30 and proved to be a source of considerable interest to the neighbourhood. The contracting parties were Mr. James Newport and Miss Emily Mills. The ceremony was conducted, in his own bright inimitable way, by the Rev. Thomas Williams, his brief address to the young couple being a model of what such words should be. On the completion of the ceremony, and after the register had been signed, Mr. Watson, on behalf of a few friends, presented the bride with a handsome silver-plated teapot in recognition of her services at the organ of the Mission Hall during the great part of the time since the work began – in doing this little duty Mrs. Watson remarked that as it was almost an universal custom in mission halls and chapels to present the first couple married in the building with a bible, on the part of herself and Mr. Watson she was pleased to hand to the newly-united pair an illustrated bible, praying for God's richest blessing on the now united lives of their two friends. Light refreshments were then served to the wedding party, and amid a shower of rice and confetti the happy couple, with their friends, beat a hurried retreat ….."* May Nutley remembered Lily Watson lending crockery for her own wedding on the 20th February, 1926.

Lily Watson also established a Reading Room in the annexe to the main hall, and it was used for several activities including Christian Endeavour (a similar association to the Boys Brigade), Bible Study and Social Evenings when refreshments were eaten.

Andover Advertiser: 9th November 1900: *"The need for a good reading room for Vernham Dean and neighbourhood has been in the heart of Mrs. Sydney Watson for some years and Tuesday night last saw the accomplishment of her desire. A short dedication service was held in the Mission Hall, which was followed by a few words of explanation by Mrs. Watson, when in addition to many wise words she emphasised the fact, and invited all present to circulate it as widely as possible, that the room was emphatically a public and a free room for the neighbourhood. This introductory meeting being concluded the people adjourned to the Reading Room, which is large, bright and cheery. There is seating accommodation* for 60 persons, and on the four large tables some 40 daily, weekly or monthly papers and magazines make a brave bid for all tastes. There is a large assortment of dictionaries, Chambers Encyclopaedia in 10 vols, time-tables etc. Those who prefer games to reading have also been catered for, one large table being set with draughts, dominoes, word-making and word-taking, and other parlour games. As at present arranged the room will be opened from 7 to 8 each week night, and to make a social hour for the girls and women of the village it will be opened from 6 to 7 every Tuesday for them …….. Henry the coloured evangelist spent Saturday, Sunday and Monday delighting all by accompanying himself on the guitar and singing American Gospel Melodies as well as by his really remarkable expositions of the work of God. Notwithstanding the continuous rain of Sunday a packed audience gathered at Buttermere in the afternoon, and the new room at Vernham had to be brought into requisition at night in addition to the Mission Hall. On Monday night the audience that gathered to hear Henry 'lecture on the Negro race – their religious, poetical, humorous, and other characteristics' – taxed the capacity of the two halls to their utmost limits. The lecture proved to be not only a splendid bit of elocution, bristling with magnificent points, masterly periods, remarkable quotations etc. but was at the same time a revelation to all who listened to it as regards the information imparted, and also of the power of a son of Africa to master language, history, poetry etc. Henry's definition of that peculiar type of humour of the true Americo-African Negro, as distinguished from the keener, colder, merely intellectual wit of some other races, and which he called 'drollery' was illustrated by many a delicious story. One of Henry's assertions, that no other race could come anywhere near the Negro in the matter of real, rightdown, rattling, infectious laughter, was certainly verified by the actual illustration of 'How a Nigger Laughs'. The enjoyment of the evening was intensified by the presence of Pastor W.H. Collins, of Wendover, whose exquisite rendering of 'My Father's at the Helm' and 'Let the Blessed Sunshine In' were alone worth a long walk. Before leaving both Henry and Pastor Collins promised a return visit at an early date".

Andover Advertiser, Friday 21st December 1900: "*MISSION HALL* – one of the gratifying results of the Gospel Mission still being continued in the above hall has been the taking of between 40 and 50 total abstinence pledges, a large proportion of these being from young men."

A 'Sunday' School was held on Tuesday evenings by Mr. Veryard, a London City Missioner, so as not to interfere with the Methodist Chapel and St. Mary's established Sunday Bible instruction. Mr. Veryard had taken 'The Firs' and also took most of the Mission Hall services. Between the wars a Sunday School was held at the Mission and there is still a register extant of children attending from 1936-1961.

Lily and Sydney Watson were an enterprising, energetic and resourceful couple, and Lily would seem to take after her father in many respects. Enos Smith (1832-1906) was a Wiltshireman who ended his days in Vernham, and devoted his time, talents and energy to the bee-keeping industry, eventually establishing a somewhat notable bee farm. He was a man of decided mechanical aptitude, inventing many of the appliances he found he required in his enterprises, and also making a large proportion of them himself. He could devise and manufacture some new arrangement to get over the fresh difficulties which his increasing swarms often presented, and the many clever auxiliaries to the hive impressed people with the scope of his mechanical skill, combined with a generous bump of perception. He was also a keen follower of politics, and served on the Parish Council to good effect.

Sydney was obviously no mean artist with his hands either, having been responsible for much of the original hall. Up in the tiny Methodist Chapel at Littledown (now closed, whereabouts of the artefacts not researched) could be seen the original collection box which was made by Sydney Watson. Another proud possession of the chapel's former custodian, Miss Chrissie Giles, is the garden seat, given by Lily Watson to Chrissie and Enid's father, and Enid's husband renovated it for her mother's 93rd birthday. The seat lived in the garden between the cottage and the chapel.

To bring the tale a little more up to date, a Minute of 13.01.90 reads: *"Mr. Sullivan gave a report on the present state and work of the assembly at Vernham and the condition and state of the property. The assembly is small yet active with a children (sic) and teenage work established. The building is in good repair and decoration and finances of the assembly are adequate and sound."* In 1996 there is a somewhat anxious Minute: *"It was noted that an adjacent bungalow in Botisdone Close had been on the market for some time. It had been heard that the existence of the Gospel Hall had in fact deterred buyers of the property ….."* Surely there is more noise from the pre-school group which uses the property than ever there would be from the congregation, and assuredly more hot air generated on Polling Day than ever issues from the lungs of the assembly. In 1996 there was a Morning Service once a month, but about 15 attenders at the Sunday Evening services, from Wilton, Oxenwood, Shalbourne, Hurstbourne Tarrant, Ibthorpe and other villages around Vernham. Some had dual allegiance and attended a Methodist Chapel in the morning and the Gospel Hall in the evening. There used to be women's meetings and coffee mornings. The 'Sunday School' is held on a Friday night and is called by the children 'The Gospel Club' with a fairly traditional base of quizzes, singing and games for the 5-11 year olds.

Over one hundred years from its beginnings, the Gospel Hall is still an integral part of the village, and a continuing witness to the foresight of its founders, Elizabeth and Sydney Watson.

The editors are grateful to David and Eileen Sullivan for proof-reading and correcting the above text, and for contributing a final paragraph:

2006: The premises are shared with Little Fingers Pre-School group to mutual benefit. Although the Trust Deed did not allow general hire of the Hall as it was to be for the preaching of the Gospel, the Trustees felt that continuance of the social benefits to the village was part of the original intention of the provision of the Hall. The Pre-School have provided valuable improvements and assistance with the upkeep of the premises. One of the greatest periods of influence in the village was during the 1970s and 1980s when many children and teenagers were again involved in the activities in and from the Gospel Hall. Some of these are now parents and send their children to Gospel Club. Others have left England and are involved in Christian and relief work around the world.

We believe that the Bible has great relevance today and to ignore the spiritual needs of people would be so sad. With the Anglican Church we believe we have a life giving message to bring and seek to continue the work commenced over 100 years ago.

Chapter 13:   THE YEARS OF THE FIRST WORLD WAR IN VERNHAM DEAN

(culled from "The Andover Advertiser")

17th July 1914: *VERNHAM DEAN'S FINE PRODUCE: IMPROVING SUCCESS OF THE FLOWER SHOW: Seeing that Vernham Dean has been handicapped through being in the valley, thereby missing many of the storms which swept the hills, and catching the frost, even more than at Hurstbourne Tarrant, the exhibits which were staged at the flower show on Wednesday were very commendable and the great wonder is how the cottagers grew all those fine potatoes, peas, beans and fruit, under such conditions. Competitors who came from Upton as well as Vernham Dean ....for this the seventh show, the officials were: (among others) President, Admiral Gamble R.N., C.B., ...there was an opening ceremony .... thanks were also due to Mr. Jennings for kindly letting them have his field, and Admiral Gamble for allowing them to enjoy his firework display .... the Inkpen Brass Band played selections throughout the afternoon and for dancing in the evening".*

The First World War broke out on August 4th, 1914.

21st August 1914: HOSPITAL SUNDAY – On Sunday Hospital Day was observed in this village in beautiful weather. The Inkpen Temperance Prize Band arrived in the village 2.45 p.m., and starting from the Pond in the middle of the village went up as far as Mr. Coleman's, back again to the Bury Dean, where they played a selection of sacred music ...."

4th September 1914: PATRIOT VILLAGERS

On Sunday a number of young men, who usually meet together for their weekly stroll, made up their minds to do their duty like men and take their stand for King and Country, so on Monday they met in the village, hired a conveyance with a Union Jack flying, and after singing a few patriotic songs and bidding goodbye to their mothers, fathers and friends they drove away quite merrily to Andover. All succeeded in enlisting in Lord Kitchener's new army. On Tuesday a number of men went from Upton and Linkenholt and no doubt men will still continue to enlist now they are beginning to understand that their country needs them. All those who have left are single young men and very robust, and no doubt will look smart in their uniform.

16th October: *FIRE: Early yesterday morning a fire was discovered at Halls Farm, Vernham Street, which is farmed and occupied by Mr. C. Mills. It is thought that the fire began in the rickyard, where the straw rick was situated; all the outbuildings were destroyed, but the house, which is of thatch roof, is quite safe, as it was well soaked by the rain. Horses, cows, pigs and farmstock were rescued.*

13th November 1914: - UPTON – FOR KING AND COUNTRY

Following are the names of men from Upton who have left their work and joined the colours since the outbreak of the war:- Pte Albert Holt and Pte Pavery Stockley, Berkshire Regt., Pte Ernest Bowley, 14 Batt R.F.A., Pte Fred Piper, R.A.M.C and Pte Jesse Stockley, Hants Regt. Pte Charles Sims, of the Wilts Regt. has been returned as medically unfit.

20th November 1914: *ANDOVER SHEEP FAIR – Entries & Prices*

(include) …. Mr. J. Mills, Vernham Manor, two-teeth rams 65s ….. Mr. J. Mills, Vernham Manor, fresh wether lambs 46s.6d., fresh ewe lambs 48s., 41s., wether lambs 39s., 51s., 48s., 49s., fat ewes 52s. 6d. ….. Mr. T.J. Coleman, Vernham, fresh, mixed lambs 49s., 40s.6d., fresh draft ewes 51s., ….. Mr. G. Maber, Lower Conholt, 2-yrs old barren heifers £10.17s.6d., the property of a farmer, barren cows £3.10s., cows £8. 15s.

27th November 1914: A CURIOUS CASE UNDER THE NEW ORDER

A SEMI-COMIC TURN WAS GIVEN TO THE RECENT LEGISLATION REGARDING ALIENS WHEN Menachem Niphdeh Walde, rector of Linkenholt, was summoned for failing to register himself as an enemy alien, and pleaded not guilty. [According to Crockfords Clerical Directory, 1903, Menachem Niphdeh Walde was rector of Linkenholt from 1886. He studied at the London College of Divinity and his first curacy was at Sowerby, Yorkshire, from 1871-1873. He then went to St. Paul's, Camden Square (1873-1875), to Wanstead (1875-1878) and eventually came to Linkenholt from Maida Hill, Middlesex. His actual nationality, incidentally, was not noted in the records].

15th January 1915: SERVING THEIR COUNTRY IN PERSIA

We have received the gratifying information from Private P. Turner, of the 2nd Dorsets, that from one regiment alone, namely the 2nd Dorsets, there are six local men who are representing their country, facing the Turks in Asia. These brave young men are Pte. P.J. Turner (Andover), Lance-Corpl. Clements (Netheravon), Pte. Dawkes (Vernham), wounded, Pte. Horne (Wallop), Dr. Bevis (Hurstbourne) and Pte. Peckover (Ogbourne).

RESULT OF WAR

For the first time since the war began Vernham Dean has experienced a little of military life. The A.S.C (Army Service Corps) has been very busy and they have been billeted at the Masons Arms and the George Inn, which has added greatly to the life of the village. We understand that they are leaving this week for good, having completed their duty which they were sent to do.

5th February 1915: *PRESENT FOR MISS WHITTAKER – On Friday at the Schoolroom Miss Whittaker was presented with a very valuable and useful present on the occasion of her departure for another sphere of labour. Miss Whittaker has been in charge of the infants school for four years, and was much respected by the children of the school and also by the inhabitants of the parish. Miss Whittaker, who has entered on her new duties in the Isle of Wight, has taken with her the best wishes of all. Mrs. Gamble presented the gift, and many thanks and cheers were given to Miss Whittaker for her past services.*

12th February 1915: **WAGES RISING!**

There are so many married and single farm servants joining the Army from this district that some of the farmers have risen (sic) the wages of their employees, which is really necessary if they wish to keep their servants on the farms. The Army is offering a much better wage to such strong and robust men if they will only accept the offer.

25th February 1915: INTERESTING WEDDING

A very pretty wedding took place at St. Mary's, Andover, on February 23rd, the contracting parties being Rifleman William Charles Minter, of the Kings Royal Rifles, eldest son of Mrs. and the late Mr. Minter, of Brightlingsea, Essex, and Beatrice May Betty, fourth daughter of Mr. and Mrs. Strange, of Bank Farm, Vernham. The bride was given away by her master, Mr. A. Lee, and wore a pretty dress of grey with white silk hat and carried a bouquet of pale pink tulips and carnations. The bridesmaids were Miss Dorothy and Queenie Strange, sisters of the bride, and Miss Dorrie Golf, niece of the bridegroom. Mr. Tom Gale was best man. After the ceremony a lunch was partaken of, given by Mr. and Mrs. Lee, after which the happy couple left for the bride's home at Vernham.

19th March 1915: *UNPAID RATES – SHOULD OVERSEERS BE DISTRAINED ON FOR ARREARS? At the meeting of the Andover Board of Guardians on Friday several financial matters came before the members which should be of interest to ratepayers ......Mr. Pain drew attention to the large number of parishes in arrear in paying the amounts due upon precepts, and proceeded to read out the list together with the amounts owing .... Mr. Hughes informed the Board that at Vernham people thought the rate had not to be paid until March 25 (laughter) .... Mr. Hughes said at Vernham the overseers had a job to get the money even after March 25.*

23rd April 1915: *TITHES AT VERNHAM – Land Dear as a Gift.*
On Wednesday at Andover there was a fresh trial of the claim for tithes on land at Vernham by the Dean and Chapter of Winchester against H.W. Prosser, of Windmills, Hurstbourne Tarrant. At the first hearing Mr. Prosser claimed that the tithe had been charged at the full

assessment, £5., instead of upon a third of that sum, £1. 13s. 4d. and he secured a verdict in his favour. The Dean and Chapter applied for a new trial, and this occupied the Court for some time on Wednesday. Mr. Bowler said this was the rehearing. The Registrar informed Judge Gye that there was a small tithe on the same property, but the Vicar of Vernham wrote that he was not at all anxious to mix himself up in the dispute, and he did not appear to be present ..........J.L. Somme, Surveyor of Taxes for Salisbury District, said the annual value of 23a. 2r. 19p. in Vernham Dean was £5. ...... George Wiltshire said he was the assistant overseer for the parish of Vernham Dean and had lived in the parish for 17 years. He knew the piece of land to which the action referred: it was a very rough piece of land, and was practically valueless. It was very hilly indeed, half of it too steep to be ploughed, and the chalk cropped up to the surface. He knew a local farmer had refused to take it. He would not like to give 30s. for the land, and he would not have it as a gift to cultivate it. Mr. Prosser said the Winchester people wanted £3. 10s. a year for land like that; tithe was an assessment upon profits .... His Honour thought Mr. Prosser must be right; a value of £5, after what the last witness had said, was out of the question .... He should like to consider his judgement in that case, and would deliver it at Winchester .... he would give them notice when his judgement was ready.

6th August 1915 *VERNHAM TITHE CASE – His Honour gave his decision in the case of the Dean and Chapter of Winchester v. Prosser, as regards costs ...... the result was judgement for the Dean and Chapter for the sum of £5. 15s. 2d. with costs.*

20th August 1915 *THE VEXED QUESTION OF TITHE*

Letter to the Editor from H.W. Prosser ends: "These are not the dealings of the ghetto, but of a professedly religious body whom we are expected to revere; I see by your issue of the 6th that although Mr. Bowler had told us in Court of the great many thousands a year these people receive, the poor vicar of the parish (the man who does all the religious work) is now to be docked of eight pence! As it is the clergy get in many instances but a small stipend; it is revolting; the persons who ought to have the tithes are the vicars, the curates, and other religious persons doing churchwork in our villages, and not go to swell the enormous income of strangers who do nothing for us. – I am, sir, yours truly, H.W. Prosser."

30th April 1915: *FLOODING IN THE DISTRICT*

The Vernham, Upton and Hurstbourne Valley. The springs in this valley have this year risen as far as Berry Dean just below the village of Vernhams Dean about 400 feet above sea level. From Berry Dean to Upton the course is very ill defined, and the water spreads over the road, which has suffered in consequence.

28th May 1915: KILLED IN ACTION

Mr. Sidney Chandler, who lately received a message from the King congratulating him on having six sons serving at the front, has now, we are sorry to say, been informed that his youngest son Reuben was killed in action in the trenches in France on April 26. Their Majesties the King and Queen have now sent Mr. Chandler a message of condolence.

28th May 1915: A LITTLE VILLAGE ARMY

A good number of our lads have lately been marching and drilling after their day's work fitting themselves for service when they get older. The Rev. J. Parmiter is greatly delighted with the boys, and he gave them an invitation to the vicarage grounds on Tuesday evening, where a good supply of refreshments was in store for them. Master Wm. Chandler and Master Albert Dudman are the leaders of this little village army which if properly armed and given a qualified instructor would become very useful to our nation in the future. Bravo Vernham.

2nd July 1915: *By order of the Mortgagees WILTS AND HANTS BORDERS. Eight miles from Andover and Nine from Hungerford: Messrs. Frederick Ellen & Son are instructed to sell by auction at the Mart, Andover, on Friday, 23rd July, 1915 at 3.30 o'clock in the afternoon (unless previously sold by private treaty) the FREEHOLD Sporting and Agricultural Estate of "HIPPENSCOMBE" Extending to about 822 ACRES OF PASTURE, DOWN, ARABLE, WOOD LAND, AND RABBIT WARREN, with PICTURESQUE RESIDENCE occupying a sheltered position, containing Three Sitting Rooms, Billiard room, Seven Bedrooms, Bath Room, and ample Domestic and Out-offices, lighted by acetylene gas. Timbered Grounds and Kitchen Garden. Farm BUILDINGS and FOUR COTTAGES. The estate is an EXCEPTIONAL SPORTING PROPERTY, some 3,000 rabbits being killed annually, whilst a large head of pheasants and partridges can be maintained. Hunting with the Tedworth and Craven. The Down and Pasture Land afford a very good healthy run for sheep and young cattle, and the Arable Land grows good crops of wheat and oats. Possession will be given on completion of the purchase. No ingoing valuation whatever. Particulars may be obtained .... (30th July) .... Twenty people attended at the Mart on Friday afternoon at the invitation of Mr. Fred Ellen, who had for sale the Hippenscombe Estate, styled a freehold sporting and agricultural property. Mr. Ellen said he had a good recollection of the year 1876 when he sold that estate, Mr. Miles renting at £525 a year ....Three gentlemen did the bidding, the first starting at £3,000, but the vendor not being satisfied with the price, declared the meeting at an end, and said he should be pleased to sell privately. It may be added that the sale was by order of the mortgagor in possession.*

2nd July 1915: *SEASON SIGNS – The hay harvest has been completed and a very satisfactory crop secured in many instances. The cuckoo is still persistently advertising his presence with strong voice, but most of the birds save their singing until the evening. Turnips are growing very rapidly, and there will be plenty of hoers next week.*

ANNUAL TREAT – On Wednesday the children attending the Primitive Methodist Sunday School had their annual treat, arranged by Mr. G. Wiltshire, assisted by teachers and friends, and it proved a complete success. Meeting at the chapel, they embarked in a large motor and trailer provided by Mr. White, of Hurstbourne Tarrant, and made a very enjoyable journey to Savernake Forest. Here they divided, some going into Marlborough to see the college and other places of interest, and others wandering through the forest to the column, or starting games. A splendid tea was provided, to which some healthy appetites were brought. Later a second meal was produced before the journey home was commenced. Arrived at Vernham shortly before 10, a large piece of cake to each was a sufficient preparation for the walk home in the summer twilight quite satisfied with the outing.

20th August 1915: *HORSE – Wanted a cheap HORSE for land work – E. Jennings, Vernham Dean*

3rd September 1915: *WANTED, Head Carter, good character. Apply J. Mills, Vernham Manor.*

10th September 1915: *LOST, last Friday evening, liver and white SPANIEL DOG; collar on, but no name – Ten shillings reward given to finder bringing the dog to Admiral Gamble, Rowe House, Vernhams Dean.*

17th September 1915: WANTED, carter FOR EIGHT-HORSE STABLE, GOOD CHARACTER AND RELIABLE – J. Herriott, Vernham Row, Fosbury.

1st October 1915: GARDENER wanted, married man, single handed, ineligible for army: wages £1 per week and cottage. – Admiral Gamble, Vernham Dean.

29th October 1915: TO ELIGIBLE MEN

We shall be glad to welcome you to the ranks of your local Territorial Battalion, now wintering in Bournemouth. The 3rd and 4th Battalion, the Hampshire Regiment, urgently requires at least 150 men from Andover and District for service in India. Join the ranks of the brave lads who lately won 6 D.C.Ms *[Distinguished Conduct Medal]* in Mesopotamia. The Recruiter for Vernham Dean is Pte. W. Alderman, Ibthorpe, who will visit Vernham Dean shortly, and who will be glad to see any men and give them all information.

5th November 1915: *THE POPLARS, VERNHAM DEAN*

Mr. Allen Herbert has been favoured with instructions from Edward Piper, Esq., (who is leaving the neighbourhood) to Sell by Auction on the Premises on TUESDAY, 23rd November, 1915, the Modern HOUSEHOLD FURNITURE, comprising the contents of Four Bedrooms, Two Sitting Rooms and Domestic Offices, with the OUTDOOR EFFECTS consisting of Seven Iron Water Tanks, Four Garden Frames with Lights, an Aviary with Seven Canaries, portable Force Pump with Hose, 18 dozen Rose Trees, a timber-built Pergola, Garden Tools and other useful items; also (included by permission) 12 Hen Coops, Three Farm Carts, Ladder, Carpenters' Tools etc. etc. Sale to commence at 11.30 o'clock. Full particulars ....

12th November 1915: VISITED BY TROOPS

On Thursday the Northumberland Fusiliers marched into Mr. Hughes' meadow for tea and a few hours rest. Later they marched away to take up a position for the night. Early the following morning, rifle shots were heard on the hills, announcing that a battle had commenced. On Friday afternoon the Battalion, with band playing, went through the village on their return to barracks.

GUY FAWKES DAY – The children here celebrated the day by burning a terrible impersonation of the Kaiser.

26th November 1915: FOR THE RED CROSS

On November 18 an enthusiastic and well supported attempt was made on behalf of the Red Cross Society. A tea, followed by an entertainment organised by Mrs. Parmiter and aided most efficiently by a large number of ladies and gentlemen, realised the magnificent sum of £9. 2s. 7d., £8. 17s. 7d. being handed over to the hon. secretary, Miss C. Randolph, for the local branch. Great praise is due to all who helped in various ways to make this village effort so successful.

BANTAMS: On Monday the district was visited by two battalions of bantams, one attached to a Durham Regiment and the other to the Scots. There were two bands to help the little men along the road and a travelling commissariat, including up-to-date cooking facilities.

17th December 1915: LORD DERBY'S SCHEME

Many of the married men of this village have joined under Lord Derby's system, and some of the single men who were employed on Munitions Works.

31st December 1915: POSTMAN IN KHAKI

Our Christmas visitor from the trenches was the well known morning Postman, Mr. T. Kent, who is home on short leave, and returns to the Trenches tomorrow (Saturday).

7th January 1916: FESTIVE GATHERINGS – *All the children on the Linkenholt Estate were entertained to a tea and Christmas tree on Dec. 30 which had been arranged for them in the big coachhouse ……… Mr. Cooper, Estate Agent ………… drank the health of Mr. and Mrs. Thomas and Family who had treated them so well ………….. thus ended one of the good old-fashioned festivals which we are sorry to see are fast becoming things of the past.*

14th January 1916: DEATHS

On the 13th October, 1915, killed in action in France, WALTER THOMAS CHANDLER, aged 26.

14th January 1916: *ALLEN HERBERT IS INSTRUCTED BY Mrs. Chandler (in consequence of the death of her husband) to Sell by Auction on the premises on TUESDAY, 25th JANUARY, 1916, commencing at 12.30, the COTTAGE FURNITURE, including 5 iron Bedsteads with bedding, Chair, Bedstead, 2 Chests of Drawers, a Nest of 22 Drawers, Washstand with Ware, several Tables and chairs, Kitchen Requisites and Ware etc., also THE OUTDOOR EFFECTS, comprising Carrier's Van with Cover, Scotch Cart with Ladders, Thill and Trace Harness, Iron Plough, Drag, Van Cloth, 2 Wheelbarrows, 3 Pig Troughs, Ladder, a 100 gallon Water Tank, several Tubs, 2 Fowlhouses, erection of Piggery and Woodhouse, several lots of Tools, 15 Chicken, a small quantity of Mangold, and Stable Manure. Further Particulars ………..*

21st January 1916: *A SMALL LOCAL INVESTMENT*

Mr. ALLEN HERBERT is instructed by Mr. Charles Rowe to Sell by Auction on the premises on TUESDAY NEXT, 25th January 1916, at 12 o'clock THE FREEHOLD COTTAGE, containing 3 Bedrooms, Sitting-room, Kitchen, Pantry, etc., with STABLE, VAN SHED, Well House, Yard in front and Garden at the rear, as occupied for several years by the late Mr. Sidney Chandler. Vacant possession will be given ……..

11th February 1916: ***PRIZE WINNING CATTLE***

At the Birmingham Aberdeen Angus Spring Show and Sale, the Angus heifer "Molly of Conholt", Heather-bloom strain, was first in the yearling class, and also gained champion and silver medal for the best heifer in the show. Another heifer "Joan of Conholt", same strain, was highly commended. Both are the property of Mr. E.A. Wigan, of Conholt Park.

17th March 1916: *ANDOVER RURAL DISTRICT COUNCIL*

The Clerk read the report of the Surveyor as under:- Messrs. Pike & Co. have not made any appointment to meet me at Faccombe. The Fowler roller has been standing at Upton since Feb. 23 on account of snow and severe weather, and the driver and assistants are employed clearing snow from roads at Faccombe, Linkenholt and Vernham Dean which are impassable on account of drifts.

28th April 1916

IN MEMORIAM
In fond and loving memory of our youngest son,
REUBEN HENRY CHANDLER, Hants Regt.
KILLED IN ACTION 26th April 1915
"Greater love hath no one than this, that he lay down his life for his friends"
From his loving MOTHER, SISTER and BROTHERS

15th May 1916: *FOR SALE – white Wyandotte-Houdan EGGS for sitting, 3s. per doz. F. Wallis, Vernham Street, near Hungerford.*

12th May 1916: *WANTED – ASSISTANT TEACHER for Vernham Dean School: salary according to experience – Application forms from J. Herriott, Vernham Row, Fosbury, Hungerford.*

12th May 1916: *SWINE FEVER CASE – James Hughes, farmer, of Vernham Dean was summoned for failing to notify swine fever on his premises on April 29. Mr. T.E. Longman, Andover, said Defendant, on his advice, pleaded guilty to a technical offence: P.C. Prior said he visited Defendant's premises, saw the pigs, and found a large store pig dead – Defendant then told him they had done fairly well up to the present and that was the only one dead. On the following Monday he was again called to the premises by the Board of Agriculture inspector, and there he saw five small dead pigs, which he said had died from swine fever. These five were part of a litter of seven pigs. Defendant said he understood the pigs had a chill; had he known that they were suffering from fever he would have given notice. A fine of £2 was imposed.*

19th May 1916: *VERNHAM STREET – About midway between Andover and Hungerford, MESSRS. FREDERICK ELLEN & SON are instructed to Sell by Auction during June, the desirable Small FREEHOLD FARM known as "HALL'S FARM" in the occupation of Mr. C. Mills, extending to 48a. 2r. 23p. of which about 17 acres are Pasture, with comfortable Farmhouse and convenient Buildings, recently erected. Particulars ….*

PROPERTY SALE – On Friday at the Mart, Mr. F. Ellen offered for sale by auction a small holding at Vernham. Mr. Ellen pointed out that there were convenient buildings in addition to a comfortable house, while the farm consisted of 30 acres arable and 17 pasture. Everything was in good order and he proceeded to offer it in one lot. After competition the hammer fell to a bid of £570. made on behalf of Messrs. R. and C. Brooks.

EMPIRE DAY 1916

On May 20th the children belonging to Vernham Dean School celebrated their Empire Day, and it was quite a unique occasion. The children assembled on the Berry Dean at three p.m. ...... Rev. Parmiter also told the children that they were about to perform a ceremony they would never forget, namely the planting of a Royal Oak Tree in the School playground, to commemorate the Great European War and also in honour of our brave men at the front .... every child had a share in the tree planting, also the teachers, managers .... their task was to put a spadeful of mould round the roots.

21st July 1916: *FOR SALE – Grey MARE, warranted quiet to ride and drive. Apply J. Mills, Vernham Manor.*

4th August 1916: *WANTED – GROOM – COACHMAN, to drive a pair or single, ineligible for war service. Apply with references, to Admiral Gamble, Rowe House, Fosbury, Hungerford.*

18th August 1916

IN MEMORIAM

Pte PERCY HICKS, the dearly beloved eldest son of Mr. and Mrs Hicks, Linkenholt, who has been posted as missing is now reported killed on the above date
At the Dardenelles, aged 20

In a distant land, in an unknown grave,
Amid the shot and shell;
We weep for you, our own dear boy,
For we loved you, Oh so well.
A light is from our household gone,
A voice we loved is stilled,
A place is vacant in our home,
Which never can be filled.

From his sorrowing FATHER, MOTHER, BROTHER AND SISTERS

8th September 1916: THE HAMPSHIRE BANTAMS (men)

Previous rejects who have been to Winchester for further examination return with varying tales of their experiences, and some consider that cattle at the December shows are treated with more consideration than are those men who have been called upon to give up time and leave business in order that the finding of the previous medical examination may be confirmed. Those who are getting some fun for their expense are the weightier among the Hampshire men, for they are invariably refused by the courteous sergeant in charge when they offer for the Bantams, while when they come to the scales the clerk is invariably nonplussed for his machine does not go beyond 15 stone 13 lbs 15 ozs. Such scales are of little use for many who are of military age, and so their card is filled in with the "x" of algebra opposite the weight. The summer bathing wrap supplied by the military is also too small for some of the country men now coming up, and a supply of larger sizes must be obtained if the military age is to be raised. Anyone attending the Hampshire Corn markets can see for himself that a weighing machine up to 24 stone and smocks up to 60 round the chest will be necessary when the military comb out the agricultural workers up to 45 years of age, but at present it is only a waste of time for those over 18 stone to make the journey. Those who live in towns have no idea how grumbling at bad times tends to put on weight if combined with plenty of fresh air and wholesome food.

15th September 1916: *WANTED young girl as GENERAL SERVANT, some experience, help given – apply Mrs. Herriott, Vernham Row, Fosbury, Hungerford.*

WANTED – WOMEN, GIRLS and LADS to Pick about 100 acres of Potatoes behind machines – Apply Cooper, Manor Farm, Linkenholt.

13th October 1916

IN MEMORIAM
In loving memory of my dearly beloved husband
WALTER THOMAS CHANDLER
Who was killed in action on October 13, 1915
And son of Mrs. S. CHANDLER

What matters it to Him who holds within
The hollow of His Hand all worlds, all space,
That thou art done with earthly pain and sin,
Somewhere within His ken thou has a place. K.C.

From his sorrowing WIFE and MOTHER

VERNHAM STREET, HUNGERFORD, BERKS.

27th October 1916: *THE NEW VICAR – Rev. H.J. Parsons, curate of St. Mark's Church, Southampton, has been appointed by the Bishop of Winchester to the Vicarage here. The parish of St. Mark was carved out of Shirley 24 years ago, owing to the westward growth of Southampton, and had a population of about 6,500. Rev. Parsons went there in 1908 to work with Rev. E.L. Franklin, who was appointed vicar at the time the separation was effected, and it will be a great change to come to a wide parish in the wilds after working for eight years in Southampton. The vicarage here is returned as being worth £260 a year at the present time.*

27th October 1916: *WOODMAN KEEPER Wanted: single-handed, must be good Rabbit and Vermin Killer: ineligible, or over 45; thoroughly trustworthy, reliable: good wages, house and garden – Apply F.J. Cooper, Estate Office, Linkenholt, Hungerford.*

17th November 1916: ROLL OF HONOUR

A list has been put up in the church of those belonging to this parish who are serving in H.M. Forces. It contains over 50 names, more than one tenth of the population. Seven have laid down their lives for King and Country: Lieut. Miller, Pte. W. Baiden, Pte. W. Thos. Chandler, Pte. Reuben Chandler, Pte. Thomas Shepherd, Driver John Seward, Corpl. A.T. Allen. This week news has come to the village that Pte. Edward Bowley, 2nd Batt. Royal Berkshire Regiment, was killed in action on Oct 24. He was shot by a sniper when carrying a wounded man to the dressing station. Our sympathy goes out to his father and mother, Mr. and Mrs. Charles Bowley, of Vine Cottage, in their loss. The news was sent to his home by Pte. Wm. Alderman, of the same regiment, who also belongs to Vernhams Dean.

17th November 1916: *HANDY MAN Wanted for General Work on Farm, go with horses if required; ineligible or over 45; work for family. House and Garden found – Apply with wages, to F.J. Cooper, Estate Office, Linkenholt.*

24th November 1916: DEATHS

Killed in action Oct. 24 Pte. EDWARD CHARLES BOWLEY, eldest and dearly beloved son of EDWARD and ELIZA BOWLEY, aged 27 years. From his sorrowing MOTHER, FATHER, SISTER AND BROTHERS. VERNHAM DEAN.

22nd December 1916:

IN MEMORIAM
In ever loving memory of my dearly beloved husband,
SYDNEY CHANDLER
Who passed away on the 21st Dec., 1915,

We loved him in life, we love him still,
But in death we must bend to God's Holy Will:
Only those who have lost are able to tell,
Of the pain at the heart in saying farewell.

From his sorrowing WIFE and CHILDREN. Vernham Street, near Hungerford.

12th January 1917: *INDUCTION OF THE NEW VICAR. On Thursday last week the Archdeacon of Winchester came to the church to induct the Rev. H.J. Parsons, lately curate of St. Mark's, Southampton, to the vicarage of Vernham Dean .... The Archdeacon and the clergy and other friends, including Admiral Gamble, were most kindly entertained to tea afterwards at Vernham Manor by Mr. and Mrs. Mills and Mr. Quick. The one cloud on the day's proceedings (as the Archdeacon said) was that Mrs. Parsons was not sufficiently recovered from her attack of influenza to be present.*

26th January 1917: *FERRETS – Wanted, several good healthy FERRETS – Jennings, Vernham Dean.*

23rd February, 1917: *COOK, good, single-handed, wanted, aged 30 to 45. Small dairy: two family: parlourmaid and housemaid kept: good references required – Mrs. Gamble, Rowe House, Fosbury, Hungerford.*

2nd March 1917: ROLL OF HONOUR

We are sorry that the name of Driver Ernest Rivers has been omitted from the roll on the church door. He joined the A.S.C (Army Service Corps) (M.T.) more than a year ago, and has been in France quite a long time. His many friends wish him the best of luck and a safe return to the district.

UPTON – A GOOD RECORD – This small hamlet can fairly claim a good record in connection with the call to defend the motherland, as no less than 22 of the young men have gone to the fray and others have been prevented from joining them by the doctors refusing to place them in the proper class for active service. Lieut. Miller, Sergt. W. Baiden, Driver John Seward, and Driver A. Parker have been killed by the enemy. Corpl. H.C. Sims, Pte. W.A. Sims, Pte. F.J. Sims, Pte. A.E. Allen, and Corpl. A. Alexander are out of action, through wounds, and all in Upton wish them speedy recovery. For the rest their friends hope for a safe return to England when the war has ceased.

25th May 1917: ***CRICKET BALL CAUSES DEATH***

The circumstances surrounding the death of George H. Ernest John Rowe, son of Mr. and Mrs. G.W.W. Rowe, of Vernham Row, are very sad. At the inquest at the Andover Workhouse on Wednesday evening, Herbert Blundy, a playmate, said on Friday, April 27, a lot of them were playing with a cricket ball on the Bury Dene. Deceased kicked the ball about, and went to school as usual on the following Monday. At night, however, he had a job to hobble home, and said: "My big toe hurts." Mr. Rowe, the father, told the coroner that his boy, the only one of seven children, was 12 years old. He understood from the boy that the ball hit his toe while he was batting. There was no sign of a mark or swelling on the toe, but early on Tuesday morning the boy called out and complained of his toe. It was then black so they poulticed it. As it got worse the nurse was called in – they were a long way from a doctor – but she said they could do no more than go on poulticing, and she did not think there was any need of a doctor ………….. (Nurse sent for Dr. Gilmour. Boy taken by Admiral Gamble to Dr. Gilmour because the latter "could not get anything to bring him over." Temperature 102. Taken to Andover Cottage Hospital on May 8 and seen by Dr. E.A. Farr. Acute blood poisoning "due to a blow from the cricket ball stopping the circulation to the top of the toe, which consequently died." Boy died May 21st.)

1st June 1917: DEATHS

On the 10th April, in France, Corporal WILLIAM ALDERMAN, of the Machine Gun Section, who died of wounds, the youngest dearly beloved son of C. and J. Alderman, of Vernhams Dean, aged 23 years. – Deeply mourned by his sorrowing MOTHER, FATHER, SISTER and BROTHER.

20th July 1917: KILLED BY A BOMB

The sad news has arrived of the death in Salonica on June 15 of Lance-Corpl. E. Alderman, youngest son of the late Mr. George Alderman, at the age of 26. Rev. L. Whitcombe, Chaplain to the Forces, has written a most consoling letter to the relations. He says under date June 16, - "I am very sorry to have to send you bad news about your son, 15229 L. Corpl. E. Alderman of the …. Royal Berks Regiment. He was shoeing a mule in the Transport Lines yesterday morning about 10 o'clock, when a hostile aeroplane came over and dropped two bombs from a great height. Your son was severely wounded by one of them, and became unconscious almost at once, and died on the way to the Field Ambulance, after his wounds had been dressed by the Regimental Medical Officer. He was a good worker, and will be greatly missed by his Battalion. God give you strength and comfort in your sorrow. I buried your son at 6.45 p.m. the same day in the British Military Cemetery close by. A permanent memorial is to be erected at the end of the war to those who lie there. Please accept my sincere sympathy in your great loss. He died at work and on duty, and the souls of the faithful are in the hands of God. May he rest in peace." The sympathy of our readers go out to the relatives in their great loss.

31st August 1917: *MAN as KEEPER with knowledge of Wood Work and Fencing, Wanted: must have good references. – Apply, Cooper, Estate Office, Linkenholt, Hungerford.*

7th September 1917: Experienced Agricultural LABOURER, and Man as SHEPHERD for Dry Flock: good wages, homes and gardens provided for good working families – Apply, with full particulars, to F.J. Cooper, Estate Office, Linkenholt, Hungerford.

14th September 1917: *WANTED, a COWMAN (ineligible) to milk three COWS and make himself generally useful. – Apply to Admiral Gamble, Vernham Dean.*

12th October 1917

IN MEMORIAM
In loving memory of my beloved husband,
WALTER THOMAS CHANDLER,
Who was killed in action in France October 13, 1915.

Sleep on dear one, in a foreign grave,
Your life for your country you nobly gave;
No friend stood near you to say good bye,
But safe in God's keeping now you lie.
From his sorrowing WIFE (Hurstbourne Tarrant)

26th October 1917: PROMOTION

We are pleased to hear that Company-Sergt.-Major Liddeard has been granted a commission in the 21st Manchesters. Being of the Regular Army one of the first to be ordered abroad, he has seen much hard fighting. Lieut. Liddeard is to be congratulated on his well deserved success.

4th January 1918: *A WEDDING took place at St. Mary's on Boxing Day by the Rev. H.J. Parsons, the contracting parties being Miss Daisy Violet Strange, second daughter of Mr. and Mrs. Strange, Bank Farm, Vernham, to Sergt. William Dillworth, Australian Imperial Forces, second son of Mr. and Mrs. R. Dillworth, Victoria, Australia. The bride carried a bouquet of white chrysanthemums, and wore a pretty dress of white silk. She was given away by Sergt.H. Giles, Australian Imperial Forces, a great friend of both bride and bridegroom. Mr. R. Maton, brother-in-law of the bride, acted as best man. The bridesmaids were Kitty, Dorothy and Queenie, sisters of the bride, and Marjorie (niece) who all wore pretty dresses of white silk and hats to match, and carried bouquets of white chrysanthemums. After the ceremony the happy couple left the church in showers of confetti for the home of the bride, where a large number of friends sat down to dinner. The presents were numerous and costly.*

18th January 1918: ***HANTS: ANDOVER, UPTON and VERNHAM:***

WINCHESTER COLLEGE ESTATE: NOTICE OF SALE of valuable FREEHOLD SMALL FARMS & HOLDINGS of 20 to 70 acres, including "BLANDY'S FARM, UPTON" with Farm House and Buildings, Several Accommodation Fields of Pasture and Arable Land, with Fishing Rights, Pair of Cottages, Important Fully-Licensed Roadside PUBLIC HOUSE known as "THE GEORGE", VERNHAM DEAN; also the well-known BEERHOUSE "THE BOOT", LITTLEDOWN, VERNHAM, which Messrs. JAMES HARRIS & SON have been favoured with instructions from the Warden and Scholars Clerks of Winchester College to Sell by Auction at "The Star and Garter" Hotel, Andover, on FRIDAY, the 22nd day of February, 1918, at two o'clock precisely in 31 lots.

1st March 1918: *PROPERTY SALE – On Friday afternoon the billiard room at the Star Hotel was filled with a business company, the attraction being the sale of properties belonging to Winchester College in Andover and neighbourhood, by Messrs. James Harris and Sons, of Winchester…. pair of Cottages, Hall's Farm, Vernham: 2r. 8p. rental £9, Mr. Thomas £200. Boot Inn, Little Down, 1r, 24p. rental £10, Berks Brewery Co. £400. George Inn, Vernham, 2a. 3r. 0p., tithe £1, rental £25, Mr. F.. Herbert £800.*

29th March 1918: *WANTED – BICYCLE for boy of 13, good make. – Apply Herriott, Vernham Row, Fosbury, Hungerford.*

5th July 1918: *DEATH OF MR. QUICK. A fine specimen of the English farmer, one who had won the respect of his neighbours for a long period, passed away at his home, Vernham Manor, on June 26, at the age of 54, and was laid to rest in the village churchyard on Saturday, in the presence of a large assembly from the parish and neighbourhood. Mr. Edwin Harding Quick had been at the manor for over 30 years, and could be best described as a quiet, consistent Christian, a true friend to his neighbours, and never an enemy. Outside agriculture he was a keen Freemason, and a firm churchman, and will be much missed in both these spheres. He was Chairman of the Parish Council and took a great interest in local affairs; a ready speaker, he was welcomed at social gatherings for his apt responses to toasts and his fund of really humorous stories. He was respected by all who knew him, and will long be regretted by many. At the church on Saturday the officiating clergy were the Rev. H.J. Parsons (Vicar) and the Rev. Alan Williams, of Sherborne, formerly in charge of Vernham …………………*

20th September 1918: *WANTED at Michaelmas, an all-round FARM LABOURER, and one able to build ricks; cottage and garden – Apply J. Mills, Manor Farm, Vernham Manor, nr Hungerford, Berks.*

WANTED an Experienced CARTER: 8-horse stable; good wages and cottage – J. Herriott, Vernham Row, Fosbury, Hungerford.

4th October 1918: *VERNHAM MANOR – Notice of Sale of 5 Valuable CART HORSES, TWO PROMISING CART COLTS, two well-built Wagons, three Scotch Carts, Self Binder, Iron Water Barrel, Shepherds House, Broadcast, Rollers, Iron Sheep Trough, Sets of Thill and Trace harness etc., etc. together with about 100 Lots of SUPERIOR HOUSEHOLD FURNITURE including Brass and Iron Bedsteads and Bedding, an ASH BEDROOM SUITE, Mahogany Wardrobe, Chests of Drawers, WALNUT DRAWING ROOM SUITE, CARVED BLACK OAK SIDEBOARD, Two Mahogany Telescope Dining Tables, Oak Pedestal Writing Table, Settee, Easy Chairs, HANDSOME INLAID ROSEWOOD CHINA CABINET, Rosewood Sofa Table, and American Organ by Malcolm, Mantel Glasses, Brussels and other Carpets and Rugs etc., which MESSRS FREDERICK ELLEN & SON are instructed by the Representatives of the late Mr. E.H. Quick, to Sell by Auction on the premises ON WEDNESDAY, 16th OCTOBER, 1918. Sale to commence at 12.30. Catalogues …...*

25th October 1918: *WANTED – GROOM single man, to drive and look after horse and dogcart and make himself useful on place. – Apply Admiral Gamble, Fosbury, Hungerford.*

6th December 1918: *BOAR PIG wanted, fit for stock. – Apply Jennings, Vernham Dean.*

……………………………………………………………………

The Andover Advertiser of 28th October, 1921, gives a lengthy report on the Dedication of the War Memorial at Vernham Dean.

A tablet to the memory of the men of Vernham parish who fell in the war was unveiled and solemnly dedicated in St. Mary's Church on Wednesday, Oct 19th, in the presence of a crowded congregation. The church was full to overflowing, over 40 children were in the gallery, and in addition there was quite a congregation gathered outside the west door. Fortunately it was a very mild evening, the door was open, and so they were able to take part in the service, as well as if they had been inside. The Church Council gave a very hearty invitation to the ex-servicemen of the parish to take a considerable part in the proceedings, and it met with a very ready response. About 40 came to the service, many of whom marched up from the village in a body to the seats reserved for them near the pulpit. One of their number was chosen by themselves to unveil the tablet and another to read the lesson …….. the church was a striking sight; the candles in the nave and chancel standards; the altar lights brightening the flowers in the gleaming brass vases; the Union Jack concealing the tablet; the two Boy Scouts on guard with heads bowed over their staves (surely no two boys ever stood so still for so long a time before); the mass of people; the crowded ex-service men in front, one here and there in uniform; the chancel full of unaccustomed folk ….. and last, but not least, in the seats of honour close to the memorial, the relatives of the men who had given their lives – all combined to make a scene which will live long in the memory of those who saw it ….. The lesson was read clearly and well by Chief Petty Officer Watts.

The Rural Dean then called upon Mr. F. Sims to unveil the memorial. Mr. Sims accordingly pulled a string, which released the Union Jack, and the tablet stood revealed in its place on the south side of the nave. The Rural Dean next dedicated the tablet ……. then went to the pulpit and gave a most touching address ……. The address ended, the hymn 'Through the Night of Doubt and Sorrow' was sung. Then the Hurstbourne Tarrant Boy Scouts sounded the 'Last Post' and the 'Reveille' after which 'God Save the King' was heartily sung by all present …….. It was a memorable service. All felt it was worthy of a great occasion, the honouring of the 17 men who gave their lives for their country.

The memorial tablet is of oak, handsomely carved with inscriptions incised and gilded. Above 'Their Name Liveth for Evermore'; below, 'To Honour the Memory of the Men of this Parish who fell in the Great War, 1914-1918'. The names are on two large panels, incised and gilded, with a wreathed Cross in bold relief.

During the last few years, it has been deemed appropriate to give the full names of the fallen and accordingly research by the late Leslie Le Mottée has given us the following, read out with deep respect each Remembrance Sunday.

Edward Alderman	William Alderman	Alfred Thomas Allen
William Baiden	Charlie Blundy	Edward Bowley
Reuben Henry Chandler	Walter Thomas Chandler	Charlie Lattimer
Cyril Roland Eyre	Arthur William Parker	Thomas Perry
Jack Piper	John Seward	Thomas Shepherd
Jimmy Silence	Tom Williams.	

A snippet from Vernham Mills: *I had been to church and the Vicar told the congregation he was to be married the next day, Monday, at Carlisle. I went home for lunch; the church bell rang out. I turned on the wireless to hear that war had been declared and that all petrol pumps would be closed.*

The vicar, in a terrible state, came to see my father, the Churchwarden. How was he to get to his wedding in Carlisle with only half a tank of petrol in his Austin 7? We had many two gallon cans, so we calmed him down, put three cans in his car so he could go and be married. He returned safely and his bride was a great asset to the parish.

Vernham Mills himself joined the LDV (Local Defence Volunteers). The shifts were 10-2, 2-4, there were several observations posts, too many posts to man in the area. Accordingly they were reduced to three: the churchyard, the dairy, and Linkenholt. Vernham received an armband – he had his own shotgun - and a pack of cartridges. Later he was given an old US rifle with five rounds of .303. The village was used to seeing German bombers flying over to bomb the Midlands towns: the area had searchlights but no guns and the Andover-Oxford area was a good path for the Germans. From the LDVs' vantage points they could see bombs being dropped on London, the sky a blaze of light.

Italian POWs (prisoners of war) came to work on farms in the area – Vernham's household had two farm workers and a cook. The cook also used to repair walls, and sometimes lit the fire to heat the church on Sunday mornings. The Italians were highly regarded in the district and soon made themselves at home – coming from smallholdings in Italy they could do most of the jobs on the farms. At one point the POWs 'acquired' some copper piping and started distilling. Vernham discovered their secret and they shared the product with him. He recalled going home on hands and knees.

Mrs. Joyce West (née Taylor) was able to contribute her memories of being evacuated to Vernham:

"At the time none of us children really appreciated the kindness of our foster families and we were bewildered to find ourselves sitting in the village hall, awaiting we knew not what, after the journey from Portsmouth. My sister and I were picked up by a girl who was the niece of my foster mother, her parents kept 'The Boot' Inn. We lived at 'The Laurels' and Mrs. Harry Brooks was our temporary mother. The walk with kitbags from the village hall seemed endless, it was a warm day and we must have presented a pretty sorry picture to Mrs. Brooks when two tired and scruffy girls turned up at her home. After leaving an 'all mod. cons' home in Portsmouth, life in 'The Laurels' was full of surprises: a candle to go to

bed, an oil lamp lit in the evening, the toilet a half mile down the garden (or so it seemed), no chain to pull but two holes across a wooden plank, with two buckets beneath. We used to read our comics in this tiny shed, but we never became ill. Everything seemed very primitive to us, especially having to have a bath in a shed outside the house in a tin bath. Baths were taken once a week, either Friday or Saturday, usually Saturday. The water was heated in an old brick boiler in a small barn. After our bath we had to run into the house just a few yards away. It was a cold run in winter. There was no running water: a hand pump attached to the kitchen sink was the only way to obtain water. It took an age for the water to come out and caused a great deal of arm ache to get the air out before the water arrived. In the house there was a kitchen range on which all the cooking was done. There was no stove such as we had been accustomed to use in town, but food always turned out well and enjoyable. However, we settled down to a new and strange life. We started school, walking there what seemed miles. The school had just two rooms, a contrast to ours in Portsmouth which had only been built two or three years ago and had so many amenities. It was really an eye opener to see this small building, and there were only a very few children from Vernham attending and others from another village. At first we did not seem to mix with these children, I am afraid to say we had a superiority complex and were inclined to lord it over the village children.

After a while 'we' and 'they' finally integrated enough to forget our backgrounds. Our headmistress at Vernham was Mrs. Moss, a very formidable lady and a strict disciplinarian. She needed to be, having more children to keep in check. After a while we older children, town and villagers, were taken from the school to have our lessons in the village hall. Our master was Philip Burnett, who came with us from Portsmouth. Like Mrs. Moss, he was strict. The boys felt the ruler on the back of their legs quite often.

Summer time always seemed sunny, and gradually we began to really enjoy ourselves. We used to help with the harvest and potato picking to earn a few coppers. Stone picking was two old pence a bucket – it took forever to fill. Every Saturday morning we went to the village post office to cash our 6d postal orders from home and buy what sweets were on offer. That was the only day we did not mind the long walk to the village. I believe there was a bus once a day from the village to Andover, but only once a week from Vernham Street stopping outside 'The Laurels'. The lady from 'Rose Cottage', (Rose Wallis) opposite our cottage, would go into town on Saturdays and bring the shopping for people in Vernham Street. Over the couple of years I was in Vernham I only went into Andover twice, and my foster mother never went at all. It was not easy for parents to visit. Some children had no visits at all, but mine did manage a few. Sometimes we would go home for a week in the holidays, but travelling was a hassle. Most of the village children had never seen the sea, which seemed really strange to us who had come from the seaside.

Our foster parents insisted we went to church each Sunday. I am afraid that we did not really enjoy the service, and most of us girls would be very inattentive and giggled our way through most of the sermon. The organ was the cause of much hilarity, we used to take it in turn to work the handle up and down for the organist (Mrs. Wallis). It was hard work but quite fun when the music stopped because we had missed a couple of pumps of the handle which came out of the side of the organ.

Mr. Frank Brooks who owns 'Flowers Farm' in Vernham Street was the nephew of my late foster parents. He always reckoned that we evacuees livened up the village ...."

Back in 1939, village life was much as usual. At the October meeting of the WI a potato competition was judged and Mrs. Lane gave a cookery demonstration. Mrs. Keith Thomson recited humorous poems and tea was served by hostesses from Conholt. Mrs. Dudley, the President, very kindly offered gifts of wool for members to knit into articles for HM Forces ..... and in November many members gave generously to the secretary's plea for wool to be knitted into comforts for HM Forces. In the wider world, however *"Luminous dog collars: in order to reduce black out fatalities among dogs, the National Canine Defence League is making luminous dog collars of a plastic material which gives out a greenish glow visible for about 25 yards in darkness ....."*

Andover Advertiser 15th December 1939: *"Death of Mr. Edward Hounslow (80). He had been in indifferent health for many years, but had only taken to his bed for the past five weeks. Some 60 years ago, when he was a corporal, Mr. Hounslow was discharged from the Army as physically unfit. He had been married three times, and leaves a widow and four children. He came to Vernham Dean as motor driver to Mr. S. Watson, founder of the Vernham Dean Gospel Hall. About 30 years ago he was appointed caretaker and became a keen worker at the Hall. He was also a trustee of the Methodist Chapel in the village and a member of the 'Hope of Andover' Tent, Independent Order of Rechabites ......"*

The war begins to bite: 22nd December 1939: *"There will be no extra allocation of butter this week, states an official of the Food Ministry, and the week's rations will have to be spread over nearly half of next week as shops will be closed on Christmas Day and Boxing Day. From Monday, 15th January, the price of bread will be increased to 1/6d. per gallon loaf. The price of a pound loaf will be 2 1/2d., and a 2 lb loaf will cost 4 1/2d. All proprietary bread 3 1/2d.*

1940 saw floods in the village, and as related elsewhere, the unfortunate Mrs. Newport had to be evacuated from her house when water reached her bed. On the social side, a Whist Drive was held in February ..... *"organised by Miss Webb, with willing helpers, to defray the expenses of buying the material for, and making, the black out blinds for the hall windows ...."* Catering for village social functions was discussed at the Food Control

136

Meeting in Andover, and Mr. G.E. Evans, of Vernham Dean, told the committee he had received applications for extra rations of butter and sugar for refreshment purposes. He had explained he was unable to supply them with extra rations. Mr. Evans was advised to inform the parishioners either to get licensed caterers to do their refreshments or to apply for a caterer's licence themselves. When the question of extra sugar for marmalade making was raised, the Food Officer pointed out that extra rations were obtainable providing the Executive Officer was satisfied that for every pound of sugar the householder or marmalade maker had purchased one pound of oranges. Ration books, however, would have to be sent to the Food Control Office before the sugar could be granted.

The 12th April saw the first birthday of the Vernham Dean branch of the British Legion. This was celebrated with a Whist Drive at the Village Hall and proved a record night with 24 tables. Appropriate prizes were presented: garden fork, rake and hoe to the men, saucepans etc. to the women. Agricultural wages reached a minimum of 48/- a week from the 30th June. Increases were also given for younger male workers and women and girls, and special rates for workers employed for tending animals. In some counties the value of allowances in kind, such as a cottage, or board and lodging, were also increased. The Bourne Valley Group of WIs was particularly concerned with canning – there had been demonstrations in Andover and the Chairman, Diana Darling, urged members to learn and teach others to use the vegetables and fruit. By now the Ministry of Food was backing a scheme for WIs fruit preservation, also backed by the National Federation of Women's Institutes. Since March 1940 330,000 members in 5708 village centres had been planning to use the fruit crop. Money had been borrowed from the Carnegie Trust to buy 100 home canning machines from America. By the 1st July there were 197 schemes in operation.

Something a little surprising at this late date: 31st May 1940: *Before Andover County Bench:*

"Absconded from Poor Law Institution. John McAlister and James Kelly were charged with absconding from the Poor Law Institution on Monday morning. They pleaded guilty ….. Mr. Jones, the master of the institution, said the men were admitted on Saturday night and should not have left until Tuesday morning. Both men said they were on their way to try to get work in the district. The Chairman remarked that they needed such men to work and sentenced them to one day's imprisonment."

And a fascinating bit of village history from the Advertiser of the 9th August, 1940: *"An Old Soldier: people of Vernham Dean and District have received news that their oldest soldier and inhabitant, Mr. William Quarrier, late Lance-Corpl. 2nd Shropshires, who is 89 years old (known locally as 'Old Bill') has once again joined the ranks of the Army. This time, however, he is with old comrades at the Royal Hospital, Chelsea, where he was introduced to a soldier who celebrated his 100th birthday a few weeks ago. Mr. Quarrier was born* at Linkenholt in the year 1850: he went to school there under his grandmother, who was schoolmistress, for about a year and at the age of 7 years he went to work in the woods with his father, where he learned to make hurdles. He continued this work until he reached the age of 17 years and 8 months, when the Army feeling got a hold of him. 'I trekked off to Aldershot and joined the Army'. He first joined the Staffordshire volunteers on August 9th, 1868. He volunteered for service in India and was transferred to the Buckingham Volunteers, sailing with that corps from England to India on December 6th 1870. After serving about 8 years in the country, he went on active service on the Afghanistan frontier, but by this time he had been transferred to the Shropshire Light infantry. Whilst returning home from the Afghanistan Campaign they were stopped and once again sent on active service, this time to the relief of Sir George Colley in South Africa in 1881. Returning home to the Isle of Wight in 1882, having completed 14 years 8 months service, he was discharged in 1883 at Aldershot. Coming back to his home in Linkenholt, he continued his work in the woods and later took unto himself a wife and went to live in a cottage at Henley. His wife died in 1918 but he continued to live in the cottage alone until last Tuesday when he was admitted to the Royal Hospital for Pensioners at Chelsea. He boasts that he has not had a day's serious illness in his lifetime. Asked how he accounted for his good health, he replied: 'Plenty of hard work and plain living. I always had a pint of beer and a pipe of baccy when I could afford it. I feel all right now excepting I get the 'screws' in my leg sometimes, and that steadies me down so I have to get about with a stick'. The good wishes of the people in the district go with him. May he enjoy his long-earned rest for some years to come".

On the 18th August the Advertiser gives a resumé of an article culled from 'Country Life' which reflects the transformation which the war had wrought to agriculture in general. It concerns the 'Miracle at Linkenholt' which Mr. Roland Dudley had evolved:

Members of the County War Agricultural Committee whose duties have obliged them to tour their counties cannot have helped feeling dismayed at the appalling state of desolation in to which 20 years of criminal neglect of agriculture have allowed much of the land to fall. Recriminations at the present time are useless. What is more to the point is to show how quickly (agriculturally speaking) the land may be brought back again to cultivation and made to grow good crops.

At Linkenholt, land reclamation has been going on for 6 years. The Wheat Act provided the original incentive and latterly, of course, the Ploughing Up subsidy has helped the work along. In all over 500 acres have been reclaimed from jungle and scrub. It must be admitted that the first batch of 50 acres was not tackled without misgiving. Local opinion was against it; 'It would grow nothing'. The old foreman maintained that he and his mate once carted 40 acres of corn in an afternoon from it. They used to ride on the wagon shafts between the stooks because, he said 'it was too far to walk'.

Today this self-same land yields in a good year 40 bushels of wheat per acre when the wheat shift comes round. It must be emphasized, however, that the fertility is kept up by three year leys on which are folded pigs and poultry – now, alas! under the ban of a few theoretical experts who are not acquainted with modern methods of maintaining soil fertility. (Shades of today, as farmers labour under the dictates of the 'elf and safety laws).

The land is not inherently poor. Some of it lacked lime though it overlies the chalk. Some of it is thin chalk soil capable of growing good barley crops after sainfoin or clover previously. Most of it is loamy clay with flints – mainly flints - on hillsides with gradients up to 1 in 7, which is about the limit of good cultivation. Doubtless one of the main difficulties with it in days gone by is that horses had not the necessary power to haul the implements required for dealing with this class of land. Thanks to the track laying tractor this trouble has been successfully overcome.

A further and also serious difficulty was the infestation by rabbits. To give some idea of this plague it may be recorded that on one field four guns killed 940 of these pests one morning. Ordinary methods of getting rid of the rabbits were quite useless. As soon as a field was cleared it was again invaded by the vermin. Obviously the only thing to do was to wire in the whole estate. It took 14 miles of rabbit netting and, though expensive, it has paid. Road intersections added to the lengths of netting required. The netting used was 4' wide 1 3/8inch mesh. It was ploughed in, in a furrow, with the bottom of the netting turned horizontally against the rabbits on the neighbouring land. Posts were 10' apart. On the boundary a strand of barbed wire was run on the top of the netting to protect it from cattle. When the rabbits were once enclosed, they were exterminated by gun, dog, trap, snare, ferret and gas.

After the reclamation of about 200 acres of the estate, which was bought in 1925, 100 acres were acquired on the southern boundary in 1936. This area had been derelict for many years but was brought in crop the next year. From the experience it was decided to purchase 483 acres on the northern boundary, including Combe wood. The wood itself occupies about 280 acres. The rest of the land was one mass of jungle: willow herb, bramble, bracken and bushes. The land to be brought into crop for this year was first wired in after possession had been obtained on June 12th 1939. Trees and large bushes were first 'stumped' i.e. the trees were cut off about 4' from the ground, so that a chain could be attached to them and could not slip when pulled by a caterpillar tractor used to haul out the stumps. The best plan is to burn the bush and tree tops as they are cut, otherwise it will be found that if there are many trees and bushes, they occupy a large space when pulled out and become a harbour for any stray rabbits which may happen to penetrate the defences. It will be appreciated that tree roots are also obstacles to the ordinary farm implements. To get over this trouble it was found that the large Ransome disc plough was a most excellent tool to use. The large discs either ride over the roots or, more frequently, cut them. It is too dangerous to use a mould

139

board plough. In bad cases a subsoiler is used to crack any obstinate roots. Of course, a Gyrotiller would do the work equally well, but it is much more expensive and one cannot always get it when one wants it. Scrub of bramble, willow herb and bracken was cut with an old grass cutter, at the sacrifice of many knives, and the debris raked up and burnt. Further harrowings and deep cultivations enabled 103 acres to be got ready for sowing to wheat on September 26th, 15 weeks after commencing operations. The wheat was sown with a combine drill slightly over 2 bushels to the acre. The variety was Carter's 'Quota' wheat. At the same time there was sown with the grain 1 cwt of sulphate of ammonia, 1 cwt of potash salts and 2 cwts superphosphate to the acre. In the spring it was dressed with 1 1/2 cwts of nitrochalk to the acre. Good judges estimate the yield at not less than 7 quarters an acre. During the autumn and winter further work of reclamation was carried out where the scrub was not so dense, with the result that 72 acres of barley and oats were sown, all of which produced good results. It is some satisfaction to feel that 175 acres, which have produced nothing for over 50 years, look capable of adding at least 200 tons to the national larder if the harvest is gathered in with reasonable good luck". (In March, 1941, Mr. Dudley was appointed Sheriff for the county of Southampton. *"By reason of his many activities in the agricultural world Mr. Dudley was exceptionally well known in this part of Hampshire, and his many friends wish him a successful but not too busy year of office ….."*)

By October, 1940, the ladies of Hurstbourne Priors had proudly made 1280 lbs of jam – voluntary workers in East Suffolk had made over 46,000 lbs, or more than 20 tons from their local fruit. Food and health occupy a prominent place in the newspapers of the war years, a committee of experts appointed by the BMA in their report on 'What to Eat in War Time' said that most adults could live in good health on a daily diet of wholewheat bread, made from flour that includes the whole of the wheat grain, cheese, milk and some fresh fruit or salad. Entries for Vernham Dean veer on the lighter side and seem to comprise vast numbers of whist drives, dances, musical entertainments of all types, mostly to raise funds for the war effort, but obviously a real boost to morale.

"Christmas Party – the Village Hall was filled to overflowing with admiring parents, foster parents and friends on Friday evening when the combined Vernham Dean and evacuee schools presented their Christmas concert. The programme opened with Little Red Riding Hood performed by the infants. Derek Bailey as the wolf caused much laughter by his struggles with Grandma's woolly coat. This was followed by 'The Singing Prince' performed by the senior girls: Muriel Cox and Dorothy Bulpit made excellent robbers, well supported by Cynthia Stacey as Queen. Joan Stallard was the dashing prince, while Joan Raynsford was a charming princess in disguise. Following this play came a Negro dialogue with Kenneth Chandler taking the lead and under his able guidance D. Neville, E Satchwell, D. Hutchings and R. Knight provided much amusing back chat. The junior boys and girls provided a spectacular piece 'Santa Claus Gets Busy'. Dorothy Wimbleton made a good Father Christmas and Myrtle Hall was a delightful fairy in this scene ….."

1941

This year saw the death of John Mills, the father of Vernham Mills. January 1941: "......
*prominent agriculturist in the person of Mr. John Mills of Manor Farm, Vernham Dean,
who passed away on Monday in Andover War Memorial Hospital after an operation, at
the age of 71. Mr. Mills had been a tenant of this farm, the owners of which are Winchester
College, for 50 years, and his knowledge of agriculture was a great asset to the countryside.
For years he was a member of the committee of the Andover branch of the NFU but he never
sought office. He represented his area on Andover RDC for a long time and was a member
of the St. Hubert Lodge of Freemasons. In his own village, where he and the members of his
family were very much esteemed, he was chairman of the Parish Council for a considerable
number of years, a school manager and treasurer, churchwarden (40 years service to the
church) and was ever ready to take a lead in things pertaining to the welfare of his village
........"*

Trawling through the newspaper's 'Andover County Bench' columns would no doubt produce
many miscreants from Vernham, but suffice to note the 26th December, 1941 at Andover
Quarter Sessions: *"Shop breaking at Vernham Dean – Saturday, before the Recorder (Mr.
W.J. Snell). Andrew Goodall, aged 23, a soldier, was charged with breaking and entering the
shop of George Evans, of Vernham Dean, on Nov 9th and stealing a quantity of cigarettes,
tobacco and matches, together valued at £7. He pleaded guilty. Joseph Hughes, aged 37,
also a soldier, pleaded not guilty to the same offence and not guilty to receiving any of the
stolen property. Both prisoners had been in prison awaiting trial since November 14th. Mr.
J. Scott Henderson who prosecuted, said he had no evidence to offer against Hughes and
he was formally found not guilty by the jury and discharged. Regarding Goodall, Mr. Scott
Henderson said that accused had been drinking the evening in question and on the way
back to camp he had to pass through the village of Vernham Dean. He smashed a pane of
glass, entered the shop and stole the cigarettes etc. He was subsequently seen at his unit
where the stolen property was found in his kit. He admitted the offence ..... had been in
trouble before ..... said he was very sorry and was willing to repay the shopkeeper for the
trouble he had caused.*

1942

February reviews the death of Charles Mills, brother of John Mills, at the age of 79.
He lived at The Malt House, just the Vernham Dean side of Upton, and had previously
farmed at Halls Farm in Vernham Street for 35 years. He fell into the fire when ill: his wife,
Ellen, screamed and Bruce Seward, also living at The Malt House, pulled him out and
smothered the flames. Mr. Mills' injuries were so intense that he died some hours later.

Another death in 1942 was that of Mr. E.A. Wigan of Conholt House, aged 73. He was the younger son of Mr. Henry Wigan and was educated at Eton and Trinity Hall, Cambridge, a noted racquets and polo player and racehorse owner. His horse, Christmas Daisy, won the Cambridgeshire Stakes in 1909 and 1910. He came to Conholt Park in 1905 and 6 years later started farming there, producing a well known herd of Aberdeen Angus. His niece, Miss H.M. Gaskell, lived at Conholt after him and added another legend to the village when she and her companion suffered burglary. (q.v.)

In a lighter vein, the village contributed well to Warship Week in March. The target for the village was £1,000, they raised £865.17.6d. with a well-attended whist drive and dance on the Friday and Saturday nights in the Village Hall. At the end of each evening an auction was conducted with various articles which had been given to help. The bidding was brisk, articles fetched excellent prices including £11.5.0d. for a safety razor. The national total for the Warship Week was £211,467.8.8d.

A proud headline on the 3rd July: *"Britain Leads the World – thanks to the intensive effort by the farmers and the combination of science, skill and hard work, this island today feeds more people per square mile of soil than any other country in the world"*.

Vernham had a right to be proud of many of its villagers, and one who comes to mind is May Webb, whose death was reported on the 3rd July. Miss Webb helped a previous vicar, now the Dean of Litchfield, when, as Revd. Iremonger he raised funds for the building and equipment of the Village Hall. Not only did she keep the accounts for that body but was one of the foundation members of the WI, serving as secretary and treasurer for many years. She was also associated with the Infant Welfare Circle in the village, and served on the Parish Council and the Parochial Church Council. In these war years she was a member of the British Legion, and a First Aid member of the local ARP.

1943

Vernham not only supported district and national appeals, but had its own unique system:

29th January, 1943: *...... progressive whist at the Village Hall ..... Mr. Elford was able to hand over the grand sum of £12.2.9d. to the 'Old Tin Box' for distributing amongst members of the forces from the village and the surrounding district. It might be mentioned that the 'Old Tin Box' is a cash box which stands on the public bar table at the George Inn, Vernham Dean, to receive voluntary contributions. It was put there in September, 1940, and at that time there were 8 serving members of HM Forces from the village and surrounding hamlets of Conholt and Fosbury. That number has now grown to 62, each of whom received in turn a postal order for 3/-. At Christmas 1941 all serving members were sent a postal order for*

5/- and at Christmas 1942 one for 7/6d. was sent to all members serving. The total money distributed from the 'Old Tin Box' since 1940 is £88.16.6d.

9th April: *A Prisoner of War ...... the glad news has just reached Mrs. M. Jones, of Bank Farm, Vernham Dean, from the War Office, that her husband Pte. E. Jones, of the Loval Regt., who was reported missing 13 months ago, is alive and well, a prisoner of war in the hands of the Japanese at Ketjo Chosen, Korea. Pte. Jones left England 6 1/2 years ago for service in the Far East. He was last heard of being reported missing at Singapore.*

The Women's Land Army had a significant presence in the village, to such an extent that they wished to form their own club. 16th April: *WLA Club needed – a successful social and dance, organised by local members of the Women's Land Army, was held in the Village Hall on Saturday. Games and various entertainments occupied the early part of the evening, followed, until midnight, by dancing to music provided by Mrs. Hiscock (piano), Mr. Hinton (guitar), Messrs. R. Cummings and Hale (accordions) and Mr. G. Abbott (drums). Prizes were given .... The proceeds, amounting to £7.14.2d. will form a fund for a local WLA Club which is to be formed in the district.*

In April of 1943 the WI was still in existence, and at the monthly meeting Roland Dudley kept the WI up to date with the agriculture question ...... *contrasting pre-war and present farming and explained the organisation and work of the County War Agricultural Committee. He included an explanation of the various fertilisers needed on farms and in gardens and the best way of using those then available. He ended by paying a warm tribute to the British farm workers, and then answered many questions ....*

June brought another challenge to the village in the form of 'Wings for Victory': .... *congratulations to Mrs. Sprackling, secretary of the village group National Savings and her committee (the Revd W.G. Pack, Mr. & Mrs. Whittingham, Mr. & Mrs. Perts, Mrs. Stacey, Mrs. Ripley and Mr. N. Smith) who got to work in earnest to smash their target of £800. The target was shot to pieces by Wednesday and their final score at the end of the week was £1,025.11.9d. On Saturday there were sports for the children and all sorts of sideshows in a field kindly lent by Mr. Bulpitt, and in the Village Hall, where light refreshments were served. The remainder of the evening was pleasantly spent dancing to the music of a radiogram. On Tuesday a concert was given in the Village Hall by members of the Grafton Concert Party and was much appreciated. On Wednesday there was a baby show at the Vicarage followed by a Whist Drive in the Village Hall after which numerous articles were sold by auction. On the closing day in the Village Hall there was a children's fancy dress parade, and the week concluded with a social for all, music being supplied by local and district talent."*

And in July .... *without subsidies, the current price of the quartern loaf would be 11d., instead of 9d. A pound of sugar would be 5 1/2d instead of 3d., and a stone of potatoes*

1/8 1/2d. instead of 1/1 1/2d. But on a happier note: ..... *in Japanese hands – after absence of news for 18 months, a telegram bearing the good news was received from the War Office on July 7 by Mr. A. Holmes of Vernham Dean, stating that his son Reginald is a prisoner of war in Japanese hands. Shortly after the outbreak of war he joined the RAF and went east. It was in February 1942 that his parents received the last letter from him. Before joining the RAF he was a baker in the employment of Mr. F. Fosbury, of Coombe. He was a keen cyclist and member of Andover Wheelers Club.*

More than half the rubber boots issued since the beginning of 1943 have been allocated to agricultural workers ...... next year's marmalade may have an apple flavour as windfall apples are being sent to the marmalade factories ..... 13th August – minimum agricultural wage now to be 65/- (80/- had been requested) ...... 6th November: lorries run on wine: more than 4 million pints of French wine have been taken by the Germans to distil into industrial alcohol for their lorries...sheets and table cloths will be scarcer than ever in 1944. The demand for them is now ten times greater than the supply.

31st December: *Mentioned in Dispatches: The King has been graciously pleased to approve that the under-mentioned, in recognition of gallant and distinguished service in North Africa, be Mentioned in Dispatches: Captain A.J. Liddiard, Res of Officers.*

1944

News of Vernham Dean seems spectacularly sparse in 1944, apart from the notice of the marriage of Vernham Mills and Betty Dowse: 22nd September: *The marriage arranged between Mr. E.J. Vernham Mills and Miss Mary Elizabeth (Betty) Dowse will take place quietly at St. Mary's Church, Vernham Dean, on Thursday, October 3rd at 1.30 p.m.* It duly took place, with Betty's sister, Grace, as bridesmaid.

The British Legion had their headquarters at the George Inn and on the 17th November the Home Guard Darts Team challenged the Legion: the Home Guard team was Cpl A. Cooke, Cpl W. Barnard, LCJ Cook, Ptes Dillworth, J. Elmer, G. Elmer, J. Stockley, A. Lewington, H. Bowley, F. Nutley. The Legion fielded: Commander Higginbotham, W. Dillworth, F. Sims. F. Fisher, P. Harding, W. Hull, G. Willmott, C. Smith, F. Harman, E. Holmes. Pte G. Elmer had the highest score at 120, the runner up was Pte Nutley 111 'shot out' ..... and a final entry for the year:

8th December. *"Stand Down" of Home Guard. Parade at Andover Recreation Ground* – 700 representatives, including those from Vernham Dean and Linkenholt.

1945

In 1945 Mr. and Mrs. Dudley lost their only surviving son: 27th April 1945: *Death in action of Mr. M.V. Dudley, Irish Guards, aged 27, educated at Harrow and Oriel College Oxford, where he read Law, but left to take a commission in the Irish Guards in 1939 when hostilities seemed imminent.* He left a widow, Barbara (née Stern) and two small boys.

Looking to the future, the Hampshire Federation of Women's Institutes were formulating their resolutions to put forward: *….. that the meeting asks for temporary legislation to forbid the acquisition of cottages in rural villages for weekend residences until the present housing situation is solved.* Also: *………. this meeting suggests that war memorials should take the form of something for the welfare of the village rather than that of stone obelisks, etc. ………that this meeting urges the Government to treat the supply of cheap electricity to rural areas as matters of extreme urgency.*

With the benefit of hindsight, it is interesting to note that government did indeed take notice of the influence of the Women's Institute movement, and in future years invited their participation in policy-making.

Needless to state, Vernham held a Grand Dance in aid of the Welcome Home Fund and put on a concert for the Homecoming Fund with the aid of the 'Ace' Concert Party from Andover. A Victory Garden Show was held on the 28th July – organised by Mrs. Dudley. In these later days it is interesting to note that there was a class for 'Those employing Labour and Professional Gardeners' in which the class for a collection of vegetables was won 1) Mrs. R. Dudley 2) Mrs. Whittingham 3) T. Walker. Fruit (4 kinds) 1) Mrs. R. Dudley. The Red Cross Fund benefited by £30.

21st September 1945: *Rejoicing. Celebrations were held recently for all in the parish up to the age of 18 years, also the children who attend Vernham Dean school from Conholt, Coombe, Linkenholt and Upton. They numbered about 150 children in all. A start was made at 3 o'clock in front of the Village Hall with a fancy dress competition, in which there were three classes ….. then paraded the village under the care of Mrs. Boyd the head schoolmistress and led by a stalwart cadet bearing the Union Jack …. returned to the village hall for tea (decorated with red, white and blue flowers) then community singing, dancing and 'The Magic Man' ….. bonfire and fireworks on the Bury Dene (superintended by Mr. J. Hiscock and Mr. J. Millar). A large field of stubble was set on fire earlier, giving a tattoo effect in the darkness.*

And finally, in 1946: 9th August: *Improvement of amenities: A sports club, with a representative committee, has been formed to organise games and social events for the residents of the district. A football team, affiliated to the County Association, will be playing this season, and it is hoped that cricket and tennis will be possible next summer.*

Ladies are invited to give their ideas….. at a general meeting of the Cricket Club held at the George Inn recently it was proposed by Mr. B. Seward and seconded by Mr. W. Dawkes and unanimously agreed that the total funds of the local cricket club, with all the equipment, should be handed to the Sports Club.

25th October 1946: *Women's Institute re-formed – a meeting was held in the Village Hall on Wednesday week to discuss the possibility of reforming the local branch of the Women's Institute.*

Village life resumed – in fact it did not really appear to stop, even falter, and unlike many other communities, very few were lost. The memorial in the church reads:

> *Erected to commemorate the 1939-45 World War*
> *In gratitude to all who served from the parish*
> *And in memory of*
> *Edward Talfourd Salter*
> *Who gave his life for freedom.*

**Annie Hayes at her
shop door, the side
of Apple Thatch,
in early 1930s**
(unknown provenance)

**Joan Linnell Burton
in the 1990s at the
same door**
(G.L. Palmer)

Edgingtons Bakery
(John Marchment)

**From David's Cottage
to Edgingtons**
(John Marchment)

The Stores - then
(Postcard SJ Bell)

**The PO, shop and
houses - now**
(David Post)

Wilfred Dawkes 1934
(Peter Dawkes

The George
- early 1920s
F.Hayes,
Parker Elmer (Landlord),
William (Bill) Walker,
Bert Walker,
Harry Dudman,
B.Stockley, G.Goodman,
B.Baring
(in front) Cyril Allen,
Joffre Elmer

Andover Advertiser

The Old Village Hall
(unknown provenance)

The Millennium Hall
(unknown provenance)

**The School
- early 20thC**
(Peter Dawkes)

**The School prior to
the 1995 rebuild**
(unknown provenance)

**The School
- today**
(G.L. Palmer)

VERNHAM DEAN
SCHOOL BUILDING ACCOUNT.

Subscriptions received, 1860.	£	s.	d.	£	s.	d.
Winchester College	60	0	0			
Rev. G. Alder	16	0	0			
W. Child, Esq.	10	0	0			
Mr. T. Herriott	2	0	0			
Rev. J. G. Gillum	20	0	0			
Mr. Herbert	1	0	0			
Mr. Batt	1	0	0			
Lady Chas. Wellesley	5	0	0			
Mr. Miles, Hurstbourne	5	0	0			
Mr. Gerrish	0	10	0			
Through Miss Child	2	0	0			
Mr. Platt	1	0	0			
Mr. Hooper	1	0	0			
Mr. Barnes	1	1	0			
Mr. Hilliard	1	10	0			
Bishop of Rochester	5	0	0			
Mr. W. Piper	0	10	0			
Collection in Church, April 1st, 1860	3	18	0			
Mr. Bartholomew	0	10	0			
Rev. R. G. Bryan	3	3	0			
Major Gillum	6	0	0			
Small sums	0	5	0			
Rev. T. Child	1	1	0			
A. B. Heath, Esq.	5	0	0			
Mr. Charles Child	2	0	0			
Bishop of Winchester	10	0	0			
Countess of Portsmouth, through Mrs. Child	5	0	0			
Mrs. Thos. Miles	3	0	0			
— Scott, Esq.	5	0	0			
Rev. T. H. Dixon	1	1	0			
J. Fosbury, Esq.	1	0	0			
Sclater Booth, Esq., M.P.	5	0	0			
Rt. Honble. W. Cubitt	5	0	0			
— Beach, Esq., M.P.	5	0	0			
Miss Fielder	0	10	0			
Box at School treat	6	10	0			
Mr. Smart	1	1	0			
Rev. Connell	2	2	0			
Friend, by Mr. A. Hilliard	0	10	0			
Mr. Lansley	1	0	0			
Mr. R. Lansley	1	1	0			
Mrs. R. Lansley	0	5	0			
Countess of Carnarvon	2	0	0			
				203	18	0

Additional Subscriptions—1861 & 2.	£	s.	d.	£	s.	d.
John King, Esq.	10	0	0			
W. Child, Esq. (2nd donation)	5	0	0			
Mr. C. Child (2nd donation)	1	0	0			
Mr. Gerrish (2nd donation)	0	10	0			
Rev. J. G. Gillum (2nd donation)	5	0	0			
Rev. T. H. Dixon (2nd donation)	3	3	0			
Collection in Church, March 24th, 1861	3	19	10½			
Through Mr. Robt. Child	0	2	6			
Mr. E. Alder	1	0	0			
Miss Gillum	1	1	0			
School Box after Lectures, &c.	1	18	1			
Proceeds of Concert	5	15	6			
W. Child, Esq. (3rd donation)	5	0	0			
Sermon preached by Rev. Dudley, at Vernham, March 30th, 1862	2	18	0			
Ditto at Hurstbourne	1	11	6			
Miss Whitear	0	5	0			
Mr. J. Fielder	0	5	0			
Mr. Thos. Miles	5	0	0			
Work sold by Miss Child	8	10	0			
				61	19	5½
Cash paid by the Rev. J. G. Gillum for the internal fittings, including the floor of School Room, not being included in the original contract				26	18	11
				292	16	4½
By amount of deficiency due from the Parish				101	3	5
				393	19	9½

Creditor.	£	s.	d.
Paid Mr. R. Lansley—see bills	393	6	9½
„ Mr. Bray, cartage of bricks	0	8	0
„ Mr. Wheeler, measuring site	0	5	0
	393	19	9½

The Expenses attending the Conveyance of the Site are included amongst the outgoings of this present year, 1862.

THOMAS GERRISH, Auditor.

It appears from the foregoing that a deficiency remains of one hundred and one pounds, three shillings and fivepence. This sum I, as treasurer, have advanced. That the supporters of the School may be able to make more liberal yearly provision than at present for the teaching and maintenance of this School, it is important that it should be free from debt, I therefore do not wish the sum repaid me, but beg to present it to the Committee and School.

J. G. GILLUM, Treasurer.

July 5th, 1862.

F. J. J. BROWNE, "NORTH HANTS TELEGRAPH" OFFICE, HIGH STREET, ANDOVER.

The School Building Account
(unknown provenance)

Culled from "The Andover Advertiser"

Apart from slowly recovering from the Second World War - what went on in Vernham Dean in 1948? Let's start with sport:

12th March: **FOOTBALL – "Short Passes"**

Our paragraph last week which referred to the Andover Club's desire to contact local juniors met with instant success. A sportsman in the district promptly recommended N. Mills, the Vernham left half-back. The Town Club acted just as promptly, with the consequence that Mills will play against Netley Sports tomorrow.

9th July: **CRICKET – Border League**

89 runs for the Last Wicket.

What we believe to be near a local record was achieved at Vernham Dean on Saturday, when A. Cooke (43) and J. Elford (46 not out) put on 89 runs for the last wicket in the home team's total of 139. However, out of that total A. Kingston managed to get five wickets for 16 runs. Longparish started disastrously, five wickets being down for less than 10 runs. C. Turton tried to stop the rot, but the innings closed for 27.

SCORES

Vernham Dean		Longparish	
P. Holmes, c Holloway, b Kingston	11	B. Wilkinson, run out	1
A. Robb, st Taylor, b Worthington	9	T. Smith, b Hall	4
S. Hall, c Cook, b Kingston	0	A. Kingston, b Cooke	0
W. Scull, c Cook, b Kingston	9	M. Taylor, c Cummins, b Cooke	0
C. Cummins, b Worthing	9	T. Tubb, b Hall	0
V. Seward, lbw, b Holloway	2	C. Turton, c Holmes, b Hall	1
R. Cooke, b Kingston	0	C. Brown, c & b Cooke	2
E. Brown, b Kingston	1	F. Worthington, b Cooke	3

E. Reynolds, b Kingston	1	G. Cook, c Reynolds, b Hall	6
A. Cooke, c Smith, b Holloway	43	J. Holloway, b Cooke	6
J. Elford, not out	46	F. Tonge, not out	0
Extras	8	Extras	4
	139		27

Bowling – Kingston 5 for 16

Bowling – S. Hall 4 for 23

R. Cooke – 5 for 1

10th July: **TRIAL GAME**

Vernham Dean Sports Club held a trial football match on Monday night in readiness for their first match against Taskers, which is to be played away tomorrow. Stuart and Gerald Hall, both old Club players, proved themselves to be still fit. It is a great pity that Gordon Elmer will not be between the "sticks" in League fixtures this season owing to the injury which he received earlier this year, although he showed his usual form in the trial game by scoring many "certain" goals. Several new young players have their chance when the Reserves play their first game against Taskers' Reserves next week. Tomorrow's probable team will be:- Elford, Hollister, Linden, G. Hall, Cummins, Witts, R. Stacey, W. Dillworth, Read, R. Smith, Willis. Messrs. C. Cummins and W. Dillworth have been appointed captain and vice-captain respectively for the forthcoming season, and they have great hopes of pushing both teams through to League victories.

17th July: **FOOTBALL – Andover and District Junior League.**

Fixtures for 18th September

Division 1	Sec A	Vernham Dean v Taskers
Division ll	East Section	Taskers Res. v Vernham Dean Res.

23rd July: **CRICKET. "MR. EXTRAS"**

In the Amport score book record of the Border semi-final tie with Vernham, won, incidentally, by two runs, is the following: "A. Wiltshire, c and b R. Cooke 22". The bowler certainly caught the ball, but not directly from the bat, for Wiltshire drove a hard return just wide of "mid-on". The latter put his hand out but the ball was too "hot" to grasp and he managed to push it on to the bowler's hand, hence the entry in the score book. This remarkable catch might have won the game, for Wiltshire was the only batsman to play a sound game in his side's innings. Vernham's remaining batsmen, after 52 were on the board for four, suffered from inferiority complex – or was it Guyettosis?" (W. Guyett 7 wickets).

PRIZE FIGHTS ………….. (from a full length column on prize fights) ……………
a letter received from Mr. G. Jones, who writes from Steelman P.O., Saskatchewan, Canada.
He stated: "I have been very interested in your writings re the old days' prize fights. I heard
a lot about the fight at Hurstbourne Tarrant from the late Mr. Gerrish who used to collect
rates during the time I held the licence of The Old Crook and Shears at Upton".

15th October   **DARTS**

A team from the George Inn, Vernham, was entertained to a darts match by the White Hart,
Burbage, on Friday night. Although Vernham were at one time losing 5-2, the match ended
5-5. A return game will be played at a later date.

5th November   **INDOOR GAMES**

A darts match between local players and the Crown and Anchor Inn, Ham, was held at the
Boot Inn, Vernham Street, on Tuesday night. It was very one-sided, ending in a victory of
5-1 for The Boot, the only two local players to lose their games reaching a total of 245 for
six darts, leaving 56 to get – and then failing to finish.

19th November   **FOOTBALL – JUNIOR JOTTINGS**

The Vernham Dean Club will soon be losing the services of a well-known player. He is the
21-year-old centre forward, Peter Linden, who is leaving the village shortly to return to his
home in Weiss, near Cologne, Germany. Peter, who has occupied the centre-forward berth
many times since last December, has been one of the strong points of the Vernham team, and
it is with regret that they will lose his services. He first came to the village in September 1947,
when he was given temporary civilian status and came to work on a local farm. A former player
of the Weiss (Cologne) Sports Club in the outside-right position, Peter now returns to his
native heath where, it is hoped, the experience gained in English football will be of use to him.
(Peter Linden also features elsewhere)

WIRTZ-FISHER WEDDING

A wedding of considerable interest took place at St. Mary's church on Saturday, the service
being conducted by the Rev. A.R. Hill (Vicar of the Parish). Miss Hilda Iris Fisher, eldest
daughter of Mr. and Mrs. F. Fisher, Woodside, Vernham Dean, was married to Mr. Josef
Wirtz, eldest son of Mrs. Wirtz, of Wurselen, Aachen, Germany. The bride was given away
by her father and she was attired in a red costume and carried a bouquet of chrysanthemums.
Her attendants were the Misses Freda and Phyllis Fisher (sisters), little Phyllis presenting
her sister with a horseshoe outside the church.

Mr. Peter Linden (friend of the bridegroom) was best man. A reception was later held at the bride's mother's home, where the toast of "the bride and bridegroom" was honoured by many friends and relatives. Their future home will be at Woodside, Vernham Dean.

And if you call owning ferrets sport ......

25th June: **NATURE'S ABUNDANCE:** From the Editor's postbag

Sir – I have a ferret going into her sixth year and six weeks ago she had a litter of eleven. While not claiming it a record this makes her total in three seasons 23. What was most remarkable two days after they were born at periods during the day there were always three laid outside her nest box and it made me curious. But of course, when I discovered eleven babies and she had only eight dugs I could see her reason for doing this. Mother and babies are all fine and fit and feeding on their own.

Yours faithfully, E.L. Conway, Upton.

....

AND OTHER ORGANISATIONS

30th January   **C.V.O's VISIT**

The monthly meeting of the Vernham Dean and Linkenholt Women's Institute was held in the Village Hall on January 24th, when Miss Wickham, C.V.O., explained the activities of the Central Organisation of the WI and gave much information to members. The two tellers, who very kindly came over from Hurstbourne Priors, coped most efficiently with the subsequent elections, and the following were declared elected to serve the Institute for the current year :- President, Mrs. Dudley: Vice-Presidents Mrs. Hill and Mrs. Higginbotham: Hon. Treasurer, Mrs Higginbotham: Hon. Secretary, Miss M. Jukes: Committee: Mrs. Bryant, Miss Dowse, Mrs. Hiscock, Miss Hand, Miss Lennard and Miss Napthine. Mrs. Fowler and Miss Foll were co-opted onto the Committee. After tea, games were played, and the Institute prepared for another busy year. The competition for the best sponge sandwich was won by Mrs. Bryant with Mrs. Banbury second.

15th October

BOURNE VALLEY GROUP – Women's Institutes at Hurstbourne Priors.

The autumn meeting of the Bourne Valley Group of Women's Institutes took place on Wednesday in the Village Hall, Hurstbourne Priors. All the five institutes, Hurstbourne

Priors, St. Mary Bourne, Vernham Dean, Laverstoke and Hurstbourne Tarrant, were well represented ..... the four visiting institutes had been asked to put on about ten minutes entertainment each ..... Vernham Dean put on "The Awkward Squad" ....

5th March **WELFARE COMMITTEE**

The annual meeting of the Social Welfare Committee was held in the Schoolroom on Wednesday of last week, Mrs. A.J. Hiscock (Vice Chairman) presiding. The Secretary, Mrs. Mills, read the annual report of the work done by the Welfare Committee. The Treasurer (Mrs. Hill) gave the financial report. The sum of £204-2-11d. has been raised, she said, and there was a balance of £11-4-6d. It was hoped to be able to raise enough funds to take the children for another day at the seaside. Then followed the election of the new Committee as follows: Mrs. Hiscock (Chairman): Mrs. Rushbrooke (Vice Chairman): Mrs. Pickup (Treasurer) and Mrs Mills (Secretary). Committee Members are Mrs. Hill, Mrs. Boyd, Mrs Ripley, Mrs Loom, Mrs. Hayes and Miss Sopp.

4th June **SPORTS CLUB ACTIVITY**

The Wednesday night dances, organised by the Sports Club to encourage dancing, and for beginners, which are held in the Village Hall have provided for a long-felt want in the district. They have so far been very popular, and provided sufficient interest is maintained it is hoped to continue them for some time to come. Music is supplied by a radiogram made by one of the members.

22nd October **RECORD WHIST DRIVE**

The largest attendance for a whist drive that has ever been seen in the Village Hall was witnessed on 13th October, when there were 32 tables in play. The organisers, the ladies of the Entertainments and Finance Committee, had only laid out 24 tables, so when the queue waiting for admission lengthened and it became evident that there were not enough chairs, tables and cards, an urgent "SOS" was sent around the village, and these were soon forthcoming. It would have been almost impossible to accommodate more people for even the stage held six tables .... the Drive was in aid of Sports Club funds.

22nd October **SPORTS CLUB**

The Entertainments and Finance Committee of the Vernham Dean Sports Club met on Monday night in the Village Hall, when there were present Mr. G. Elmer (Hon Secretary), Mr. L.Hay, Mr. and Mrs. P. Dawkes, Mrs. H. Stacey, Mr. W. Dillworth, Mr. J. Cooke, Mr. S. Hall (Hon. Treasurer) and Mr. N. Smith. It was announced that there was a balance in hand of £19-15-5d. This was considered very satisfactory, in view of the fact that only two events had been organised since the present Committee was elected. The increasing difficulty of obtaining dance bands for Club dances was discussed at length, as was the advisability of introducing beer, etc., at such events. It was decided, after various viewpoints had been heard, not to do this. Commenting on the success of the last Drive, Mr. J. Cooke suggested that in order to attract large numbers of players, high value prizes would have to be bought. To this the Committee agreed.

30th July **WOLF CUBS**

The 15th Andover (Vernham Dean) Wolf Cub Pack was recently honoured by a visit from Brigadier D.C. Rawson (District Commissioner) and Miss Paddy, (Assistant District Commissioner). The Cubmaster of the Pack (Mrs. Rushbrook) was handed her Warrant by the District Commissioner, and the Assistant Cubmaster (Mrs. Dawkes) also received her Warrant. The Pack was inspected by the District Commissioner and complimented on their turn-out and proficiency in signalling.

19th November

In aid of Wolf Cubs and Children's Welfare

GRAND GALA DANCE

9 p.m. to midnight

VERNHAM VILLAGE HALL

SATURDAY, 27th NOVEMBER

GERRY ETWELL'S BAND

Professional Exhibition of the "Can-Can", the

Dance that Thrilled the Nineties

Novelty Dances and Competitions with Prizes

Admission 3/-

Beer and refreshments available

15th October **BRITISH LEGION A.G.M.**

The local branch of the British Legion held its Annual General Meeting in the Village Hall on 7th October, when there was a fair attendance of members. Members expressed their appreciation of the work of Mr. F. Sims, the retiring Secretary, who has held the post since the Branch's formation in 1938. The following officials were elected: Chairman, Comdr. P.H. Higginbotham: Vice Chairman Mr. W. Dillworth: Hon. Secretary, Mr. A. Green: Hon.

Treasurer, the Rev. A.R. Hill. During the meeting the apparent lack of interest by members in Legion activities was mentioned by the Chairman, but no suggestions were forthcoming to stimulate this. The Legion have hopes of winning the Watershed Group Darts Competition for which they are entering a team this season.

22nd October **VILLAGE SCHOOL**

Controlled Status – the Village School, which is shortly to be redecorated, has now been officially recognised as having Controlled Status. A new stove has already arrived, and will shortly be installed in the main classroom.

Vernham has never been short of people willing to express their views:

10th December **LOCAL FARMERS EXPRESS VIEWS**

At County N.F.U. meeting: MR. CULLEY AND LABOUR QUESTION

…………………… two Andover members, the Chairman (Mr. G.H. Culley) and Commander Higginbottom (sic) took part in the discussion on planning and housing. It had been pointed out that while agricultural cottages were free from development charges, farmhouses, at the moment, were subject to them. Commander Higginbottom expressed himself strongly on the subject. Planners seemed to be one of the biggest menaces that they would have to face in the future, he added ……….

FOOD ORDER RESOLUTION …………. N.F.U. should give three months' notice to the Government that if the Food (Seasonal Allowances) Order was not rescinded, farmers would not comply with it. There had been 14 votes for and a similar number against. Commander Higginbottom, the mover, was trenchant about "the ridiculous fashion in which farmers are messed about by the Ministry of Food in having to collect and distribute the rations and fill in the necessary forms". He added that even though farmers might refuse to carry out the Order the men would still get the food ……………… Earlier, an amendment that the Commander's suggestion should be referred to Branches was lost.

24th December **CHRISTMAS PARTY**

About 80 children attended the Christmas party given by the Social Welfare Committee in the Village Hall on Friday. The hard work of organising whist drives and dances during the past year, which the Committee had undertaken, was well rewarded by the happy time the kiddies spent, and everyone who helped deserves congratulation on the party's success. The event started with a sumptuous tea, with sandwiches, cakes, jellies, etc., in abundance, after which parents and friends joined the children and all enjoyed the film show of cartoons and the Baksi-Woodcock fight, the latter causing much interest. Later, shrieks of delight heralded a well-disguised Santa Claus (Mr. J. Hiscock) complete with sleigh piled with well-filled sacks, and above the noise the Vicar (the Rev. A.R. Hill) did his best to announce names as presents were drawn out. Besides this present, each child received a cracker, a balloon and an orange. During the evening sweets, made and given by Miss Lennard were handed round and enjoyed. Three cheers for Father Christmas, called for by the Vicar, ended the party too quickly for many of the youngsters. One child was heard to remark; "Father Christmas has come early this year, hasn't he, Mum".

THEY WON THEIR CHRISTMAS DINNER

At least one local family made sure of their Christmas dinner several times over by securing prizes at fur and feather whist drives in the district. Mrs. H. Stacey, of Upton Road, Vernham, secured a pheasant at a Shalbourne drive and two rabbits at Oxenwood. Mr. H. Stacey also won a cockerel at Oxenwood and a pheasant at Vernham Sports Club's event. His son-in-law, Mr. Reynolds, who played as a lady in the latter, carried off the first prize which was a pheasant. A very successful week.

And a few other oddments ....

Tut tut, Colonel Whittingham (14th May)

COLONEL'S CAR LEFT NEAR DRILL HALL

Andover Borough Magistrates Court

Monday – before the Major (Mr. H. Guard), Mr. W.J. Anstead and Mrs. Russell. A fine of 10/- was imposed on Col. Frederick H. Whittingham, Vernham Dean, when he admitted a charge of having left his car standing in Eastfield Road without having the necessary lights during the hours of darkness. P.C. Roulston told the magistrates that on the evening of the 9th April he was on duty in Eastfield Road and saw the Defendant's car standing outside the Drill Hall without lights. He went inside and spoke to the Colonel, who admitted that he had forgotten to switch the lights on. Col. Whittingham did not appear in Court but sent a letter explaining the circumstances. He was on duty in the Drill Hall that evening, and he considered that no inconvenience or danger was caused to the public as the car was standing within the radius of lights on the road. He had been, the letter stated, the holder of a driving licence for 30 years and his record was as yet entirely clean.

21st May **FOR SALE – GRAVES 3-valve Wireless set:**

in good condition, working order, what offers? – Brooks ......

13th August **FOR SALE, 1938 MORRIS 9 2-seater Tourer:**

good running order, overhauled before laid up in November: four good tyres, two nearly new, £300 or near offer ....

27th August **CHURCH LIBRARY**

The Vicar of the Parish (the Rev. A.R. Hill) has recently formed a Church Library, which is a welcome addition to local amenities. About 50 fiction, non-fiction and children's books from the Vicar's own collection are available, free, for parishioners.

Over fifty years later there are many descendants of the same names living in the parish today as there were in 1948 . Some are mentioned below.

9th July   **PASSING OF MRS. BOWLEY**

The death occurred on Wednesday of last week at Bank Lane, after a short illness, of Mrs. Eliza Bowley. Mrs. Bowley was well liked and respected. She was one of the oldest inhabitants, having attained the age of 83. Living in and around Vernham all her life Mrs. Bowley had many friends. The funeral took place at St. Mary's church on Saturday, and it was requested by Mrs. Bowley that no-one should be dressed in black. The family mourners present were: Mr. H.W. Bowley (son): Mr. and Mrs. F. Bowley (son and daughter-in-law): Mr. and Mrs. R. Wyld (son-in-law and daughter): Mrs. T. Annetts and Mrs. W. Ryder (daughters): Mr. and Mrs. S. Hearn: Mr. R. Bunce: Miss B. Bunce: Mr. D. Annetts and Miss P. Ryder (grandchildren): Miss Sandra Hearne (great grand-daughter): Mr. and Mrs. T. Ryder: Mr. and Mrs. E. Fisher: Mrs. C. Hunt and Mrs. G. Walters (nephews and nieces): and Mr. J. Fry. Among the many floral tributes was one from the local branch of the Women's Institute and one from the President (Mrs. R. Dudley).

155

Vernham Dean Gillum's Church of England Primary School

150 years on – and flourishing and expanding.

The school boasts about 100 pupils, the still recognisable original buildings have been augmented and altered, temporary classrooms situated on the playground have been and gone, new land taken in, landscaping, play areas ….

There had been several 'Dames Schools' in the area before Sidney George Gillum realised his dream of a Church School for the children of the village. Sidney Gillum, born in 1835 and educated at Peterhouse, Cambridge, graduated with first class honours – and a distinction in Hebrew – in the Theological Tripos. His contemporaries from that time remembered him with affectionate regard "as a kindly friend, a trustworthy oarsman". He was ordained in 1859 and "at once threw himself heart and soul into parish work". He served his first curacy at Vernham Dean from 1859 to 1862. There would be no scope for his prowess in Hebrew or with the oars in this agricultural chalkland village whose shallow bournes only flow in winter, and intermittently, but the creation of the village school must have absorbed his energy.

The school building account, (see reproduction) makes interesting reading. Winchester College itself (owner of much of the land in the area) donated £60, but it is Revd Gillum himself, as Treasurer, who makes the largest initial contribution of £20, with a second donation of £5. The note at the foot of the account reads: *"It appears from the foregoing that a deficiency remains of £101.03.05. This sum I, as treasurer, have advanced. That the supporters of the School may be able to make more liberal yearly provision than at present for the teaching and maintenance of this School it is important that it should be free from debt, I therefore do not wish the sum repaid me, but beg to present it to the Committee and School"*. This sum came from his own pocket.

After such a magnificent bequest it is only fitting that the school should still retain his name in its title. All touch was not lost with Revd Gillum: in 1910 five visitors came to the school: *"They were very interested as their father, Revd Gillum, had partly built the school"*. The National Society's Archive has a file on Vernham Dean, but unfortunately the earliest material dates from 1880 and there is no information relating to the actual year of the founding of the school. It is thought to be 1865 (not as printed in 'Hampshire Treasures')

The school opened in a predominantly agricultural area, with its accompanying disadvantages of an agricultural population, in turn subject to the vagaries of weather, disease, the demands of the agricultural year and family duties, leading to somewhat intermittent attendance on the part of the pupils. The nearest town was ten miles distant, transport minimal, teachers understandably reluctant to accept a position so far from amenities. The water supply was scanty, often suspect; in summer drought was a common problem. The area as a whole reflected the economy of Britain: the agricultural depression of the 1880s, with external migration figuring noticeably. The Education Acts and the subsequent legislation covering all aspects of child education and care came slowly into the village, but come they eventually did. Declining rural population threatened the school's very existence in the 20th century, but sheer persistence paid off, followed by an expansion of the village with new housing starting in the 1960s. During the latter half of the 20th century the economic base of the area was completely transformed with improvements in transport, education and housing. The land is still farmed constructively, the village still surrounded by large estates, but the school now draws from all sections of society, parents from a large catchment area choosing to send their children to a village school to avoid the overcrowding in Andover and to avoid the street mentality of the urban milieu. *"Our children are not streetwise"*, said a former Head Teacher, Pat Horne *"and it is a cultural shock when they go on to secondary school"*. But the results attained by the pupils speak volumes for the hard work and concentrated effort of the staff, backed up by a vibrant 'Friends of the School'.

The school's log books and Managers' Reports, allied to snippets from the *Andover Advertiser* illustrate superbly, and mirror precisely, the fate and fortunes of a village school in rural Hampshire over the last century and a half.

When the school started, religious instruction was the most important part of the curriculum, fees were charged, and it must be remembered that the call for child labour took children out of school at certain times of the year. Illness and epidemics often interrupted the children's education, as did the weather. *"We never had wellingtons or raincoats as they do now, and if it was wet or snowy we couldn't go"* a comment true in the 1860s and still true for many years into the next century.

The 'feudal' influence was still strong. In the 1860s the Childs held sway at Vernham Manor (though in fact tenants of Winchester College, not owners of the manor). John Fielder Child in particular gave time to the school:

15th May 1867: *John Fielder Child took First and Second classes to dictation and arithmetic.*

20th November: *Miss Child came in today and took the first class to arithmetic.* Miss Child made herself responsible for much of the needlework materials for the school and monitored the girls' progress.

Diocesan and later HMI reports on the school are frequently somewhat damning:

August 1866: *The children are in very fair order and seem to have had pains bestowed on their religious education ... they are still inaccurate .... the arithmetic seems to require particular attention.* (A recurring theme.)

1868: .... *the children are still very backward.*

1871: .... *the school has passed a fair examination in reading and writing, but only 5 out of 31 individually examined have passed in arithmetic.*

The Education Act of 1870 made a great difference to schools. They were subject to inspection and great importance was given to attendance, but the general tone is not set to change for several years.

1874: .... *school is doing pretty well, but Reading and Writing are too often only just passable and Arithmetic is weak in all above the first standard. The infants presented to me struck me as very old looking and on reference to the Admissions Register it appeared that nine of the members were over age ....*

1875: .... *the results of the examinations show a considerable change for the worse in all respects. Attainments very low and children careless and inattentive.*

The arrival of Julia Osborne in 1876 produces better results: 1877 .... *the children are under good discipline and a decided improvement is shown in the general character of the work ....* and 8th July 1881 .... *this school has been much neglected but is now entering unmistakeably on the path of improvement ....*

An illuminating comment from the Head Teacher on the 11th April 1882: *Children seem more intelligent this week.* (Good spring weather?) A frustrated teacher writes in 1883: *It is difficult to get distinct articulations and overcome the provincialisms .*

(In the late 1990s, a father is told firmly before a PTA meeting at a local secondary school: *"Dad, don't you dare open your mouth. Don't speak AT ALL"*. Dad, who speaks beautiful Queen's English, would apparently have harmed irrevocably the daughter's standing among her glottal-stopping peers. Dad obeyed. *"They can speak as they like at school"*, he said, *"but they understand I demand correct speech and pronunciation at home"*. No doubt peer pressure was as strong then as now).

To return to the 1880s, circumstances are taken into account: .... *considering the many drawbacks this school labours under the average of the attainments is decidedly creditable.* In fact, in 1885: ... *this school has reached a high state of efficiency, both in attainments and discipline. 1890: ... ... the school is in very good order ... ... 1895* (Scripture Report) *... ... ... this school passed an excellent examination. The children are throughout very bright and in first rate order.*

1901: *... ... this year's course broken by illness and changes in staff.* 1902: *..... this is a difficult school to conduct successfully.* 1903 (Scripture Report) *... ... ... this school has special difficulties with which to contend. These have been considered in the markings ... ...* 1911: *..... the new Head Teacher found the school in a very backward condition and the children ill-behaved ... ...*

1914: *... ... pleased with the efforts though the work still very poor ... ... 1920: ... ... improvements in tone and discipline, trying conditions but backward and not very intelligent ... ... a careful study of the Memorandum on the Methods and Aims of Rural Education will be found helpful in preparing schemes and timetables ... ...* At a visit of an Inspector, the Vicar explained that backward conditions were caused by frequent changes of teacher, general abilities were good and behaviour satisfactory. 1922: *... ... ... for a year this school has been without a permanent Head Teacher ... ... difficult to find a suitable candidate. Meanwhile duties are ably discharged by a young supply teacher, fresh from a Training College, who has not only succeeded in maintaining the school in working order but has made great improvements in certain very important directions.* 1928 *... ... ... work now reached a creditable level.*

and 21st November 1931: *... ... a detailed inspection ... ... shows that the general standard of attainment is well above the level reached in country schools of this type ... ... character training of the best kind. This is already a good school. Under the present highly competitive direction it should become one of the outstanding schools of this district.* 1933: *... ... this is now a very good rural school. It affords proof (if proof were needed) that children in a remote country village are not necessarily shy, awkward and tongue-tied. These children speak clearly and confidently, are well-mannered, have learned to read for information and as far as was seen, have retained in an intelligent shape what they have read or been taught.*

How are the mighty fallen, however, for in 1939: *.... Much disturbance, continual change of staff .... six head teachers since 1935, level of work low ... insufficient effort, lethargic and disinterested.* 1944: *HMI very critical of the state of things left by Mrs ... ...* 1947: *.... favourable general behaviour. Miss ... ... should apply for training under Emergency Training Scheme. Lack of responsiveness of children ... ... need speech training and dramatisation to attain fluent speech.* But 1948: *.... very encouraging, some children to be 'A'.*

So much for well-nigh 100 years of the school. Fast forward now to the end of the century to the Ofsted Report. From the Andover Advertiser of the 22nd August 1997: *Vernham Dean Primary School provides its pupils with a good education .... teaching is never less than sound at the 73-pupil school .... head teacher Pat Horne singled out for her 'secure, caring and committed leadership'.*

Returning now to the early days, apart from fluctuating teachers the weather played havoc with comfort and attainment. 22nd March 1867: *..... sat the few children that came as close to the fire as possible to keep them from crying with the cold.*

In contrast: 19th June 1868: *........ the heat of the room is so oppressive that I have resorted to the plan of putting one or two classes out of doors under the shade of the school.* 24th June 1870: *...good attendance, the weather being very fine.* 10th November 1870: *..... commenced fires in school, the weather being very severe.* 1871: *..... snow. School closed January 9th to 13th.* 22nd October 1880: *........ Miss Child gave permission for the fire to be lit .... was obliged to have it put out, the smoke poured out of the holes in the stove.*

The stoves were continually unsatisfactory and it must have caused a welcome diversion when on the 3rd December 1893: *......... the woodwork under the stove caught fire ..... took all the children in the classroom and sent for the blacksmith who took up the ignited boards.*

The saga of new grates, mended stoves and fixed chimneys continues in like vein to the present: 26th October 1906: *......... drew attention to want of new stove in classroom ....* 29th March 1912: *.........the contractor has not been able to supply any more coke through the (Miners) Strike, so fires have not been lit this week. But attendance 94%.* 9th November 1916: *.... bitterly cold. Mr. Maber called to take Harold and Wilfred home at 2.45 as it was snowing fast and they have a long way to go so have cancelled their marks.* (A bit fierce this, since they had been at school most of the day. The Mabers lived at Lower Conholt Farm, off Ankers Lane). 1917: *....... the Vicar promised to lend some wood from the church until a supply was brought.* 16th December 1919: *........... stove smoked so much had to have drill and games outside instead of scripture.* 30th September 1925: *....... temp 48 degrees F in infants' room. Children sitting in their coats, having exercises and going to the fire in turns.....* January 12th 1931: *........ Revd Iremonger discussing buying a stove to heat the north end of the room.* 1933 *........ Heavy snow .....* 6th June 1939: *CARETAKER LIT FIRES.* 12th January 1940: *......... the worst weather conditions since the severe cold of 1894. A hot drink of Horlicks is now supplied daily to the children at a half pence per beaker. Horlicks of Slough provided free on loan 48 beakers, cabinet, copper jug and plunger 4 oz x 1 oz aluminium measure ....* 1942: *....... snow 3-4 feet deep in drifts.* 24th November 1944: *........ children collected wood for the fire as no-one is able to supply the school with bavins.*

Snow in recent years has caused less trouble, but the modern plumbing suffered from the cold. 1987: *New toilet block frozen up. Remained frozen for the week. Children sent home.* 1988: *still have to turn fire off during gales.* 25th January 1990: *.... all roads into Vernham closed at one time* (fallen trees) and 13th February 1991: *..... frozen pipes.* And current villagers will never forget the latest flooding of the 1990s, when the school looked as if it was surrounded by a moat, and Portaloos were supplied the length of the village street.

Weather in all its guises slowly played a less significant role in the pupils' progress. Another initial factor of very great importance was health. The virulence of scarlet fever, measles, whooping cough and influenza ebbed and flowed through the years and the introduction of school medical care is amply illustrated in the log books:

May 1868: *..... measles. Only 17 at school.* 17th May: *........ measles spreading. Closed school for a fortnight.* 14th October 1870: *..... the attendance is greatly affected by an outbreak of scarlatina in the village.* 2nd November, 1871: *.... small pox in village, school closed 12 weeks. Re-opened 29th January.* 1872: *... average attendance 33. I find the children have lost greatly in all subjects in consequence of the long vacation.* 9th February *......... average attendance 41. Parents are fearful lest an outbreak of the disease should show itself again.* 23rd February: *......... average 51. A few more of the children have come back again but not in any great numbers. In fact they appear to dread the idea of again entering the school.* November 1874: *........ whooping cough.* 14th January 1881: *....... some children away on account of bad boots and chilblains.* 20th February 1885: *...... several children absent on account of a 'breaking out' on the skin.*

In 1885 there is the first mention of the 'Sanitary Inspector'. Some parents did not welcome this innovation and kept their children at home when he was expected. He then adopted other tactics.

25th June 1885: *......... inspector came without warning.* 1st February 1888: *..... several children still absent with coughs and colds. Mr. Gibson (local surgeon) has ordered many to stay at home.* 1892: *..... mumps.* 1st February 1892: *..... 57 children absent, nearly all of whom are ill. Only 47 present.* 2nd February: *....... school closed by Medical Officer.*

A sign of the times is found in the Andover Advertiser for 23rd October 1896. Andover County Bench: *........... James W....... of Vernham Dean was summoned for a breach of the Vaccination Act by failing to comply with a magistrate's order to have his child vaccinated within a month ......a fine of 10/- + 7/- costs.*

12th October 1899: *......... reopened after 10 weeks. Whooping Cough has been very bad indeed.* 24th June 1902: *........ broke up for a week's holiday for Coronation* (Edward VII, whose crowning was then postponed due to appendicitis). *School closed by the doctor till*

30th July, due to small pox in the village. (Part of a countrywide outbreak said to be one of the worst in medical history).

30th October 1908 sees the first mention of Medical Inspections: .... *5-11 year olds 11th November.* 7th December: .... *weighing machine received for school.* 7th May 1909: .... *doctor inspected some children. He was here all morning.* 21st November 1910: .... *several stayed (behind) to have teeth and eyes seen to in Andover.* 12th May 1911: .... *Dr. Walker examined the children born in 1898 and 1906. Several of the children in the upper division stayed away as he was here.* 19th May: .... *Dr. Walker paid surprise visit as several stayed away on date of medical examination.* 14th July: .... *Dr. Walker surprise visit and examined all the children. 96% attendance.*

Inspections led to further necessary innovations. 12th November 1911: .... *fireguards sent for both rooms.*

23rd January 1913: .... *took weights and measurements of whole school.* 25th November: ..... *Dr. Farr suggests each child has his own pen and pencil – done.*

NURSE is first mentioned in January 1917. She visits regularly and examines heads, attends to weights and measures, conducts examinations on a regular basis, sometimes accompanied by the Medical Inspector. 1921 brings further specialist attention: 25th January: .... *eye clinic. Two boys to have glasses.* 16th October 1925 gives mention of Mr. Ward, the dentist: .... *46 children had teeth examined.* 19th October: ..... *Mr. Ward comes again.* 30th November: .... *gives treatment to ten children.* 27th October 1930: .... *17 children received dental treatment.*

3rd December 1930: .... *Medical Officer reported two cases of tonsils and adenoids and one of spinal curvature, provisions for treatment being made by the LEA.*

Even in 1931 there is still antagonism towards the medical inspections: .... *I have been informed that the School Nurse is to pay a secret visit on Friday.* 1931 also introduced mention of Dr. Simpson, AMOH, who examined seven backward children in connection with the Otis Intelligence Tests, and in 1934 another step forward: 12th December: .... *48 children now being supplied with milk.* i.e. 1/3 pint of milk under the new National Milk Scheme. In 1935 the MOH takes swabs in connection with a case of diptheria. 1936 sees a Dental Clinic being held in the empty school house, when 37 children had teeth extracted in two days.

It is not until 1938 that mention of school closures for infectious illness ceases, and 28th May 1941 sees all local children receiving the first injections for diptheria immunisation with the second injection on the 25th September. Modern systems are now in train: physical defects gain greater attention. By 1946 28 are receiving school milk and 25 have midday meals. 4th July 1961: ... *Dr. Fenn of Great Bedwyn – 18 children had polio injections.* 1969: ...... measles injections. It is interesting to note the decreased virulence of scarlet fever in the comment in 1959 as by this date ...... *the rule about contact with scarlet fever was no exclusion unless concerned with preparation of food.*

15th October 1982: .... *snow. Dentist commented on the very high state of mouth hygiene he discovered during his visit.* Yet even in 1984 there is a case of a mother refusing consent for her daughter's medical examination.

In theory, at least, the years brought complete control over the welfare of a school child. Battle was joined, between child and the school authorities, eventually to great effect.

The other side of the coin was dirt – on person and clothes. Few houses had their own wells, the water supply was often suspect and scanty. Families had to fetch water from the village pump.

28th January 1892 first makes reference to the situation: .... *cautioned two families that the children must be sent clean to school. They are a disgrace to the school they came so dirty.*

9th May 1893: .... *cautioned two families who send their children very dirty, that they must be sent home if they do not come free from personal dust .... they are really disgraceful and the parents seem not to care in the least.* 27th March 1896: .... *one family cautioned that unless they send the children clean they must be sent home.* 7th February 1908: ..... *one boy sent home with ringworm* (from now on a regular cause for exclusion). 1909: .... *sent home two children because they were dirty.* 15th February 1909: .... *one very dirty family moved to Andover.* 1910: .... *sent one home as he came so dirty.*

But 1922 sees the most meaningful attack on all manner of dirt and infectious conditions. 31st October, 1922: the year of the 'young supply teacher, fresh from a Training College' who not only succeeded in maintaining the school in working order but made great improvements in certain very important directions. The worst feature of the school was the squalid and unsavoury condition of the children, and against this the supply teacher and her colleagues waged steady and continuous warfare. Their efforts to secure reform were soon apparent and the majority of the children became less objectionable than they were. .... *but a good deal remains to be done ...... cleanliness of person is an essential part of good discipline and the cultivation of habits of self-respect is difficult in a school where the majority of children are dirty and untidy.* A retaliatory comment in the Managers' Report later in 1923 said they .... *would back up teachers in any measure they took to ensure the cleanliness of the children. At the same time they felt that to describe the majority of the children as dirty was hardly accurate ....*

Many and often were the exclusions for 'dirty heads' and the consequences could prove even more unsavoury. 24th February 1924: ……. *the Headmistress and Miss Maber absent from school from 10 a.m. – 12 in order to go to Andover as witnesses against Mrs* ……… *who came to school (her daughter having been excluded with a dirty head) and behaved in a disorderly manner. Mrs* ……… *was fined 2/6d. and warned against future misbehaviour.*

28th April 1925: ……. *Harry* …….. *sent home to have his nits removed from him. Mrs.* …... *came to the schoolhouse and demanded to know why her boy had been excluded.* 4th May: ………. *Harry* ….. *still excluded as his head is not yet clean.* 7th May: ……… *Mrs* ………… *came to the school house for a second time in the dinner hour but I refused to see her as she was inclined to be very rude, saying she was sent to me by the wife of one of the Managers.* 11th May: ……. *Harry* …….. *returned, hair cut short and attended to.* 30th September: ……… *ALL CHILDREN CLEAN.* Victory – for the moment. 'Dirty heads' still have entries in the log books. In 1951 there is trouble with a case of ringworm. The mother denied the fact, sparks flew, but eventually it was agreed that the doctor should see him.

Nits never really go away. 3rd March 1983: ………. *following persistent problems with headlice, a film shown about them and their control* ………… *children during the day and parents during the evening.* 1984: ………… *serious outbreak of headlice infection.*

The staff and school authorities had other battles to fight apart from the weather, illness and infection. With children drawn from a predominantly agricultural background there was the demand for their labour, and girls were kept at home in cases of the mother's illness or absence in the fields, to care for the younger children.

Absenteeism:

11th April 1866: ……… *Jessie* ….. *one of the Third Standard, has left school to work in the fields during the summer months.*

15th October 1866: ……… *very few children in attendance as yet, owing to the great demand for juvenile labour which there is in this district at this season of the year.*

16th August 1867: …….. *closed for harvest holidays.*

30th September: ………. *many children still in the fields.*

28th July 1871: ……. *the attendance of the children is very fluctuating, they attending (sic) on an average not more than 3 1/2 days per week each.*

15th March 1872: …. *away in consequence of 'Bird Keeping' which generally in the spring of the year helps to thin a school in an agricultural parish.*

19th April: ……… *discharged Emma ……… who is required at home to mind the baby while her mother goes out to field work.*

21st July 1872: ……… *children needed at home to look after infants during hay harvest.*

14th January 1879: ……… *Isaac ….. present this week who has been absent since June to assist his father at ploughing.*

10th March 1880: First mention of the School Attendance Officer. There is little change at this stage although matters are arranged on a more formal basis.

12th July 1880: …… *Took two boys P ……….. and B ……… as half timers (cow keeping a.m.).*

5th November 1880: ……….. *C ……… is still at work for Mr. H. in spite of visits and threats of Attendance Officer.* (Mr. H. was a highly respected farmer and influential figure in the neighbourhood, whose name was also associated with the management of the school.)

24th November 1880: ………. *Mr. Stagg, Attendance Officer, called this morning for names of absentees or irregular children.* 29th November: ……… *John ……. returned to school this morning having been absent since 2nd July, during which time he had been employed by Mr. C ……… his return is due to the visits and threats of the Attendance Officer.* (Again, Mr. C. was a person of standing in the village).

7-11 October 1881: ……….. *some of the children attend very irregularly. It is difficult to get them on through this.* 27-30th December: ………. *could not give any holidays on account of so many being given in early part of school year. Am afraid many children will not make 250 attendances on account of the school being closed so long and harvest.* May 1882: ………. *absentees due to raspberry picking on the down.* July 1883: ……… *strawberry picking.*

29th November 1883: ……….. *the Attendance Officer taking names ….. does not seem to make the slightest difference. On the contrary, it seems to get worse. Average only 60, numbers on book 84.*

However: 11th May 1885: ………. *Clara ……..'s father was summoned for not sending the said Clara to school which seems to have produced a good result upon the other parents.* 25th June: ….. *Inspector came without warning.* 21st July: ………. *Ernest ……... and Fred ……….. are being employed by one of the School Committee, to work when they ought to be in school, having only just passed Standard III.* 24th September: ……… *children still absent in the fields.* 27th October 1887: ……… *gleaning not over yet.* 29th November: ………. *punished Ernest ……... for playing truant.* 12th November 1895: …… *cautioned several parents that the children must not be kept home 'beating' for the sportsmen.*

31st January 1896: Andover County Bench: .... *George ......was summoned by George Stagg, School Attendance Officer, for not sending his son to school.* 28th February 1896: Andover County Bench: .... *William .... of Vernham Dean summoned by George Stagg, Attendance Officer, for a breach of bye-laws under the Elementary Education Act by neglecting to send his child (not named) to school.* 23rd October 1896: Andover County Bench: .... *James .... summoned by Mr. Stagg, for not sending his child, J .... to school. A medical certificate was handed in but the Bench were unable to understand it .... case adjourned to await a further certificate from the Medical Officer.*

29th July 1911: .... *school closed 28th as haymaking had begun.*

12th September 1913: ...... *some children employed by farmer.*

8th March 1915: .... *Bertie ...... left for work last week. He is nearly 14 and the new bye law makes it possible for boys over 12 to leave for agriculture.*

4th June 1915: ...... *Attendance officer took name of Gordon .... who has left to work on the land but was not given legal permission.*

Absences due to agricultural demands became fewer, but there is a note from 22nd June 1922, that a summons was issued to three parents, reason not stated. The Second World War saw a resurgence of agricultural comments. 5th May 1941: .... *school commences at 9.30 a.m. as the local farmers have not adopted the new summer time.* 3rd – 20th October: ..... *part summer holiday.* Children are asked to help local farmers with potato lifting. In 1942 holidays are postponed to enable the children to help with lifting again. The local farmers seem more inclined to follow the due processes of law as (1945) .... *letter from Mr. H ...... (farmer) asking for Raymond ..... to be released at 3.30 p.m. each day to be referred to Mr. Cooke (Juvenile Employment).*

2nd October: .... *Mrs. C .... called with parents' consent for six boys to do potato picking – all done very officially.*

25th October 1946: Vernham Dean Parish Council Meeting – *some discussion took place on the closing of the school so that the children could help with the potato picking. The children considered that the farmers should have been consulted before this break was made because with the lateness of the harvest many were late to begin potato picking and in consequence the extra labour provided by the school was lost to them.*

Allied to agricultural absences are the agricultural perambulations, the response to the autumn hirings, the poverty, the desperate moves to other areas in search of work,

the emigrations to Australia and New Zealand. **Nowhere are the economic conditions more pitifully mirrored than in the Head Teacher's often despairing comments:**

26th March 1874: ………. *several of the parents of the children are migrating to the North of England, taking their families with them.*

1st May: …….. *several of the children have left to proceed to New Zealand with their parents, who have emigrated.*

12th October 1886: ………. *Several children absent – Weyhill Fair.* This was THE event of the agricultural year in the area, a hiring mecca, a must for everyone who could get there. The result, most years, was the comment: *"Many children have left".*

10th October 1891: ……….. *several families are moving from the village and we lose the children in consequence.*

2nd May 1892: ……… *a family of four have left the school as they are leaving the village. This is the fifth family who have left the village since the last examination – 13 children in all.*

8th October: ………. *several families have left the village this week and others are moving in.*

17th October: ……… *admitted 7 children this week who came to Vernham last week.*

17th October 1898: …….. *a good number left the place this Michaelmas including several of the best scholars.*

27th April 1900: ……… *two families left the village.* 3rd June: …… *three fresh children admitted.*

The Diocesan report for 1900 includes the comment: *"I hope that the employers of labour will endeavour to prevent the drift to large towns of boys taught in this school".* The vacillations continued, however: 14th April 1909: …………. *several families leaving the village the last three or four months with four or more children in them.* 13th October 1911: ……… *Weyhill Fair, so attendance 88%.*

Linkenholt School closed in December, 1939, and the five pupils attended Vernham, although due to lack of transport from that village there was much absenteeism. The Second World War saw an influx from Stanshaw School, Portsmouth, and the Village Hall was used to accommodate the vastly inflated number of pupils. In 1945 some came over from

Combe, in a car provided by the Berkshire Education Authority. Buttermere School closed in December 1944 and a request came in September 1945 for those children who had had no schooling since its demise. A note for 29th October says: *"Buttermere transport agreed, but they came October 29th and walked the whole way"*.

In 1946 there were 21 infants, 24 juniors, 17 seniors – 62. 5 still came from Combe, but by 1947 the Combe children seem to have gone to Faccombe and *"several children are boarded out because of transport difficulties"*

Other frequent entries in the Log Books reflect the social structure of the village, the interests, entertainments and commitments of an isolated community. Church, chapel and, later, the Mission Hall provide the bulk of the diversions. An early entry is rather touching:

2nd April 1866: .... *have a great number of children coming in late on account of their stopping to gather Spring Flowers.*

6th July 1874: .... *half holiday Monday in consequence of a Benefit Club being held in the village.* One gains the impression that Benefit Club and like occasions offered a chance to tuck in without stint – and usually with a bun to take home at the end.

5th July 1875: .... *school closed on Monday afternoon in consequence of a Sick Benefit Club holiday – their Annual Holiday: the parents of most of the children being members.*

There are regular Chapel Sunday School meetings – 13th April 1880: *Annual Tea Meeting.*

22nd April 1881: .... *was obliged to close school on Monday afternoon owing to Sunday School anniversary. There would not have been 20 children present.*

26th April: .... *Sunday School Tea – changed time to finish at 3 to prevent them staying away.*

27th May: .... *Tea meeting at Littledown – Band of Hope at Hurstbourne Tarrant – afternoon attendance not good.*

The theme continues - 1882: .... *Tea meeting at Littledown – 1/2 of the children absented themselves to attend it.*

1883: .... *Club, as usual, caused disruption.* July: .... *Annual Club again, also strawberry picking – Church Sunday School Treat.*

168

18th April 1887: ……….. *anniversary at Primitive Chapel and tea for children consequently half holiday.*

25th April: …… *anniversary at Wesleyan Chapel but the children who are members came much better than that of the Primitive* ………….. (was the tea not so good? Or perhaps the sermons longer?)

A change of theme on the 18th July 1888: …….. *several children are absent this afternoon because one of their schoolfriends gave a birthday party.*

A pitiful entry: ………. *three boys left school today on account of their being sent away to an orphanage.*

26th July 1889: ……. *attendance lowered to 45 by children going to a circus in Andover.* Even worse in 1890, the 25th July: ………… *circus in Andover, only 21 out of 47 on books present.*

16th February 1891: ………. *the three children admitted last week only came three days and were then taken to the Union,* (the workhouse) *their father having left them on the very day they came to school*

14th July 1897: ……….. *holiday on Wednesday as all the Dissenters go to Andover on that day.*

Caustic comments abound. 12th October 1897: ……. *Daisy* ….., *Alice* ……., *Tom* ……. *and the C* ………. *family seem to stay away when they like.* And an annoyed head teacher writes on the 20th June 1902: ……….. *wrote to Fosbury Attendance Officer about irregular children who belong to that parish.* 28th May 1903. An equally miffed Inspector: *"I shall be glad to be informed whether the Wiltshire children are absent with reason or not".*

In the first decade of the new century Lily and Sydney Watson established the Mission Hall, and Sydney Watson became famous for his outings for the youth of the village.

22nd July 1904: …….. *A good many children gone to Southsea for treat.*

There were other excuses for a holiday – in 1907 the induction of the new vicar earned them a half holiday, and in 1908 there was a holiday for the Flower Show.

13th February 1911: ………… *Fred* ….., *Reggie*…….., *James* ……. *and Percy* ……. *arrived late for their mark this afternoon, having followed the foxhounds in their dinner hour.*

Resignedly, on the 9th March: ………… *gave children play vacation from 11 a.m. to enable them to see meet of foxhounds at Woodside as last meet several children stayed away from school altogether.*

Empire Day, royal occasions, funerals and Jubilee festivities afforded holidays on a regular basis.

22nd June 1914: ………… *owing to a Military Review taking place this afternoon several children absent.* It would be interesting to know the details of 1st July 1914: ……… *owing to a non-conformist demonstration being held in the village this afternoon only 62% present.* One of the few references to the war is on 15th May 1915: ………… *all the Walkers have been absent today as their Father came home from the Front.*

3rd December 1917: ………… *an aeroplane came down during playtime this afternoon so allowed the children an extra quarter of an hour to see it start again.*

Ascension Day was taken seriously. 9th May 1918: ……… *Church children attended church.* (It is remarked elsewhere that most of the children were "dissenters").

Peace celebrations were held on the 18th July 1919, with sports and tea in the school. Holiday was given on the following Monday afternoon "after clearing up." 2nd December 1919: ……… *a fine spread given by Mr. & Mrs. Mills (at the Manor) in honour of their son Vernham's 10th birthday.* (Vernham Mills was unable to attend the village school due to poor health, and was educated at home). The various manors still exerted considerable influence – 14th January 1921: ……… *Mrs. Huth* (Fosbury Manor) *is giving tea and a Christmas tree to all the children on the Fosbury estate.* Sir Eastman Bell carried on the tradition – 20th December 1938: ….*Mr. Rose from Sir Eastman Bell came to check numbers for the Annual Children's Party.*

There are fewer and fewer mentions of junketings of this sort as the century goes on and leisure patterns change. Suffice to finish with the 20th November 1947: ……… *school closed. Princess Elizabeth's wedding.* 18th June 1953: ………. *to Odeon to see 'A Queen is Crowned'.* Finally – 15th July 1957: ……… *half holiday to celebrate A. Robb's boarding scholarship to Marlborough Grammar.*

A chalkland village with little or no open water bestows at least one blessing – there is no mention of infantile paralysis (polio) in any of the accounts. Death itself seems rare, at least among the children – or is it so common that it is not usually mentioned?

26th October 1877: ………… *have withdrawn Rose Stroud from the register, being dead.*

6th – 10th March, 1882: …….. *marked off two scholars on register this week. One has returned to Reading, the other deceased.*

By 1917 death is being treated differently in the account. 8th May: ………. *George Roe is to be buried today. Many of the children are attending the funeral by request. The cause was 'acute blood poisoning due to a blow from the cricket ball stopping the circulation to the top of the toe, which consequently died'.*

28th May 1919: …….. *Queenie Strange died. 2nd June: …….. funeral. Half the children attended.*

16th April 1920: …….. *Vivash children lost their mother.*

21st July: ………. *chapel children attend funeral of Sunday School teacher Mrs. Hounslow.*

30th June 1931: …….. *Rita Filmore (11) run over by a car on Saturday and has died in hospital.*

2nd July: ………. *upper classes attend funeral.*

1948 – the last entry about the death of a child. 10th March: ……… *Margaret Stella Bennett, ill from February 6th at home then Sarum Isolation, then Salisbury Infirmary, died.*

Deaths – epidemics – weather – absences – inconstancy of teaching – what else was there to afflict a village school? Before compulsory schooling, which was only gradually enforced due to many circumstances, often beyond a rural person's control, teachers were confronted with children of all ages, ranging from completely illiterate to scholarship potential. Vernham was no exception. Inspectors commented that the infants *"seemed very old"* and proved their supposition by checking the register. Children were not always sent as early as they should to start lessons. Classes were often huge (1870: 100 in residence, 131 on register). Fluctuating attendance, parents only sending the children to school for half the week – here are some of the cases the teachers had to confront:

14th June 1875: …… *admitted Jane …….. aged 13. She is only fit for the infant school.*

16th January 1889: ……….. *admitted Emma …….. who is 12 years old but knows nothing of learning, so is obliged to be placed with First Class Infants.*

16th November 1891: …….. *admitted four fresh scholars from Upton School. 2 of these, 10 years old and 9 years, are only fit for Infant Class.*

19th October 1909: ………. *2 new children from Hippenscombe. Can only come in fine weather.*

15th November 1930: ………… *three hawker's children have been admitted this week. The eldest child of 10 knows nothing – not even her letters and Miss Maber is taking her with the infants for RRR with the child of 8. They will rejoin their classes for other lessons.*

17th November: ……… *gypsies absent.*

Late entry and the backlog of illiteracy duly dealt with, the school buildings themselves were a bone of contention. The rooms were overcrowded with inadequate ventilation and inefficient heating, *"offices"* at best makeshift, no piped water and only one or two buckets of water allowed per day for the entire school. The desperate cold in winter has been covered elsewhere, but it may come as a surprise to learn that flush toilets were not available until 1961.

An irate entry 21st April 1926: ……… *I, the Headmistress, now have to employ a man to see to the Teachers' Lavatory.*

The longest running saga must be that of water. Or lack of it. 27th March 1903: John Herriott wrote to Winchester College (ground landlords): …… *re school's drinking water from rainwater tank condemned for drinking by County Surveyor. Request to allow School Mistress to take water from well in garden opposite the school, lately occupied by Mr. Stone.*

16th January 1905: letter from the Clerk of the Andover Divisional Committee (Education) to Winchester College: ……….. *in reporting on this School HMI says there is only one closet for the girls and one for the boys, both in a dirty and unsanitary condition.* The Reverend F.J. Leeper in response to a communication from this committee said: *"The Winchester authorities have been applied to for a piece of land for the erection of new sanitary buildings but no reply has been received. I understand from one of the other Managers of the school that they have not sufficient ground to enable them to build new offices but that if the College would grant them a small portion of the wasteland adjoining the School they would be able to find the necessary money for erecting the building. I shall be glad to be informed if the College are able to render this assistance to Vernhams Dean."* The Managers, for their part, had set up a subscription list to pay for new offices and repairs which raised £31.3s.6d. The Diocesan Church Schools Association subscribed £30, and Bellons Charity £10. Other contributions came from A.H. Huth, Esq, Revd A. Williams, Revd Gillum, Mr. J. Mills, Mr. Herriott, Mr. Wallis and Mr. Wiltshire, and a Church Collection which amounted to £2.13s.6d.

The school itself ran a jumble sale on 15th August 1916 to raise funds for much needed blinds. £10 was taken, £7.10s.0d. after expenses. 1912 and 1917 saw subscription lists being set up for repairs. 27th December 1917: ………. *the Correspondent was asked by the Managers to apply to landholders to assist them with the expenses of carrying on the school.*

The results were:

Admiral Gamble £2: Mrs. Huth and E.A. Wigan, Esq, £1 each: Revd H. Parsons, J. Herriott, J. Mills and G. Wiltshire all contributed a guinea, 10/6d came from J. Coleman and "Jennings", another guinea from Major Marshall and a final 10/- from Revd A. Williams. A footnote saw £1 being contributed by Mr. Quick (of the Manor).

Skirmishing for land and the necessary money for new offices dragged on for years. The need for piped water was as acute and the entries about water supply are legion.

The requests continued. 15th June 1925: ………. *a letter to be sent to various people asking for help with a £130 repair bill.*

From an LEA letter 24th October 1930: ………. *the supply of drinking water may be considered inadequate as it is dependent on water drawn from a private well. The answer shot back:….. that this has been the custom of the school from its foundation, but that the Managers were arranging for twice the usual amount of water being on hand in the future. Mrs. Davis should receive 6d. a week for bringing two bucketfuls a day. Receptacle should be covered and if possible a tap attached to it.* They compromised, the only receptacle available was an enamel pail and lid.

27th September 1932: ………. *at the last analysis the water was found to be contaminated.* No action was taken until official notification of this arrived, and on the 15th January 1933: ….. *Revd Iremonger says the well water has been analysed and has been found to be quite right. In future the caretaker will draw water from this well, as before and not from the parish well, 1/2 mile away.*

21st July 1933: ….. *but since the water is contaminated, all used in school is boiled before being drunk.*

There was a case of diptheria in 1935 which gave weight to the plea for better water. A comment was made that if the school had taps it could render the school liable for water rates and there was precious little money around. It was painfully obvious from the deliberations over sanitation that one of the main problems was money.

6th October 1936: .... *the Parochial Church Council suggests a 6d. fund for the school. It raised £6. 11s. 0d. ...... in view of the use of the school by Linkenholt children the people of Linkenholt to be asked to contribute towards the repair of the school building: churchwardens to be approached.*

1944: A new Education Bill, whereby the authorities would secure to the Managers half the cost of any improvement to the school. It was estimated that £1,000 was needed to improve and modernise the school, still under church jurisdiction and the rule of Managers. An appeal fund for £500 was set up. Mrs. Dudley, of Linkenholt Manor, gave £50 and each Manager was responsible for raising £100. Discussion in the Parish Council revealed a wish on the part of some parents that the school should be surrendered to the LEA. One wonders if they felt this would involve a cessation of pleas for money from the Managers, but the Managers *"thought it would be inadvisable because of the uncertainty of any good accruing therefrom"*. By 1946, however, £4,000 was needed for repairs and it seemed inevitable that Vernham would metamorphose into a 'controlled' school. It comes through plainly that finance was the reason for altering the status of the school. More money was needed for urgent repairs than could be raised by an impoverished community; the 'gentry', hitherto a well-tapped source, now perhaps in equally sore straits.

After the war pressure was put on the authorities for wash basins and a water closet: by 1949 the County Architect proposed wash basins and flush sanitation. Meanwhile the archaic system sludged on: 1950 Hants Cleaning Services were to empty the buckets twice a week. If the septic tank overflowed and it not dealt with, the Managers would tell the Education Authority and the school would be closed until the matter was settled. On the 10th October 1950 the MOH visited the site to see the situation for himself with the result the Education Authorities suggested a new school altogether. The Managers pointed out that the site chosen would be quite impracticable as the bourne would flood it. If the authorities would only bring the sanitary arrangements up to scratch then there would be nothing wrong with the present buildings. There was another pause, with Racasan (lavatory cleaner) delivered in 1951 for the bucket equipment. 9th May 1952 displayed a landmark: .... *Mr. Lester called about mains water.* On the 11th June the County Surveyor called to measure the playground and water main for tap water to be put into the school, and on the 20th September 1954 measured up for installation of washbasins. By 1955 there were three washbasins for the children's use in the bigger lobby, a sink and tap in the larger room in October and – 20th February 1957: the School Architect called with a view to connecting the lavatories up to water. Mains water had been in the village for some considerable time and by June 1960 there was a definite promise to attach the lavatories to water. The Parish Council was also agitating for decent sanitation but it was still being discussed on the 8th November....... however it all ended on a triumphant note: .... *all building operations completed: lavatories, staff toilet and wash basins, hot and cold water systems for staff and scholars.* (1961).

Yet more about money

Initially, fees were charged and the log books reveal considerable hardship:

11th June 1866: ... ... *Emma and John ... . are obliged to leave the school because they cannot afford to pay the school fees.*

3rd December 1877: ... ... *returned seven children who did not bring the required school fees.*

7th December ... ... *attendance much lower this week, only 48, partly owing to the increased school fees.*

16th February 1887: ... . *sent to Mrs. C ... . for school money as none had been paid for more than a year. Promised that she will pay it by instalments.*

To encourage attendance, Mr. John Child, on the 26th April 1871: ... . *visited on Wednesday and presented prizes to those children who had attended the full number of times to entitle them to examination.*

An ironic comment on the 11th October 1872: ... ... *holiday. Regaled by the committee – tea and cake. 88 partook. Average attendance during the week 65.*

Under the Elementary Education Act 1880 education became free from the ages of 5-10, and the Free Education Act 1891 provided for the state payment of school fees up to ten shillings per week. (Source – Wikipedia)

One gains the impression that the school relied heavily on local philanthropy in the early days, now translated as the modern 'Friends of the School' but just as vital. As now, events were organised to raise funds. 9th November 1899: ... . *holidays given until next Wednesday as a bazaar is going to be held for the funds of the school.* To give perspective, in 1904 an infant teacher received £45 p.a., the Parish Council paid 1/0d. rent per month for the meeting, and 5/- for their Annual Meeting.

The Managers did not mince their words. 30th August 1904: ... ... *there is great poverty. Most of the residents of the village are of the labouring classes. Very few indeed who might be termed gentry.* The Managers at this stage were seeking money for new closets and it was hard to get. In 1907 Mr. John Mills reintroduced a proposal for a fund be started to give prizes to the schoolchildren for good conduct and attendance. The Education Authority stuck closely to their schedule of allowed costs and there were many difficulties in finding cleaning and caretaking volunteers at the current rates. Fund-raising continued and in the spring holidays in 1932 a concert made £16.11s.7d. (handed over to the Managers) and a Nativity play took £13.5s.4d. The annual School Party Tea of 20th December 1934 had been provided out of the proceeds of a Whist Drive and Dance – sandwiches, jelly, fruit cakes and crackers.

Whist Drives, jumble sales, concerts – and, in 1940, the 20th December: ……. *tea possible because parents and friends presented rationed butter and sugar, also cake and milk.*

The school kitchen was opened on the 29th October 1945 and 52 dinners were served: …… *the meal was excellent and the behaviour of the children exemplary.* There was, however, no let up in the relative hardship. 2nd April 1951: ………… *dinner money raised by 1d. a meal.* 2nd March 1953: …. *school dinners increased from 2/11d. to 3/9d. per week, 2d. per child per day. This made a difference of 9. These 9 brought midday lunch of sandwiches.* Money was still tight on the national front; a suggestion for a cycle shed in 1953 brought forth an instant response: *"restrictions on capital expenditure".*

It is with some diffidence that the Editor approaches the next section:

PUNISHMENT. The boys and girls who figure most often in this category have many relations still living in the area today. It is yet another aspect of rural life, and cannot be ignored. Perhaps the children, grandchildren and great-grandchildren of those mentioned will not recognise their ancestors? Surnames have been omitted.

5th March 1868: ………. *was obliged to severely punish a child for saying bad words and swearing.*

2nd February 1869: …… *expelled from the school today Ann* ……… *because her parents obstinately refused to conform to one of the rules of the school.*

14th October 1869: … .. *kept several children in for talking which I am sorry to say is very prevalent in the school, but I hope to soon rectify this habit.*

7th June 1871: ………… *expelled Eliza* ………*for not conforming to the rules of the school, and unruly behaviour.*

26th July 1877: ………… *punished Robert* ………*for swearing.*

15th February 1878: …… *had to punish Isaac*…….. *and David* ……*for insubordination. Isaac* …. *tried to kick governess's legs.*

16th – 20th January 1882: …… *sent Frank* ………*home for obstinate and continued refusal to obey orders on Monday. Jan 30th – Feb 3rd:* ……. *allowed Frank* ………*to return to school Tuesday having apologised for his conduct and promised to do better for the future which promise he has kept.*

176

8th December 1883: ……. *punished Ernest ……… For telling me a lie.*

So far, so good: the usual misdemeanours in school. It would be interesting to have a copy of the early rules so as to understand parents' attitudes.

A more serious note is sounded on the 23rd February 1887: …… *a complaint is made today that the boys on their way to and from school have broken all the window glass in two cottages belonging to Mrs. Mills.*

Punishment was not always accepted. 21st June 1911: ………. *Fred and Lionel …….. sent to Oxenwood School on Tuesday as former was punished at school on Monday.*

23rd July 1913: stone throwing again ………. *complaint received that three boys threw stones on the way home from school and injured another boy's leg.*

Out of school misdemeanours hit the 'Andover Advertiser': Friday, 21st September 1917, page 4:

"Full of mischief – two youths of Vernham Dean pleaded guilty to wilful damage on July 13th to the extent of damaging a galvanized bucket, valued at 2/-. P.C. Prior says Mr. W…….. informed him of the damage done to the bucket which he kept in a field at Upton Hill. A ………… replied when questioned about it: 'I threw once or twice at it, and hit it once. B ……… also threw'. B …… said 'I threw once or twice and hit it once'. A ……….. added: 'It is a piece of mischief'. B…….. subsequently said: 'We haven't anything else to do'. (Plus ça change?) Each defendant was fined 5/-, 4/- for Court Fees and 1/- for damage. June 1924 sees four strokes on each hand for a boy who stole, a girl receiving three strokes. An excerpt from a small piece of a rescued punishment book shows that the children from one family alone merited six punishments out of twenty-one, with one more boy not far behind.

The 1920s sees P.C. Todd busy with the boys. 30th March 1926: …… *12 boys damaged one of a farmer's ricks during dinner hour.*

A slight variation on the 9th November: ……. *R …….. and J……… thoroughly caned for disgusting behaviour in the infants lavatories.* The same month R ……… *was caned six strokes for playing truant on Tuesday afternoon. He was refused admission to Oxenwood School on Wednesday.* This lad seems to get quite a large proportion of the punishment meted out. 30th November: …… HM *had to take R …….. to the football ground to find a letter that had been sent by the Director of Education to his father. The boy had received the letter from the Post Office, torn up the envelope, and hidden the letter instead of taking it home. The letter was taken to the Correspondent to the Managers ……..*

1928: trouble with the GPO for four boys who had damaged the insulation on the telegraph poles with their catapults, and with the AA for damaging the signs.

As a contrast to complaints of children coming dirty to school, 1930 sees a visit from Mrs ……… after school hours, complaining that her son, C………… aged 5, had been given chalk and a BB pencil and had made the sleeves of his shirt dirty in school.

4th July: ………… Mrs. ………… *still complaining but was told the child must learn to keep himself clean.*

On the other hand: 25th June: ……… *received a note from Mrs S………… complaining that Miss Maber had told G ……………, aged 6, that his jersey was dirty. Examined the boy, and found that evidently a meal had been spilt down the front of the boy's jersey and sent word by the elder girl that the boy must come in clean clothes to school.* 26th June: ……… *G ……… came to school in the same jersey in the same filthy condition and was excluded until clean.* 27th June: …… *returned to school clean.*

There are a few notes on confrontations with parents but a vivid entry of the 20th October, 1938, warrants inclusion: ………… Mr. ………… *'stampeded' to school 4.15 p.m. to fetch his children, A & B. A. was being kept in by Miss McIntosh for making a noise and B marched in and said that A 'got to go' to a bazaar so she was kept in too. Mr. ……………… demanded his children. Mr. Carre (Vicar) was present and saw all that happened. He recommended that Mr. ……… would get what he wanted if he came in a decent manner.* 21st October: ……… Mr. ……… *came to school this morning and apologised for his manner yesterday and asked me to see about his daughter, A, who is very difficult.* 22nd October: ……… *spent afternoon answering questions Mrs. Carre asked me about the above matter. Everything now answered satisfactorily.*

A few cases of petty crime get as far as the Juvenile Court, the majority seem to be settled within the village. Every village has its bad apples and Vernham suffered from time to time. The last entry relating to misbehaviour is an entry from Miss Holland, a former Head Teacher. 1964: …. *Miss Holland complaining about youths riding powered cycles, writing obscenities on school building, using foul language and general misbehaviour. There was a right of way through the school grounds. Despite many efforts it resisted removal.* 7th May 1966: ……… *there is a development plan for the village so the Right of Way cannot be moved at present.* In fact, it was not removed to outside the school grounds until 1972.

Vernham's current existence in the top range of primary schools is a fitting tribute to its many years of hard graft. It will do no harm to mention some of the success stories. Surely in this connection it is harmless to mention the pupils' actual names.

June 1883: 82 children presented for examination. Five left to go to work having been given Certificates of Proficiency.

10th July 1885: 99.4% passed the exam.

6th May 1898: Commenced working three children to compete for Junior Scholarship.

10th July 1925: Kenneth Seward passed the Scholarship examination, being the first boy in Vernham Dean to pass this examination.

31st July: Kenneth Seward gained a scholarship to Andover New Grammar School.

28th July 1926: Alan Seward gained a scholarship to the Andover Grammar School.

In 1927 pupils do well in an RSPB essay, two gaining medals, two more succeed in 1928 and the school as a whole is 'highly recommended'.

16th January 1929: Gwendoline Holmes and James Hughes gained a certificate from the Royal Sanitary Institute for an essay on 'Why cleanliness is the first law in health'.

1st July 1929: Frances Harding gained a Certificate from the National Milk Publicity Council for an essay on 'Milk'.

11th July 1930: Margaret F. Holmes gained a County Scholarship.

21st July 1931: Margaret Brewer gained a Junior County Scholarship.

19th December 1932: the Hampshire Challenge Shield, awarded for the best six nature essays by the RSPB, had been won by the Vernham Dean CE School. Prize essays: Joan Coleman, Betty Dillworth, Lilian Coleman, John Jeanes.

23rd July 1933: Eve Filmore won a Junior Scholarship.

4th August: Joan Coleman awarded a scholarship to the Farming Institute at Sparsholt.

5th July 1936: Charles Bulpit and Betty Edgington – scholarships to Andover Grammar.

28th June 1937: Percy Dawkes awarded scholarship to Andover Grammar.

Just before World War II preparations were made for all over 11 to attend the Andover Senior School. War put paid to this and all the books had to be unpacked again. In September 1946 the re-organisation occurs and 23 are transferred to Andover secondary schools. Attempts are continually made for scholarships but it is not until the 6th June, 1953, that a success is actually noted. Robert Hiscock was awarded a scholarship for Andover County Grammar: *"the first scholarship to be awarded for many years"*.

1955: John Holman won a County Grammar School scholarship.

21st June 1958: A. Robb, at 10 years 4 months, awarded a Boarding Scholarship at Marlborough Grammar.

May 1959: Alan Brown gained Grammar School Scholarship.

13th June 1960: Keith Shepherd awarded a Grammar School place.

1962: Keith Armstrong passed for Grammar School.

1963: Lynda Shepherd gained a Grammar School Scholarship.

1966: Gillian Hoare selected for Grammar School education.

1969: Simon Hoare and Jayne Raynsford selected for Grammar School education.

1970: Elizabeth Waghorn and John Easton to Grammar School.

1971: Paul Phillips, Sally Dancer and Sharon East selected for Grammar – Sharon was an under age candidate.

1972: Paul Borchersen to Grammar School.

By 1974 mention is being made of the John Hanson Comprehensive School and Common Entrance is taken. In 1980 Amrita Seneviratne went to Cheltenham and in 1994 Paul Wallington gained a scholarship to Dauntsey. James Herriott went to Dauntseys a year early, and four passed into Godolphin, one to Wells School of Music. It might save current villagers' embarrassment if the tale stops at this stage – but success continues.

A change of emphasis: a team reached the final of the TSB General Knowledge Quiz in 1986: they finished second out of 78 entrants, one point behind the winners. To finish this part of the saga note must be taken of the 21st April, 1994, when for the first time the boys won the football at the Andover County Schools Sports Association competition at Barton Stacey. Edward Sclater was the captain: they beat Clatford in the Final 13-3 and … …

1997: 1st July. Ofsted Inspection begins. Bernard Major's Romany caravan was rented for the Inspectors. 10th July: …… *Vernham Dean is a very good school*.

In the beginning, the school was very much a church concern. Along with the emphasis on religious education, the current vicar visited regularly and often took lessons, as did the Childs, then resident at Vernham Manor. When necessary, managers stood in – but they were inclined to close the school in cases of teaching emergency rather than undertake the lessons themselves, being more accustomed to the plough than the pen. Teachers came and went – some with great rapidity, others stayed twenty years. Pupil teachers and monitors assisted, with varying success.

The emphasis on content varied gradually. In 1883 Eliza Avery cut down on the needlework, putting more time into grammar. In 1891 there was a notable entry: …… *began arithmetic on paper*. In 1896 'Drawing' seemed to be for boys alone – cookery lessons began for girls in the upper classes in February 1895. By 1911 the girls in the Senior Division were: …… . *taken in Drawing instead of Needlework, the lessons to be continued every Wednesday*. The same year, on the 27th March: …. *gave lessons on filling the census paper*…. presumably to assist possibly illiterate parents? Emphasis on different subjects ebbed and flowed over the years. 5th February 1932: …… *cookery course begins: 8 girls, one month each in cottage*. 3rd-12th February 1933: …….. *12 children having a fortnight's dairy course*. The curriculum continued to reflect the needs of rural children, with an agricultural bent, and the needs of those who went into service. The atmosphere still seemed somewhat feudal. 7th May 1934 – Mrs. Dudley (of Linkenholt Manor), a School Manager, promised *"a well-filled work basket to the girl showing the best needlework by Christmas."* Mrs. Dudley had been appointed following a directive that all the schools under the LEA should have a woman on the board of management.

By 1937 officialdom is well established: the school was officially *'Vernham Dean Gillum's Mixed & Infants School 338'*. Electric light was installed in the school and turned on on the 14th October 1946. There were talks about the prospects for domestic science and manual training, possibly a garden. There were hopes for an extension into the adjoining grounds for PT and games. In July 1946 when the Seniors went to Andover, the school was re-organised into a Junior Mixed and Infants Primary School.

A quick resumé of recent years: Head Teacher Pat Horne retired in 2001 and Louise Herbert took over at the end of that year. After many years of planning and mountains of paperwork, pupils moved into the re-vamped school in September 2002. Pat Horne was invited back to perform the official opening on the 2nd December, 2002, with Tim Cook, a long-serving Chairman of Governors. Louise Herbert left in 2004 and was replaced by Stephen Bennett.

Let's finish with entries from each end of the 20th century:

Friday, 25th May 1900: (Andover Advertiser) *MAFEKING – this little village celebrated the relief of Mafeking with a tea, given by Mr. E. Quick and Mr. and Mrs. J. Mills to the children of the National School. They marched from the school to the Manor, where they were regaled with tea, cakes, bread and butter, and other good things. After games and races, etc., they returned to the Manor and, having sung 'God Save the Queen', and given hearty cheers for Baden-Powell and Lord Roberts, each child received a bun and returned home.*

Pupils in 1900 might recognise some of the events of 1990:

25th January: the school closed early because of storm force winds.

February: Simon Rose, a fourth year pupil, won the inter school cross country event.

21st March: all the children went to Marwell Zoo as part of topic work on conservation.

23rd March: Vernham Dean School won the local inter school football league.

29th March: the school participated in the Andover Country Schools' Music Festival.

April: the Linkenholt Open Clay Shoot raised £1,400 for the school. The main school building was carpeted completely. The second football team came third in a large inter school six a side tournament at Barton Stacey.

May: *"We constructed a 'mini beast' area in the school grounds".*

June: *"We built a pond for conservation in the school grounds".* The children took part in the Country Dance Festival at Amport. They danced at the Playing Fields Fete on the Burydene. Dressed as Celts, they took part in a celebration at Danebury as part of a history topic.

July: Eight children took and passed their cycling proficiency test with P.C. Thomas. The school rounders team came third in an inter school tournament. The older children went to a leavers' service at Winchester Cathedral. A leavers' service was held at St. Mary's Church.

September: Harvest Festival Service at St. Mary's Church. The children took the food to the old people of the villages.

October: the older children dressed up as Victorians as part of their topic. The Juniors went to Sparsholt College of Agriculture as part of their science work.

November: the school held a coffee morning and sale.

December: Canon Michael Benton called to see the school. Visit to the Watermill Theatre to see the pantomime. School play, Snow White and the Seven Dwarves.

Perhaps not so different in essentials?

Parish Councils came into being in 1894 to take the place of the old Vestry System, forming the fourth leg of Local Government: County Boroughs, County Councils, Urban and Rural District Councils – Parish Councils. Parish Councils were composed of duly elected councillors who really were the men and women in close contact with the people. They were accessible and could voice the opinions and desires of the local inhabitants, perhaps better and more intimately than any of the other branches of local government.

Andover Advertiser, Friday, 7th December 1894:

THE PARISH MEETINGS: *the great experiment of local government in rural England began on Tuesday night, when in every parish was held the first parish Meeting. In villages with over 300 inhabitants it acted as the preparation for the Parish Council.*

And on Tuesday, 4th December 1894
in the Schoolroom at Vernham Dean at 7 p.m.
a meeting was held
for the election of Six Parish Councillors.

40 electors were present *'including all the largest ratepayers'.* The Overseers were W.A. Cook and R.J. Coleman. Mr. J. Homer-Powell was unanimously elected Chairman. Of the ten nomination papers, three were declared to be invalid – and

CHARLES ALDERMAN	RICHARD JAMES COLEMAN	
WILLIAM ALFRED COOK	EDWIN QUICK	ENOS SMITH
DAVID WATERS		

were elected, with JOHN HERRIOTT nominated as District Councillor. Descendants of these people still live in the village today.

At the very first meeting of the Parish Council, held at 7 p.m. on Saturday, 15th December 1894, with John Herriott and James Manners present as representatives of the school managers, R.J. Coleman was elected Clerk and W.A. Cook as Treasurer. It was agreed with the School Managers to provide fire and light for every meeting of the Council held in the classroom at 2/6d. and at every parish meeting of the whole electorate 10/-.

One hundred years later, in 1999, while the Village Hall was being rebuilt, history repeated itself as all events had once again to be held at the school. No note of the charges are to hand ..... without doubt a little more than 12/6d, approx 65p.

At the first meeting it was agreed to purchase a reading lamp for not more than 17/6d. Later there came the first of continual calls for a Parish Map. Councillors also asked for a Parish Chest:

24th October 1895:

…. Long, deep, wide – 2'0" x 1'6" x 1'6" with two locks, two handles dovetailed, stained and varnished …. The estimate was for 18/-, but the Clerk was told to get a quotation from any local tradesman for a galvanized iron chest the same size.

Sculling through the Council Minutes from the earliest days to recent years gives a bird's eye view of the village during the late 19th to the late 20th century. Fascinating concerns are highlighted:

Monday, 13th April 1896: *Mr. D. Walters proposed steps be taken by the Council to prevent shows, roundabouts, Vans or Stalls from pitching in the Village Highway. Seconded.*

And – a recurring feature: *proposed to write to various owners of property calling attention to the dilapidated condition of the Village Well and ask them to assist in pulling (sic) the well in repair. Seconded.* Water and the pond are covered in another chapter, but form a frequent item on the Council's Agenda.

22nd July 1896: *Wheat carting commenced this day.*

14th July 1897: *Mr. and Mrs. Watson offered to erect a lamp in the village at their own expense in commemoration of the Queen's Jubilee on condition that the Council will keep it lighted. This was negatived by 4 to 1. They thanked Mr. and Mrs. Watson but 'do not see their way to undertake the conditions. The Council will not object to Mr. and Mrs. Watson erecting the lamps if they will undertake the lighting'.*

There is still no lighting in the village today, villagers managing with the aid of the 'Parish Lantern' (the moon) and a multitude of security lights which spring into action at the footfall of a hedgehog.

13th February 1899: *carried unanimously, that the rating of the cottages should be made more equal …… resolved that the Overseers rate the Owners of Cottages instead of the occupiers and allow them an abatement or deduction of 15% from the amount of the rate …..*

5th July 1899: the first mention of the Bourne Valley Light Railway, detailed in an earlier chapter.

7th June 1900: *... in the event of peace being restored in South Africa the Chairman should call a meeting to consider what steps should be taken to celebrate the event.*

1901: *The Queen Victoria Memorial Fund, collected by Messrs. Herriott, Quick and Wiltshire, amounted to £3.16s.8d.*

4th March 1901: *An application be made to the GPO for the establishment of a Telegraph Office at Vernham Post Office.*

Tuesday, 10th September 1901: *.... resolved that the offer of the Telegraph Department be accepted and that the Parish Council provide the necessary guarantee.*

29th October: *.... resolved that the guarantee for the Telegraph Office at Vernham be signed.*

25th March 1902: - delay in opening the Telegraph office – complaint.

(27th January 1904: Captain E.H. Gamble sent a cheque for £4.12s.3d., the amount of the loss on the year's working of the Vernham Dean Telegraph Office, which loss had been guaranteed by the Parish Council).

Tuesday, 6th May 1902: ………. *consider steps to be taken to celebrate Coronation of His Majesty.*

27th May: …….. *resolved a dinner on Coronation Day at one o'clock: Ale to be provided, not to exceed one pint to a Man. 2 bottles of Mineral Waters to be provided for abstainers. Tenders to supply dinner per head and provide Roast Beef, Boiled Beef, Roast Mutton and Veal, Mutton Pies, Veal and Ham Pies, and Cold Ham, also obtain tenders for Tables and seats for 220 persons. Proposed Divine Service in church on Coronation Day. Proposed obtain a Band for the day.*

Tuesday, 10th June: …….. *2 tenders. Mr. Bell 2/6d. per head: Mr. Timms 1/5d. Accepted Mr. Timms at 1/5d. and 1d. per head for cheese. Accepted Mr. Bell's tender for Mineral Waters at 9d. per dozen. Mr. Morris – ale at 1/2d. per gallon. All to bring own plates, knives, forks and glass. Mr. Bell's tender for tea at 5d. per head. Coronation festivities postponed till Wednesday, 2nd July 'if the Band would come on that day'* ……*a Coronation Fund set up* ……*Sports Committee.*

It was at this stage that women first seem to figure, in the sports committee and the tea committee.

The coronation of Edward VII was postponed from June to August because of the king's illness (appendicitis) but ...

Tuesday, 19th August: .... *the Accounts for the Coronation Festival. Sum collected was £38.10s.8d. and it balanced ...... apart from Mr. Mills 9/9d., so £39.0s.5d...... the Burbage Band played ...... and lunch for the band cost 10/-.*

In 1903 the balance of £1.2s.9d. from the Coronation Fund was given to the School for prizes: for good attendance and two prizes in each standard.

In consideration of the drunkenness in the village, the Parish Council request the Licensing Authorities to reduce the Licenses in the parish by two.

From 1903 there was a demand for allotments, which involved years of submissions and discussions and, mirabile dictu, in 2006 the question arose again.

Section 19(2) of the Motor Car Act 1903 provided that the County Council shall cause to be set up signposts, denoting dangerous corners, cross roads and precipitous places where such sign posts appear to be necessary .... *it was proposed that the road Vernham Street/ Littledown was dangerous, being narrow and having many sharp turns and the Council consider a post should be placed above the Pillar box and opposite Mr. C. Mills's farm.*

25th August 1903: ..... *it was proposed to hold meetings in the Public Reading room .... Resolved to ask the school committee to reduce the charge for the use of the schoolroom and provide fire and light when necessary .....*

22nd June 1904: .... *accept offer for use of the schoolroom for 12/- per annum. Mr. Beck proposed that the meeting express its sympathy with the Passive resisters of this parish, in as much as they have had to suffer in having their goods distrained upon for non-payment of that part of the Rate which is used for sectarian purposes.*

1905: Mrs. Watson – the co-founder of the Mission Hall – was elected a member of the Parish Council. This looks like the first woman member.

29th March 1906: ...... *petition to the Board of Education asking them to appoint a schoolmaster at the Vernham Dean School, the reasons being threefold:*

First The School Misstress and assistants absolute lack of controll over the children

Secondly Unsatisfactory progress made by the children attending the school

Thirdly Great Dissatisfaction prevails amongst parents owing to any complaints made to Managers having no effect
(the spelling is as given in the PC Minutes).

14th May 1906: .... *the School Committee to meet parents of children at a Parish meeting so that the parents may lay their view before the Committee.*

5th November 1910: .... *letter to be written to the Education Committee asking a schoolmaster to be appointed instead of a school mistress in place of Miss Bowles, who was retiring.*

24th April 1911: Coronation Committee .... *to prepare a dinner for adults over 14 and tea for all those under. Dinners to be taken to aged people who could not attend. Tenders to be invited from caterers to consist of Roast Mutton and Veal, Mutton Pies, Veal and Ham Pies, Roast Beef and Boiled Beef and Cold Ham with Two kinds of Vegitables (sic).* There was to be a collection towards this:

Contributions: Mr. Wigan £5: Mrs. J. Bell £1.1s.0d: Mr. Guy Knowles £1: Agreed that Mr. Baiden's tender for dinner at £1.7s.0d. per head be accepted. Mr. Bell's tender for tea at 6d. per head to be accepted. Mr. Hayes price for 20/- for the tent to be accepted. Drinks: Minerals at 9 1/2d. per dozen for 30 dozen. 300 glasses at 6d. per dozen. 25 gallons of beer at 1/1d. per gallon. 300 tickets to be procured for the Dinner and 100 for the tea. (This provides for 100 more than at the Jubilee celebrations).

26th October 1922: .... *record the Parish Council's high appreciation of the service rendered to the parish by Rev. Parsons in the interest he took in bringing about measures whereby the dificalties (sic) in the election of parish councillors for the parish of Vernham Dean were overcome.* (what on earth had been happening?)

30th July 1931: ..... *to see what demand there was for houses under the Rural Housing Act.* Sites suggested: opposite the Bury Dean, by Poplars Farm, the top of Bulpit Hill, and opposite the Post Office. It was decided to recommend the site opposite the Post Office.

29th March 1932: .... *Chairman said he did not think they stood much chance of having any cottages erected ....*

12th December 1932. A MOST UNUSUAL ENTRY IN THE PARISH MINUTES viz .... *J. Mills suggested a letter be sent congratulating the council on the good state of the roads* ....

26th November 1934: .... *proposing to get information on an electricity supply for house lighting ..... and ...... a complaint was lodged that nothing had been done about the extermination of cats during Cat Week, as it has been heard that poison was available.* Letter from the Wessex Electricity Company – they did not see any hope of electricity in the near future.

1936. Letter from the RDC re Air Raid Precautions. A letter from Mr. Stacey, the Secretary to the Men's Club, asking for PC support for fire-fighting equipment. It is considered out of the Council's due restrictions (sic – presumably jurisdiction but what a lovely effort). A draft was received concerning Air Raid Precautions Schemes for Rural Areas. More information was required. 15th March 1936: ...... *Air Raid Scheme rather confusing, it was decided to discuss it at a future meeting.*

May Webb seemed to be the second woman elected to the Council. Celebrations for the Coronation were discussed.

19th April 1936: discussion on housing shortage. Letter to be sent to the RDC requiring 12 cottages.

18th June: .... *rent of houses, if built, would be 10/- per week inclusive of rates. This was considered too high, but houses were urgently needed, and letter to be written to Winchester College to see if they would consider building some houses in Vernham Dean in place of some not now available on their property* ..... (Winchester College had procured a great deal of land in the area several centuries before as endowment for their foundation. This land was eventually sold piecemeal during the latter part of the 20th century).

13th September: .... *necessary to ascertain demand for housing. Seven applicants, of which three at Vernham Street.*

29th September: the RDC said it was not possible to build houses to let at less than 10/- a week.

1938: - Under the new Agricultural Housing Act, a letter to go to the RDC for information as there was a shortage of suitable houses.

7th July – the RDC replied that if the new Housing Bill became law the rent for agricultural workers would probably be 3/- or 4/- a week exclusive of rates. The Parish Council were to state how many they could fill, and give suggestions for sites.

15th March 1939: five applications had been sent in for agricultural housing, but there had been no reply. A demand was to be made to the RDC for agricultural housing.

25th April: the Parish Council to suggest sites for houses under the Agricultural Housing Act – suggested field opposite the Pump House: Vernham Street – Mr. Mills' field: Smith Close, and in Mr. Davies' meadow opposite Flowers Farm.

18th August.: the Council had chosen a site the same side as the pump house, instead of opposite, for the erection of cottages, also two in Mr. Davies' meadow and two on some land just below Mr. Davies' house BUT: 30th October …….. *the housing question would have to remain over while the present crisis lasts*. (WWII)

30th March 1943: ….. *DECIDED 18 houses should be demolished and 50 houses built*.

20th March 1944. ….. discussion on the new cottages erected in the parish for agricultural workers. Very disappointed at the way they were built. With any future building by RDC the Parish Council should be consulted.

31st July – ask RDC for a date on which they would start on the site already purchased by the Council.

13th December 1944 – still no date for building.

23rd March 1945. A letter from the County Education Office asked why the School Manager elected by the Parish Council had not attended a Managers' Meeting for two years. Mr. Hughes asked why was the meeting held at the vicarage and not at the school? The Vicar replied he had the Linkenholt Manager in mind, to which Mr. Hughes replied: *"But they have a car"*.

Mr. Hall said he would like to see the school taken over by the County Council as none of the parents were very happy. The Vicar said he did not think it would benefit the children. He was conscious of difficulties but would await a report from the School Surveyor and Architect.

15th May, 1945 – query – when would school meals start for the children?

1946: *Tempery (sic) houses and site discussed. Objections could not really be made as a) it would be of no use and b) the chief concern was to get houses*. (This probably refers to prefabricated buildings).

Discussion on Victory Celebrations:

Monday, 29th April ……. *enquire from the Food Office what extra food was going to be allowed for the Victory Celebrations*.

1st November 1946: - discussion on the way in which Council houses let – should publish the names of the proposed tenants. …….. *if and when Mr. Evans could get the information he would produce it*.

13th December: *... proposed tenants for council houses and pre-fabs produced. The Council approved of Mr. Evans' list without any amendments. Chairman and Clerk to see Mr. Arnold* (Winchester College) *with a view to obtaining some of the Bury Dene for playing fields …...*

6th August 1947: .... letter from Sanitary Inspector re collection of pail closet contents – Hants Cleansing Service prepared to undertake collection of night soil providing minimum of six householders – min. 5d. per bucket.

1949: More discussions about building sites – Bury Dene? Subject to expert advice. Top of Bulpit Hill? The football field on the right past the S bend? Complaint re empty cottage at the bottom of Conholt Hill…...... *no cottage should be left to go to ruin in times like these.*

1950: Re. Council houses – plans of new houses to be made available to the Parish Council.

5th May 1950: …… *something must be done to improve the state of the postal system as on occasion letters posted in the Andover Post Office in the afternoon have not been delivered until the following afternoon…...*

By this year (1950) the Parish Council's wishes regarding council housing are being supported by the District Council, but there were objections on the 2nd June because the site under consideration was rated as agricultural land. However, by 11th December there is a decision to be made about the number of bedrooms in council houses, and six new houses are to be built.

13th April - Miss Lennard wants improved comforts in council houses – RDC to be told.

14th December - complaints re electricity points in council houses to be sent to the RDC.

1952 – the six council houses to be known as Dene Terrace.

14th March – six names of needy cases for council housing to be submitted to the RDC.

4th June – the matter of boilers and fireplaces in the council houses to be investigated.

11th July – further words on boilers in the council houses.

During this year there were also concerns at the line of the National Grid pylons, and Coronation celebrations were discussed.

10th April 1953: …. *untidiness – resolved to write to the RDC that the village is in A disruptibl State – the Parish thinks that the Road Men are not Properly Spervised….* (sic)

29th March 1954: …. *possibility of more council houses after next August.*

Trouble on the Berrydene – much feeling in the village because Vernham Mills had wired in a large portion. Within living memory the land had been open to residents and it was to be regretted that without notice much had been enclosed for pig pens and now a milking ground. It was a unanimous decision that it spoilt the amenities and the approach to the village. The Chairman was to write to Winchester College, pointing out the local feeling and requesting them to approach Mr. Mills with a view to making some arrangements for the Berrydene to be re-opened as formerly.

9th July: there would be no allocation of houses in 1954.

3rd October 1954 – search for a Clerk: ……….. *Chairman said he was endeavouring to obtain someone suitable but without success. Mr. Stacey felt that one of the younger men in the village ought to take up the work, but realized there was probably no willing person who was capable of properly carrying out the duties.*

8th October 1954 – a letter went to the RDC suggesting a site for further building opposite the present houses in Hatchbury Lane.

11th February 1955: Mr. E.P. Woodgrave was to serve as Clerk. The Parish Council was to ask for eight council houses. Mr. Adams was to ascertain the owner of the land Hatchbury Lane/Bulpits Hill. Mr. Brooks was tenant of the land and was not willing to vacate because he could not spare it. The owner, Mr. Gray of Baddesley, was willing to sell. The decision was to ask the RDC to procure the field, compulsorily or otherwise.

27th May. The RDC would not take action on the proposed site and other sites were to be pursued.

18th July: Messrs. Hiscock and Miller were not unwilling to co-operate in the housing site search, but circumstances did not permit a decision. Mr. Trott's field at Woodside was to be viewed, but a decision was made on a portion of the field at the rear of Dean Terrace. Winchester College to receive a letter.

9th January 1956. The RDC said there could be no housing as there were no subsidies, but the Surveyor would view the site.

At the Annual Parish Meeting on the 12th March there was a complaint of the apathy of the School Managers and it was felt the school needed much improvement. Neither had the

Parish Council representative been called to a meeting since February 1955: the Clerk was to write to the Vicar.

6th May: Lack of discipline had been alleged at the school but Mr. Evans had paid a surprise visit and all was well. There was still a general opinion that the children's behaviour was bad, particularly at meals. Mr. Adams agreed. There was prevailing dissatisfaction and Messrs Evans and Bulpit were to convene a meeting of the School Managers and present a report. On the 16th July it was reported that the School Governors' meeting had been held and some improvement had been apparent.

7th July 1958 …… *uncultivated council house gardens – defaulting tenants should pay an extra 10/0d. a week rent until the situation is rectified. ….. Proposed RDC usually attends to the situation and a letter suffices.*

1st February 1960: The school toilets were very unsatisfactory, there was a lack of proper sanitation. A letter was to be written to the Medical Officer in the strongest possible terms, with copies to RDC and the School Managers.

7th March : ……… *letters intimate that the County Council have every intention of dealing with the problem in the programme of modernising local schools.*

2nd May: Mr. Hiscock thought Mr. Juckes' field, uncultivated for three years, would be a good site for housing e.g. four old persons' bungalows. The RDC were to explore through the owners.

4th July – the RDC considered the entrance to Mr. Juckes' field inadequate. The field at the rear of the George Inn would be more suitable but the Council asked the Chairman to press for the acquisition of the field at the rear of Hatchway Cottage.

5th September – the site at the rear of the George Inn was purchased, with numbers of houses to be increased to six.

7th November – the bungalows to be one-bedded to qualify for government subsidy. This was essential in order to keep rents at an economic level

And – 1961 – improvements in the electricity supply

1962 – precedence must be given over strangers to old persons in houses now too big for them, local persons, those who have lived locally years ago, and those in tied cottages.

6th January 1964: Mr. Jones, the RDC member for Linkenholt, said the village map was in course of preparation and Vernham Dean was one of the most important of the local villages earmarked for development. Details were to be obtained.

1st March 1965. Michael Shepherd asked if there was any possibility of providing a playing field. Several people had put the question to him and the Bury Dene had been mentioned as a possible site. It was agreed in principle that a playing field is a necessity.

1968 – building of "The Dell"

6th October 1975 – permission for 23 houses at the rear of 'The Homestead'.

25th October 1976 – the new road to be named Shepherd's Rise, after Michael Shepherd, who had worked tirelessly for the village.

1977: Jubilee celebrations

25th July: 8 dwellings proposed on the site adjacent to the Gospel Hall. This was opposed on grounds of access, density and not in keeping. On the 22nd August the decision was deferred.

19th September – Jubilee fund £460, of which £250 appropriated towards a hard standing on the playing field.

5th December – approval for the future Botisdone Close to the rear of the Gospel Hall.

9th April 1978. There were no objections to eight dwellings on the land adjoining 'The Dell' as long as the roads were put in place first.

3rd July – re Botisdone Close: ……… *must keep mature beech even if it means re-siting dwelling. Recommended the imposition of a tree preservation order.*

20th December: Parish Council decided 'No' to street lighting.

On the 9th October 1978 typed Minutes appear. This was a great relief to anyone researching the Parish Minutes, although the early hand written work is a joy to behold.

1978 seemed a point at which it was wise to stop delving into the Parish records, which have proved a goldmine in that they give the flavour of the village over the years. Now in the 21st century the same concerns are to the fore as the previous two centuries, with greater emphasis on housing and planning permission. Water – namely the abundance during storms, is a continuing wrangle, electricity and sewage make regular appearances. As in 1894 a cross-section of the village is represented on the Council, which does sterling service in its attempts to preserve and develop the unique flavour of the village.

Imagine, if you will, the countryside in very early times: for the most part scattered farmsteads, slowly consolidated into hamlets and villages. From the days of the hunter gatherer, to primitive agriculture, to barter, trading and all the attributes of a developing civilisation, Vernham Dean and its surroundings were little different from any other rural setting in England: you cultivated your plot, if you had one, or hired yourself out to a local farmer or lord. You might be a small trader, blacksmith, baker or carrier. Leave aside for the moment more fortunate people, landowners and landed gentry, and consider the social and economic conditions of those who lived to a very great extent a hand to mouth existence.

There was no social security. Almsgiving was inadequate, for with social dislocation and the void left by the dissolved monasteries, hospitals and chantries. there was precious little provision for the needy. In later years it could be added that enclosures may have deprived some of the free grazing, and industrialisation killed off many cottage industries.

It therefore fell to individual parishes to care for the 'impotent poor' and as long ago as 1536 the 'Beggars Act' (27Henry9c.25) established the duty of the parish in this regard. A string of Acts followed whereby the parish in the shape of churchwardens, although they had previously had some responsibility, now took on more secular duties in addition to ecclesiastical ones: recording births, marriages and deaths, maintaining the roads, raising a quota of men to serve in the militia. 1572 saw the formal establishment of the office of Overseers of the Poor which permitted levying compulsory poor rates in parishes and towns, and by 1601 the raising and distribution of poor relief fell into the hands of the parish. Parish Poor Rates, essentially, were designed to help those who were unable to help themselves. The Overseers were answerable to the parish vestry and the Justices of the Peace – an Act of 1640 provided that Overseers were chosen from substantial householders in each parish and should, together with the churchwardens, set and maintain the poor 'on work' and levy a tax on the inhabitants. Officials elected from the parish had to include a constable who would report regularly on matters of crime and disorder, while the churchwardens had to keep an eye on the body of the church and the minds of the parishioners. Quite a burden for all concerned, and by 1662 the Act of Settlement was devised so that a person's relief was tied to the village of birth, and defined the ways in which a parish was responsible for its poor. Any stranger settling in the parish was to be removed at once, by order of the Justices, unless he rented a tenement of £10 annual value or found security to discharge the parish of adoption from any expenses it might incur on his behalf. Alternatively a stranger had to bring a certificate from his own parish which undertook to receive him as soon as he became a liability on the new parish. By 1687 it was decided he could settle permanently if he had such a certificate. Bastards, incidentally, adopted the parish of birth. It was more usual for the father to be made responsible by bond for the upkeep of the mother if marriage were unlikely.

In Vernham Dean we have examples of people being returned to their 'parish of registration'.

1841: Hannah Wells, Mary, Jane – from parish of Vernham Dean to Southwark.

1851: John Dennis (38) charged to Vernham Dean. Amy 37, Charles 3, Mary Ann 1. John born Hungerford, under-carter in Shalbourne to Joseph Cundell two years, then carter to Mr. Barnes four years. Married Amy 1846 at Vernham Dean. Andover Workhouse. Removal to Shalbourne.

So much for the official structure and organisation of poor relief. It is painfully obvious that being poor was considered a stigma, and any form of provision was in the way of a punishment. The fear of being 'sent to the workhouse' still lingered on well into the 20th century.

1575 saw the establishment of 'Houses of Correction' where each county had to provide two or more such houses, plus a stock of implements for setting the poor 'on work' and for punishing such 'as be inhabiting in no parish or be taken as rogues'. Workhouses were set up from 1695 where poor people could work for their living. This system lasted until the Poor Law Amendment Act of 1834 – conditions were vastly different from the previous centuries with a great increase in the national population. A new system introduced unions of parishes run by boards of elected Guardians – the Andover Union was constituted from various parishes, including Vernham Dean. The infamous story of the Andover workhouse need not be repeated here but it is a particularly abhorrent example of provision of relief in its most unpalatable form. The workhouse was erected in 1836. A list of Overseers in the *Andover Advertiser* of Friday, 17th April 1868 include:

Linkenholt	Robert Henly, Henry Henly
Vernhams Dean	H. Bilbrough, W.H. Lansley
Parochial Constables	Linkenholt George Shuttle
Vernham's Deane	James Poore, Sylvanus Marchment.

An Overseer was empowered to raise tax 'assessments' or 'rates' in order to meet demands for poor relief. He had to decide the merits of appeal for poor relief, to temper mercy with knowledge that the rate payers would demand explanations of expenditure. The pauper, however, could take his case to the Justice of the Peace: the Quarter Sessions were the Court of Appeal in Poor Law matters, the JPs the superintendents. The Overseer had to check the likelihood of incomers becoming a burden on the Poor Rate and superintend their removal to the parish in which they were legally settled. Overseers were usually middle-aged yeomen, husbandmen and craftsmen rather than labourers or cottagers.

It was only gradually realized that poverty was due to unemployment and other factors often beyond the control of the system and that a tightening up of rules had no effect on prevailing conditions. Changes had to be made, necessitated by the increased mobility of labour, poverty caused by low earnings, irregular employment, large families, sickness, widowhood and old age. By 1847 the Poor Law Board had representation in Parliament and an attempt was made to separate the different groups – children, the sick, lunatics and vagrants, and to establish district schools for pauper children and asylums for the afflicted.

Our village suffered the same as many other basically agricultural villages, and the 'Swing Riots' of 1830 had particular relevance here. It was a time of hunger, deprivation and unemployment. Smouldering fires of bitterness caused by the 17th century Poor Law were fanned by provisions of the Speenhamland system which allowed low wages to be supplemented by parish relief. This encouraged farmers to underpay, knowing that labourers would receive money from the parish to bring wages up to bare subsistence level. The numbers applying for relief rose and this placed a heavier burden on the parish, causing bitterness and resentment among those who contributed to the Parish Rate.

The 'Swing Riots' concentrated on varied demands: an increase in wages sufficient to support a family, the ending of the use of machinery so as to increase the work available, a guaranteed rate of poor relief which would be fair and honourable. Landowners were to be forced to lower farmers' rents; the clergy to abolish or lower tithes so that the farmers could afford increased wages: justice and equality under the Law – universal suffrage – annual parliaments – secret ballots.

Families who had been used to meat, bacon and cheese were now reduced to bread and potatoes. The standard of living was lower than it had ever been for farm workers, and a wife had to provide on wages of 7-9 shillings a week. The Napoleonic Wars had caused a boom in agriculture, highly profitable for landowners and farmers: prices went up, not wages. Returning soldiers then swelled the ranks of the unemployed. In addition, the accelerating rate of enclosure of land had deprived cottagers of their few rights on previous common lands.

Three years of poor harvest, the bitter winter of 1829 and the introduction of the threshing machine added fuel to the flame and it took little more for 'Captain Swing' to blaze over the southern counties of England. The first riot was on 28th August in Kent, but rioting reached Hampshire on the 10th November 1830.

'Captain Swing' was a mythical person who sent signed letters to farmers and landowners, threatening action if they did not raise wages and destroy their machines. Hand-threshing had occupied four months of the year, and the machine was seen as a bitter threat to winter work. Better wages and regular employment were the only means by which poverty and hunger could be kept at bay. Desperate labourers visited farms and large houses, with the aim of destroying agricultural machines, securing agreement that wages would rise – usually to 2/- a day, and soliciting donations of food, drink and money.

Vernham Dean was not immune from the disturbances, most of its inhabitants relying on agriculture. A report in The Times relates:

'A mob visited Henry Fermor's farm at Vernhams Dean again today. They threatened to do more mischief if they did not get money. Under this threat Mr. Fermor handed over two half crowns. The mob also went to William Child's premises where they destroyed a threshing machine and forced Mr. Child to give them a half crown for their work'.

The best documented case in Vernham Dean relates to Jacob Wiltshire. He was 25 years old, single, a farm labourer and shepherd. He was 5 ft 7 1/2 inches with fair to ruddy complexion, brown hair and weak grey eyes. He could read and write. He was charged on the 21st November 1830 *'with divers other persons, riotously and tumultuously assembled together, and feloniously and with threats, demanded and received from Darius Bull, one sovereign, the said Darius Bull being put in bodily fear of injury either to his person or property. A sentence of death was recorded commuted to transportation for life'.* (Chambers)

Darius Bull, the tenant of Vernham Manor at the time, appeared to have had regrets – or was perhaps appalled at the severity of the punishment for the young man and petitioned the authorities to have mercy.

'Allow me to say his character is quite irreproachable in every respect, particularly in regard honesty, industry and civility. He being brought up extremely well. I mean for a person in his condition of life, for this he is much indebted to his parents for no one have had better, and very few so good, as a proof of which I have never known or heard of one of them guilty of the least dishonest act ......, the said Jacob Wiltshire before his committal on the above charge always bore a character of an honest hard working and industrious man and was also the son of parents who alike bore most excellent characters the father and grandfather of the said Jacob Wiltshire having been in the almost constant employ of your Petitioner the said Darius Bull for the last thirty years and upwards and it was only from a sense of duty to the public and for the protection of property that he was induced to prosecute the said Jacob Wiltshire for the above offence'.

In spite of numerous signatories to the petition, Jacob was transported. He arrived in Australia but in common with many other transported individuals, his one aim was to get home and he wrote to the Colonial Secretary in Sydney:

'Mr. Thompson, Sir, Pardon me for taking the Liberty of a Drass you but mi torobles cales mi to Do so I rived by the Ship Captain Cook in the year 1833 Santanse Life for Riating &

Mesheen Braking I saw the news-paper with menn that was triad with mi they have goot ther Liberty ….. George Hopegood was tried with me at Winchester and for one afance he as goot his Liberty and as been to see me to write to your honor hoping you willin for me if I may Expect mi Liberty in a short time or not. Jacob Wiltshire.'

His pardon was granted at the end of 1839. It was too late. He died on the 26th February 1839 in the General Hospital at Bathurst, Australia.

In total at the trial in December 1830, 101 were sentenced to death, 3 executed and 117 transported. The savage response to the riots was a reflection of the paranoid fear of revolution in the landowning and ruling classes, who saw large-scale public protest as a threat to their security. The Magistrates were well pleased that 'Captain Swing' rioters were apprehended. Darius Bull received £40 for his part in the affair.

Distress continued in rural England for by 1832 most of the wage increases had been eroded. Throughout the 19th century rural labourers remained the worst housed, fed and paid in Britain. It took the better part of another 80 years for the most notable inadequacies to be addressed.

As mentioned before, illegitimate children could be a charge on the parish unless paternity were proved and the putative father made to pay.

Andover Advertiser, Vol 5, No 236, Friday, 11th July 1862, page 4.

County Bench, Friday July 4 1862 BASTARDY ….. *John Cummins, of Linkenholt, labourer, was summoned by Mary Beavis, of Vernham's Deane, ……. Ordered to pay 1s. 6d. per week towards its support, together with the costs.*

Vol 5, No 261, Friday August 15th 1862:

BASTARDY. John Kelly, labourer, of Oxford, was summoned by Jane Alderman, of Vernham's Deane, to show cause why he should not support her illegitimate child, of which she alleged he was the father. The defendant admitted the paternity of the child and was ordered to contribute 1s.6d. per week towards it support, and also to pay the costs of the application.

Andover Advertiser, Feb. 20th, 1863, County Bench: *SWEARING – Maria Wiltshire, of the parish of Vernham's Deane, applied to have an order made on George Digweed, of Newbury, for the maintenance of her bastard child, of which she alleged he was the father ……2s a week and costs.*

October 23rd, 1863, County Bench: *Margaret Baverstock of the parish of Vernhams Deane applied for an order on Thomas Baverstock (her cousin) of the same parish, for an order for the maintenance of her bastard child. The Defendant admitted the paternity of the child, and consented to have an order. Order made for the payment of 1s.6d. and costs.*

And again the Cummins seem to be in trouble:

Andover Advertiser, Friday, 12th June 1868: County Bench.

Lucy Ann Fisher, a young woman residing at Vernham's Deane, appealed to the Bench for an order on John Cummins, a labourer, living at Linkenholt, towards the support of her illegitimate child of which she alleged him to be the putative father. The defendant pleaded not guilty and the evidence given by the complainant not being corroborated in any material particular and it also showing that the conduct had been a very lax description the Bench decided to dismiss the application upon which the complainant's father (who was in court and had been called by her as a witness) evidently unprepared for the result, said that as the Bench would not make an order he was determined that the parish should keep both the mother and the child.

Drunkenness and poaching were other matters before the Courts.

Andover Advertiser, Friday 5th February 1869. County Bench: *POACHING*

John Kent, of Upton, Labourer, was summoned by Samuel Medhurst, of Vernham Dean, woodman, for trespassing in search of conies (that meant adult rabbits, only the young were called 'rabbits' at that time) *upon land in the occupation of William Child, Esq., situated at Vernham's Dean. The Defendant pleaded guilty to the charge and begged to be leniently dealt with as it was his first offence. After a suitable reprimand he was ordered to pay a fine of £1 including costs.*

Charles Alderman, of Vernhams Dean, was summoned by P.C. Brockway, of that parish, under the Night Poaching Prevention Act, for having on the 12th ult, suspected of coming from land where he had been unlawfully in search of game. Convicted in the sum of £1 penalty and 8s.6d. or in default to be imprisoned for one month with hard labour. Allowed one week to pay the money.

William Child frequently figures:

Andover Advertiser, Friday, 21st February, 1868: County Bench: Master and Servants Act. *Josiah Bray, labourer, of Vernham's Dean was summoned by William Child Esq of Vernham's Dean, for misconduct in service by leaving the same before the term of his contract had expired. The Bench, after some discussion, considered that a yearling hiring was not made out, and thereupon did not pursue further with the case.*

On to drunkenness:

Friday, 23rd July 1869: County Bench: *Drunk and riotous. An information was laid by Supt. Campbell, against John Elford, of Vernhams Deane, labourer, for being drunk and riotous on the public highway at the above parish. P.C. Davidge proved the offence. Committed to Winchester Gaol for seven days hard labour.*

John Elford seems to have the knack of getting into trouble:

Friday, July 23rd 1869 (again) column 2.

STEALING A JACKET – John Elford, a labourer, was charged of stealing on the 28th June last a jacket valued at 3/-, the property of Lot Chandler, of Vernham's Deane, Lot Chandler deposed: 'I am a labourer. The prisoner and I were together at the George Inn on the day in question, we both had a lay down, and about half an hour afterwards I got up and asked the prisoner to take care of my jacket and stop till I returned. Before I have got back I met the prisoner in the village with my jacket on, I passed him, and did not see anything of it afterwards. I saw the prisoner the next morning but nothing passed about the jacket. I was the worse for beer'. Mordecai Cook deposed that he lived in Vernham's Deane and bought the jacket off the prisoner for 1s.6d. and a pot of beer. P.C. Brockway deposed to receiving the jacket from the last witness, which he took to Lot Chandler, who identified it as his property. The Bench sentenced the prisoner to seven days imprisonment with hard labour.

……. whereas Anenisas Hughes, charged with stealing a spoon, was sentenced to 21 days imprisonment with hard labour and Amos Holmes, for poaching – 'an old offender' again of Wm. Child's property – fined £2. plus costs.

Andover Advertiser, Oct 4th, 1895 Bench: a labourer sent to gaol for a month and in leaving the box said *it did not matter as he should be in the hospital all the time for he was double ruptured.*

On the 19th October 1900, County Bench: Henry Tarrant, labourer – trespassing on land in occupation of F.R. Child ….. in search of conies. P.C. Downes saw him put down two gin traps. Fined 40/- and 10/- costs, in default 21 days, the Bench describing him as hopeless.

Andover Advertiser, 23rd October 1914: *VERNHAM GIRLS IN TROUBLE.*

Andover County Bench Children's Court: before Col. Harmer and J.C. Forster, Esq. *Winifred Sheppard (14) and Edith Ryder (9) were summoned for stealing two brushes of the value of 1s.1d. from a travelling van on Oct. 6. The girls' mothers were present to answer the charge, and pleaded guilty, although they said they did not know what their children did in their absence. David Schaffer who, on being questioned, said he was an*

English Jew, deposed that he was a licensed hawker of a travelling van, and on Oct 5 he and his brother were in Vernham about 5.30 in the evening. At the tail end of the van there were two baskets containing hardware, brushes, etc. The brushes produced were in one of the baskets. Witness noticed two children hanging on the tailboard and next he saw them running away each of them had a brush. He ran after them, and overtook Sheppard, who gave her friend's name for her own. She told him she did not have a brush, but afterwards pointed out the one in the hedge and said: 'There it is'. The girl's mother then came up, and while he was talking to her his brother came along with the other brush. They were deep baskets, so that brushes could not possibly fall out – John Schaffer told how he saw a brush in the hedge ten minutes after he had last seen it in the basket. P.C. Cooper stated that at 6 p.m. on Oct. 6 in consequence of information received he visited the defendants at their homes. Sheppard told him that as they were following the van went over a stone, the brushes jumped up, and they took one each. When they saw the men they ran away and put them in the hedge. Ryder said they had one brush each, she laid hers in the hedge on one side, and Sheppard put hers in the hedge opposite. He brought them to Andover police station where they were immediately bailed out. Mrs. Ryder informed the Bench that she had never known her girl to steal anything. She was away at Winchester at the time. Mrs. Sheppard said hers had always been a good girl, and she had never had cause to complain of her children, who had been well brought up. The Chairman asked the children if they knew the seriousness of the offence which they had committed, and then quoted them the following couplet 'He who takes what isn't his'n, when he's cocht will go to prison'. On their promising to be better girls in the future, the mothers were each bound over in the sum of £4. to be of good behaviour for six months.

The foregoing related to the official channels of social provision and law enforcement, but what were people doing for themselves?

Diana Coldicott, in her address to the Spring Symposium, 26th April 2003, Hampshire Field Club, put Friendly Societies in a neat nutshell:

Looking at rural societies, they were all established and run with three main aims: firstly societies were there to provide some insurance against sickness for their members, both cash benefits when they were not earning after illness or accident and also medical treatment from the society's doctor. Secondly, societies paid the funeral expenses of their members – and there would always be a good turnout of members following the coffin. And thirdly there was the all important social dimension of the friendly societies. Members met for club nights, usually once a month in the local pub, and then once a year there was the Feast Day (sometimes called the Festival) which was a real red letter day for the whole community.

The majority of the societies were founded in the years immediately after the passing of the Poor Law Amendment Act in 1834 .... This act removed the care of the poor from the parish and led to the building of central workhouses such as the notorious one at Andover, and friendly societies were a natural reaction by working men to a new situation. Poorly paid though most of them were, they founded societies to make what provision they could to help one another in times of sickness, accident or death and thus try to avoid the harshness and stigma of the new poor relief. As one man said at the time: 'We must look out for ourselves and provide for a day of sickness and old age now there is no parish to look to'.

Diana Coldicott kindly searched her Xerox of HRO Q16/3/1/1-2 which is a list of the many Friendly Societies in Hampshire that were enrolled at Quarter Sessions 1830-1846 (as per Act of Parliament). Vernham Dean does not appear, so its origin must be post-1846.

There is a nice illustration in the Andover Advertiser of the 5th July, 1879:

FRIENDLY SOCIETY

The Vernham George Friendly Society held their Annual Feast Day on Monday last. Members met at two o'clock and partook of lunch, and afterwards marched to the church headed by the St. Mary Bourne band, and listened to an excellent sermon, preached by Rev. Mulcaster. After the service the Club called on Mr. Child (Manor Farm) who is an honorary member, where abundance of the right sort was waiting for them. After drinking the health of Mr. Child, the members returned to their room, where an excellent dinner was waiting for them, the chair being taken by the Rev. Mulcaster who was supported by Messrs. Child, Barnes, Neale, Smart, Vivash, Hutchings, Worrell etc. After justice had been done to the inner man, the Chairman proposed success to the society, dwelling at great length on the value of such societies. The Reverend gentleman concluded by giving the members some good advice and hoped they would finish the day's enjoyment as men ought to do, and set an example to their neighbouring club. Mr. Stroud responded, and was pleased to be able to say that the society was in a very flourishing condition. Three hearty cheers were given for Mr. and Mrs. Stroud for the capital dinner provided. The St. Mary Bourne band gave every satisfaction ....Payments – Sick Pay £41.10s., medical attendance £18.10s., clerk and stewards, £3.10s. for band and refreshments to members £10.10s, the sum of £20 and the interest £6.19s.8d. have been added to the amount previously invested, making the total payments £100.19s.8d. and leaving a balance in hand of £11.2s.8d. so the total value of the society is now £314.17s.4d. The reading of this report was received with ringing cheers and was considered very satisfactory in every respect. Mr. Miles then proposed 'The Health of their Medical Officer' which was well received by the company and was responded to by Dr. Gilmour. The other toasts were 'The Visitors', 'The Band', and 'Host and Hostess' after which the club visited the residences of the principle inhabitants in the village, and returned to the clubroom to supper about 8 o'clock, and so ended one of the most successful club festivals held in this village for many a year.

And some years later:

Andover Advertiser, 23rd May 1894, Page 8, Col 8 *VERNHAMS DEAN*

Club Festival – The Vernham George Benefit Society met on Monday last to celebrate their annual festival. The members assembled at their clubroom at 10 a.m. and after the roll had been called over and the usual business transacted they marched in processional order headed by the Burbage Brass Band and their new colours, to the parish church, where an appropriate service was rendered by the Rev. F.J. Leeper, who gave the large congregation some very excellent advice. After the service the members proceeded to the Vicarage and the band played a selection of music on the lawn. They again formed into order and marched to the Manor Farm (for many years the residence of the Child family) and there the band again performed. On leaving the Manor they at once proceeded to the clubroom to discuss the most important item in the day's programme, namely the dinner. The clubroom was nicely decorated with flowers, etc. and a splendid dinner was placed on the tables by Mrs. Stroud. The Misses Stroud and other lady friends very kindly waited on everyone present. Dr. Gilmour presided, and was supported in the chair by Mr. G. Miles and Mr. G. Stagg, the other visitors included Mr. E. Quick (of the Manor), Mr. J. Miles, Jun., Mr. F. Clarke, Mr. Morris, Mr. Coleman, Mr. Evans, Mr. Liddiard, Mr. Green, Mr. Dobson, etc. On the removal of the cloth the Chairman proposed the 'Health of Her Majesty the Queen and the Members of the Royal Family' which was received with three such hearty cheers as only true Englishmen know how to give. 'The Health of the Club' was then proposed and the Secretary's statement of the financial affairs of the society was read. The members have not been so healthy as usual during the past year, therefore the amount of sick pay is larger than common. The Secretary's statement is as follows:- Receipt – Balance in hand at beginning of the year £25.13s.5d., monthly contributions, fines and entrance fees, £74.5s.9d. Interest on money invested £6.19s.8d., donations from non members £5.3s.5d., total £112.

There are many references to a society, under various names, in Vernham and further research would be valuable. One particularly fascinating snippet must be included from an 1871 edition of the Andover Advertiser:

Great Robbery of Club Money – a daring robbery has taken place within the last few days at Vernham's Dean. It appears there is a club held at the George Inn, kept by Mr. Stroud, and the cashbox and documents were kept there. The box was missed on Wednesday morning, and on a woman named Piper, who lives near, going into her garden about eleven o'clock she found it lying on the ground, under the eaves of the house. On examination it was found that the sum of £37.19s. had been taken, 1s.4d. and the papers being left. The robbery has caused great stir in the village, and the police are busy in trying to discover the thief ......

Andover Advertiser, Friday 28th July 1871: *Vernham Dean*

It will be remembered that a short time ago, we announced a large robbery of money from a box kept at the George Inn, Vernham Dean, and since that time diligent inquiries by the police have been made, but hitherto they have been fruitless, therefore as the visible powers have failed to detect the thief, the dark art of the wizards and witches has been called into requisition by a large number of the inhabitants, and the mode adopted to find out the robber is as follows: a Bible is opened and the wards of a key placed on particular verses, and the book is fastened with a garter. The ring of the key is then placed between two persons' thumbs horizontally, the Bible still being pendent. The verses which the key touches are repeated and the names of suspected persons mentioned. When a name is called out if the key remains unmoved they are innocent, but if it moves slightly out of the horizontal so as to cause the Bible to fall, they are guilty. What is stranger still is the statement made that in every case the key turned at the sound of the same name. To complete the absurdity, a 'cunning' man at Newbury was consulted with a view to ascertain the thief. That necromancer said the money would be returned at a time now past, but with all the aid thus sought the heinous robber is still at large. We would scarcely have thought so much sheer superstition was extant in the latter half of the 19th century.

An amusing reference of 1878 refers to Vernham George Friendly Society *hoping they would set an example to their neighbouring club.* One presumes this refers to Hurstbourne Tarrant, there was definite rivalry between the villages, even the in 1990s newcomers to Vernham Dean could detect a certain frisson when Hurstbourne was mentioned. But Mr. Child seemed to have no such distinction, as the Andover Advertiser for Friday, 26th July, 1878, page 5, column 5 reports:

Hurstbourne Tarrant. A report of the Hurstbourne Tarrant branch of the Hampshire Friendly Societies celebrating their 5th anniversary. W.C. Child took the chair as Mr. Hillier, chairman, was absent .... The various members of the Child family did not seem to maintain any distinction, possibly because they had land interests in both parishes.

There are numerous references to a 'Coal and Clothing Club'. A letter in the Winchester Archives makes it clear that John Fielder Child had been landed with the Treasurership of the club:

Mr. Leeper declines to take part in the matter – or anything else, it seems, for the good of his parishioners and the poor Vernham people. There are many of the latter, and a poor plight they are in. I wish, with all my heart, that it was otherwise.

30th December, 1887 (Winchester College Archives again) ...... J.F. Child thanks the Bursar ..... *for 40 years or about this Club has been established and has always worked on the principle advocated by you. The Clergyman at Vernham gave up the management last September for what reason I know not. The members pay 1/- each and every month. In December contracts for delivery of 1.2 tons are entered into, the farmers drawing it in gratis. The price is generally about 20/- a ton. The residue, with bonuses added (thanks to Winchester College) to be spent on articles of clothing at any shop they (the members) like to choose. I had an interview with one of the (now) most influential inhabitants, Mr. Homer-Powell of Row Farm who will assist in the club being carried on as heretofore. I have promised to assist him for the present. I should add tickets are issued to the shopkeeper, who is chosen to supply the goods.* (The parson referred to here is Revd Leeper). In another letter of the 13th December, 1888, John Fielder Child, writing to the Bursar at Winchester College, reminds him of the usual donation which the College makes.

This interesting series of letters from Vernham people to the Bursar (uncatalogued in HRO at the time the research was undertaken) have tantalising snippets about the Coal and Clothing Club viz 8th December 1890, coal is wanted for Mary Ann Hughes, Elizabeth Wilshire, Mary Ann Wiltshire, Ann Taylor, Jane Smith, Ann Hall, Jane White, Ann Kingston. In the 1860s clothing and bread were equally distributed, with numbers in the high 50s being quoted. Numbers decline after 1881 (60) with a sharp fall in 1882 to 35 recipients. Thereafter the numbers decline steadily, in the 20s in the 1890s, and in the 20th century from 21 down to 8 in 1938.

The club still seems to be going strong in 1916, and there are also details of 'Miss Bull's Charity' (HRO 110M 70 PK1) from 1868 onwards, mainly concerned with shirting, flannel and calico. There is a list of all recipients from 1868 to 1891 in two account books, and represents a charitable bequest by Miss Thirza Bull of Reading in 1864 to the poor of Vernham Dean, her family having been resident at the Manor for some considerable time. The interest on £112.16s.8d. in Consol. £3% annuities to be *given away to the aged poor, in bread or clothing, before Christmas annually at the discretion of the Trustees, they having urged to the recommendation of the Minister and Churchwardens'*.

A letter from L. Buckland & Son, of Andover, December 1943, says *that as no order has been given it is presumed money will be given as goods are in short supply.* The last account was for 1942, but in 1938 provision was made for: *Sheeting, Mrs Job Ray: Nightdress: Mrs. John Seward, Upton: Flanellette Mrs. Richardson, Upton: Sheeting, Mrs. Russ, Vernham: Winceyette Mrs. Bowley, Vernham. Two blankets Mrs. Geo. Smith, Vernham: One blanket Mrs. Tom Fisher, Upton: Sheets, Davis.*

The various charitable societies and trusts of Vernham merit considerably more research: the names change but it seems that several schemes run in parallel or are amalgamated. A somewhat hazy picture.

A 'Men's Club' was started in the Revd Iremonger's time (1930s) and the rules were very precise:

1. Members of the club shall be over 16 years of age.

2. The subscription shall be 4d per week, payable on Friday evening in advance. Entrance fee 6d.

3. The Club shall be open from 6.30 to 9.30 p.m. on Monday, Tuesday, Friday and Saturday, except on Shrove Tuesday, Good Friday and Christmas Day, and at other times that the Club committee or the trustees may determine.

4. A committee of four shall be elected at the annual general meeting of the Club, which shall take place in January. The committee shall have power to add to their number, and to make bye-laws which shall be binding on members of the Club.

5. Any member whose subscription is more than two weeks in arrears shall be fined 3d., and any member whose subscription is three weeks in arrears shall cease to be a member of the Club.

6. The charge for cannon and bagatelle shall be two pence for half an hour.

7. Gambling, or playing any game for money, is strictly prohibited.

It is not strictly a benefit society, more a social club for men who might otherwise gravitate to one of the many pubs or beer houses in the area. The 'Vernham Dean Men's Club Roll of Members' for February, 1933, makes interesting reading, including as it does men from all social ranks in the village from Roland Dudley (of Linkenholt Manor), to The George landlord, Mr. Elmer, to farmers, hauliers and labourers.

Why did Friendly Societies as initially constructed die out? Perhaps we have to consider the emigration of younger men, alternative provision, and membership of larger organisations; then finally state provision in 1909 with the introduction of the old age pension for the 70+ age group.

However, there was, and still remains, an element of provision on a purely voluntary basis, viz a reference to a Welfare Committee in 1948 'Annual Meeting of the Social Welfare Committee' which apparently raised money to take children to the seaside, etc.

In the 21st century Vernham can be proud of its efforts on behalf of its village over the last few decades – money was raised to erect a new sports pavilion on the playing field.

The Millennium Hall replaced the old village hall and on the 29th January, 2006, the church re-opened after a year of repairs, all monies for the above raised by village effort and grants from official bodies.

Rarely does a national appeal arise without an event arranged in the village to raise funds – typically the amount raised by Matthew Rose and his family and friends following the Boxing Day Tsunami of 2004.

Sources:

The Andover Advertiser

Hampshire Record Office

David Kent: Hampshire Papers: Popular Radicalism and the Swing Riots in Central Hampshire.

Jill Chambers: "Hampshire Machine Breakers".

The Times

Derek Tempero: "They Only Stole to Live".

The Ghost Vicar of Conholt Hill, and Other Spooky Stories.

There are several variations of the Ghost Vicar of Conholt Hill story, but most follow roughly the same lines.

In the times of plague, about 1665 (during the reign of Charles II), the vicar of the parish persuaded all the villagers who had been in contact with the disease to go into isolation in a closed camp, or in some versions a pest hospital, on top of Conholt Hill, near Chute Causeway. The vicar promised to bring them regular supplies of food, and for a while he did. Then he became afraid of catching the disease, so stopped. There is an alternative version, which has the vicar dying alone of the plague on Conholt Hill, while taking food to the villagers. Either way, no food came. Those villagers who did not die of the plague starved to death. In the version where the vicar fled he caught the disease anyway, and died. His grief-stricken ghost can be seen climbing the hillside to where so many of his flock died.

Now for the history: in the 1660s Vernham Dean was not a separate parish, it was part of Hurstbourne Tarrant. Hurstbourne has kept a list of parish vicars since 1546. This is the result of one of Henry VIII's little laws that have helped historians in later ages: he ordered every parish to keep a register. The act was passed in 1538. Hurstbourne got round to implementing it only 8 years later. From 1637 until 1646 Christopher Teesdale was the vicar, and then from 1646 until 1653 the vicar was Pastor Henry Gough: from 1653 until 1663 there were several Puritan pastors. In 1663 Christopher Teesdale (one of the above-mentioned Christopher Teesdale's sons) returned and remained until circa 1671. His successor, Edmund Sparke, was inducted on the 1st June 1672. *Madge: Hampshire Inductions (1918) p 26.* The outbreak of bubonic plague in the 17th century started in 1665 but had more or less died out by 1666. So was Christopher Teesdale the 'wicked vicar'?

However, there is a small village in Derbyshire called Eyam, 6 miles north of Bakewell. In 1665 a box of laundry was brought to Eyam by a traveller. The laundry was infested with fleas, and the epidemic started. Eighty per cent of the people died here and there could have been a terrible outbreak in Derbyshire had the village not had a courageous rector called William Mompesson. He persuaded the villagers not to flee the village and spread the infection, but to stay until the plague had run its course. His wife was one of the victims and her tomb is in Eyam church. Mompesson preached in the open air during the time of the plague. Every year a commemorative service is held on the last Sunday in August where he preached. During their 'siege' the villagers dropped money for provisions into a well so as not to spread the infection on the coins. In the words of James Stewart in the film "The Man Who Shot Liberty Valance" – "When truth becomes legend, print the legend".

Reported sightings of the rector or a monk on Conholt Hill were fairly frequent, although there have not been many recently, unless you know better. Before the First World War a carter, tired after a hard day's work, stopped at the bottom of the hill, but was helped to the top of the hill by a friendly arm under his elbow: when he turned to thank his helper, there was no-one there. In 1917 a churchwarden and his wife (not living in Vernham Dean) were travelling home from Hungerford by horse and cart one summer's evening. On the way up the hill the husband got out to assist the horse up the hill, and then quickly got back in, muttering about not being as young as he used to be. His wife noticed a tall hooded figure walking alongside, which disappeared when they got to the top of the hill. She remembered years earlier her nanny telling her about the ghost of Conholt Hill. Another churchwarden's wife was going home up the hill in a dog-cart when a figure appeared. On this occasion the lady had a young man with her, who jumped down and chased the figure towards the Causeway, where it disappeared. The figure wore a pointed hood or cowl. A theme seems to be developing here, involving churchwardens' wives, but next come temperance meetings, and lady cyclists.

The founder of the shop that preceded Habel's store in Andover, a Mr. Pond, was returning from a temperance meeting in the local chapel when he saw a tall hooded figure. He threw a stone at the apparition which passed right through it. The figure promptly disappeared, but then so would most people if a stranger started heaving rocks at them.

In 1949 a lady cyclist on her way to Fosbury saw a figure dressed in a long flowing robe. The robe was white from the waist up: the figure disappeared into the trees. There is no record of what colour it was below the waist. A few years later a male motorist reported seeing a tall robed figure carrying a back pack. The motorist checked for on-coming traffic, as taught in the Highway Code, then looked back at where the figure had been, but it had disappeared.

During 1994 Eric Levell wrote this story in his "Country Days, Country Ways" column in the Andover Advertiser. His grandfather started work as a plough-boy in the fields at Conholt when he was about 7 years old. At dusk, his grandfather would be lifted off the horse by the carter, who sometimes asked if he was afraid of the ghost. Eric's grandfather whispered "Noooo" then ran all the way down the hill.

Only a short while ago, a lady motorist was driving down Conholt Hill one July evening. It was a typical English summer's day. It had rained without stopping all day, the rain was torrential and coming in sideways, the wind was blowing gale force, and walking up the hill wearing trousers, a white jacket and panama hat was a vicar. He appeared completely oblivious to the terrible weather. They made eye contact, he stared impassively at her, and she felt a cold chill come over her, but drove on. When she looked back he was gone. Perhaps the ghost has changed his cowl for a panama.

There is another ghost story

Nick Brown was told it by James Haigh – it goes as follows:

The sound of a horse's hooves (one animal) with associated jangling and clattering of paraphernalia, is to be heard progressing down Anker's (or Conholt) Lane from the Conholt direction – the progress of the horse then reaches the Vernham-Upton road, passes along then turns left up towards the church – the sound then turns right to pass the dairy and then left again to join the Upton-Linkenholt road. The passage from there on is via Netherton Bottom out to the A343 and northwards towards Newbury.

The timing of these sounds is from late at night through to the early hours of the morning, and in real time – i.e. as if a real horse were really making that journey. I believe that the time of year is shortly preceding the anniversary of the 1st Battle of Newbury, although I am not aware of whether this is an annual event or not. Apparently the identification of this route/event came about from the observations of people on the route who coincidentally remarked on the late night horseman/woman, and agreed to listen out – once the first person had heard the sound, they 'phoned the next on the route and correlated the time from first call to last.

I have no idea who these folk were, nor when this 'passage' was identified, and it may well be anecdotal nonsense! However, when pressed as to how was it known to be a Cavalier going to war the answer was apparently that there was the jangling of swords, etc, which you would not normally associate with horse-riding.

Yet more spooks and things that go flash in the night

The George Inn seems to have a few ghosts. Twenty years or more ago the landlord said a figure had been seen in the bar after closing time. He insisted that it was not a lock-in or a reveller asleep in the corner who had been overlooked at closing time. The son of a more recent tenant saw a figure in his room, and the next tenant's grown-up daughter came down to the bar one night and spoke to a strange figure, who when it turned to look at her had a very distorted face. Interestingly, that tenant's dog refused to sleep downstairs.

Deer's Leap (see Civil War section below) has a room that always seems cold when entering it, and some dogs refuse to go into it.

Recently people have reported seeing strange lights while walking along Hatchbury Lane and Hungerford Lane. Hatchbury Lane continues from Hatchbury Terrace and Hungerford

Lane is the track on the left further up Bulpits Hill, just past Haydown Leas. There have been several reports: the lights are usually seen after midnight. It appears to be a lantern being swung from side to side. Some of the people who have reported seeing the lights are late night dog walkers. Others offer no reason for being there at that time of night.

Knyghtes Mere, at the top of Ankers Lane, is supposed to have a carriage and horses buried at the bottom of it, but as it never dries up, no-one has been able to check. Some local horse-riders say that their horses do not like passing Knyghtes Mere, although dogs do not seem to be affected, and they are supposed to be very aware of things spiritual.

The Domesday Book

First some brief background details to the Domesday Book. William I (The Conqueror) commissioned the survey while at his Christmas Court in Gloucester in 1085. It was completed during 1087. The Greater Domesday, which included Hampshire, did not record details of individual cattle, pigs, sheep etc. These were recorded in the Little Domesday, which only covered the counties of Norfolk, Suffolk and Essex. There is another document, Exon Domesday, which gives details of livestock for Cornwall, Devon, Dorset, Somerset and Wiltshire but nothing exists for Hampshire. Possibly the volume of data for the rest of the country was too great for the monks, or the data was out of date by the time they came to write it down, so it was thrown away. Winchester is omitted totally from the Domesday survey but a later survey was carried out circa 1110. *(This and another survey of Winchester in 1148 are studied in ed. Biddle 'Winchester in the Early Middle Ages 1976)* In the 11th century the capital of England started to move from Winchester to London, but the King's Treasury, and hence the real centre of power, remained in Winchester under the supervision of the Bishop of Winchester until well into the 12th century. London is omitted as well. Before the Dissolution (1539) Winchester was a monastic cathedral: St. Swithin's. The Dean and Chapter were brought into being by Henry VIII in 1541, when the last Prior of St. Swithin's became the first Dean.

The following information is taken from the 1992 Penguin translation edited by Dr. Ann Williams and Professor G.H. Martin. Although there is no entry for Vernham Dean as such, in the Domesday Book Hurstbourne Tarrant is covered in detail.

Hurstbourne Tarrant was in the Basingstoke Hundred (Hundred – an administrative subdivision of a shire, with fiscal, judicial and military functions) – of Hampshire. The Penguin Domesday translation is in italic:

The King holds Hurstbourne Tarrant in demesne. Demesne: a) land whose produce was reserved for the Lord, rather than any tenants, so the King had the profit. b) manors (held directly or indirectly) from the King by the Lord of the Manor. *It belonged to King Edward's farm.* This refers to the pre-conquest times – the king being Edward the Confessor. The Normans ignored the reign of the last Anglo-Saxon king, Harold II. The commissioners who collected the facts were ordered to assess ploughlands and the number of ploughs etc. both before and after 1066 William claimed to be Edward's nominated successor. The Domesday Book compared the estates in 1086 with the period before 1066.

They did not record the number of hides – the standard unit of assessment for tax, notionally the amount of land that would support a household. As this was one of King William's personal holdings tax was not important. *There is land for 16 ploughs. In demesne are 2 ploughs; and 24 villans, and 12 bordars with 15 ploughs. There are 10 acres of meadow, and woodland for 20 pigs, for the herbage 20s.* Villan – villager, a peasant of higher economic status than a bordar, technically not a freeman, as he was subject to the authority of the manorial court. Bordar- a cottager, of lower class and not as wealthy as a villan. 20s was twenty shillings or one pound.

Vitalis the priest holds the church of this manor, with half a hide, and there he has 1 plough with 2 bordars, and 1 acre of meadow, and the church-scot which is valued at 14s. These 3 manors, Basingstoke, Kingsclere, and Hurstbourne Tarrant render 1 day's farm. Church-scot – church tax, an annual render in kind paid to the Church. Day's farm: – not an agricultural term in this context, but the amount of produce that would support the King and his retinue for one 24 hour period. 14s: fourteen shillings or 70p.

It would seem that Hurstbourne Tarrant was a small village, with 24 families with a reasonable income and status, and half that number of poorer families. There is no mention of any slaves. They had their own priest, and sent a fixed amount each year to the King. In the 11th century this would have almost always been produce, by the 13th it was often money. Providing they did this, they would usually have been left alone.

Linkenholt also appears in the Domesday Book. In the Hurstbourne Hundred, it was held by the Church of Gloucester, the Abbey of St. Peter to be precise. In the reign of Edward it was held by Eadric and was assessed at 5 hides and was worth 100s (£5). By the time of Domesday Emulf de Hesdin had, with the permission of King William, given it to the Abbey. It was, in 1087, assessed as 1 hide, with the remainder in demesne. There was land for 5 ploughs, with 2 in demesne, and there were 4 villans, and 8 bordars with 2 ploughs. There were 6 slaves, with 7 acres of meadow, and woodland for fencing. The tax assessment was £4.

Andover according to the Domesday Book had six watermills, used to grind flour. Later on, others were built to process wool. Sheepskins were made into parchment, there was a leather industry, and in 1175 Andover received a charter from the king allowing the traders and merchants to hold a market.

Members of Parliament

In 1884 George Hicks (1879-1954) of Flowers Farm, Vernham Street, was admitted to Vernham Dean School. When he left school he became a bricklayer. He was later a trades unionist and a Labour Party politician. Mr. Hicks was General Secretary of the Amalgamated Union of Building Trade Workers for twenty years from 1921, and one of the leaders of the 1926 General Strike. He was President of the Trades Union Congress 1926-27 and a member of the General Council of the International Federation of Trade Unions. Elected as Member of Parliament for Woolwich East in a 1931 by-election, George Hicks served as a junior minister (Parliamentary Secretary to the Minister of Works) in the wartime coalition government.

In 1295 Andover sent two MPs (Johannes Oriold and Richardus Lotyn) to a parliament, and did the same in 1302, 1305, 1306 and 1307, although usually different men to each parliament. However, owing to the high cost no more MPs were sent from Andover until 1587, in the reign of Elizabeth I. In medieval times, unlike now, it cost an individual quite a lot of money to be a Member of Parliament. A notable Andover MP was one John Smith, who was the Chancellor of the Exchequer from 1699 until 1702 and then became Speaker in 1705. In 1708 he was a signatory to the Act of Union with Scotland, thus becoming the first Speaker of a British Parliament. In 1708 he stood down as Speaker, but remained an MP for a few more years.

When Oliver Cromwell died in 1658, his son Richard Cromwell became Lord Protector for a few months until the restoration of Charles II. Richard Cromwell summoned a parliament in January 1659 and Andover sent Gabriel Beck of Westminster (sic) and Robert Gough of Vernham's Dean. Not a lot else seems to be known about Robert Gough. He may have been related to William Gough, who was a Major-General in Cromwell's army, in charge of Hampshire. William Gough was a signatory to Charles I's death warrant, and died in 1679. As a result of Gladstone's Third Reform Act in 1885, coupled with the Redistribution of Seats Act, separate constituencies with populations of less than 15,000 were abolished, and Andover no longer had its own MP.

The Civil War

The above item leads nicely on to the Civil War (the Charles I against Parliament civil war). There were many battles in the area, and a running fight through Andover, a scene sometimes re-enacted on Saturday nights. This occurred in 1642, when Cavaliers, retreating from Marlborough to Winchester, were attacked by Parliamentarians on their way to Newbury. There was a battle at Devizes in July 1643 and on the 20th September came the first Battle of Newbury. Then on 29th March 1644 there was a battle at Cheriton, near Winchester. The siege of Basing House started in November 1643, and it finally fell to Cromwell's army in

October 1645. On the 18th October 1644 came the Battle of Andover (actually held near Monxton) and they finished off on the 27th with the Second Battle of Newbury.

The house currently known as "Deers Leap", according to several sources, was used as a field hospital by the Parliamentarians at this time. It appears to have probably been built in the early 17th centuary, so would have existed during the Civil War. It is said that there used to be a plaque on the chimney breast recording this fact. However, without examining the plaque there can be no certainty of its authenticity. The plaque disappeared many years ago. The house was formerly known as "The Homestead". Such field hospitals certainly existed in other parts of the country, so on the balance of probability, this was also one.

Less credibility can be given to the claim that the playing fields "The Burydene" were a Civil War cemetery. There is no recorded evidence of a battle, or even a skirmish, in the near area, and anyone who has tried to work the ground will know there are far too many flints to dig very deeply. An alternative spelling of Burydene is "The Berrydene".

Conholt Park

Although not actually in Vernham Dean or even Hampshire, Conholt Park is considered part of the village. Conholt Hill dominates the view to the south, and coming back from Andover via Tangley, on seeing the house, one feels almost at home. Conholt House as it now stands was built in 1810-11, as an addition to an older 18th century property. In the 1950s the older part was demolished.

The estate covers nearly 2,000 acres. The site has been occupied for nearly a millennium, but not a lot seems to be recorded about the earlier period. During the Second World War, the records that existed were taken to London for "safe keeping" and were bombed. There are records of small farms in the 13th and 15th centuries, when it was owned by Battle Abbey, but nothing about any substantial buildings.

In the mid 17th century a man named Daniel built a house which has since been completely destroyed. In the 18th century Sir Philip Meadows, when he was 95 years old, built Chute Park House over the road from where Conholt Park House currently stands. In 1737 Sidney, the son of Sir Philip Meadows, changed his name to Pierrepont, and succeeded to the estate of the Duke of Kingston, whose sister he had married. Chute Park House burned down, and Sidney built Conholt Park House. On his death it passed to a grandson, Henry, whose only daughter married Ford Wellesley. It then passed to Philip Pierrepont, who had no children, so it passed to Mr. Norey, who changed his name to Meadows. He leased it to Lady Wellesley, and then it was sold to Edward Wigan, a shipping magnate in 1904. In the 1881 census the head of the house was Lady Charles Wellesley, whose occupation was stated to be "widow of son of duke". There were twelve servants: a housekeeper, a lady's maid, a cook, two housemaids (one upper and one lower) a kitchen maid, a laundry-maid, a butler, a scullery maid, a footman, a house boy, and a domestic gardener. None of the servants had the same surname. Estate staff and gardeners did not live in, so were counted elsewhere.

In 1943 Miss Henrietta Gaskell inherited the estate. Apart from the aircraft crash (see below) Conholt Park did not figure much in the news until 1988. Miss Gaskell was then 90 years old, and lived in the house alone apart from a 67 year old companion, Miss Marjorie Mills.

On Saturday March 26th 1988 the ladies had gone to bed when, about 2.00 a.m. on Sunday morning, Miss Mills was awakened by a noise. She tried to switch the lights on but burglars had cut the power lines. She got up, and confronted two men who panicked and ran off. Miss Mills locked the door and tried to telephone the police: the lines had also been cut. The burglars then returned, broke down the door, and dragged Miss Mills around the house. They then woke Miss Gaskell, and demanded to know where the keys to the safe were kept. She refused to tell them, but gave in when the burglars threatened to shoot her pet Labrador, Bruno.

The ladies were handcuffed to the stairs, while the burglars ransacked the house removing paintings, silver, jewellery and antique furniture, worth at least £10,000. Miss Gaskell had removed her watch and ring and hidden them under the stair carpet. At one point the burglars, who are believed to have been Irish, asked the ladies if they would like a drink of whisky, (or should it be whiskey), to calm their nerves. Miss Mills replied: "No thank you, we would rather have a gin and tonic". This was provided, together with cushions for the ladies to sit on. It is not recorded if ice and lemon were included with the gins.

Once the raiders had gone, at about 5.30 a.m., Miss Gaskell remembered a tool box under the stairs. The ladies then spent five hours sawing through the banister. They let themselves out of the house and, still in their night-clothes and handcuffed together, started walking down the drive. An estate worker, Bill Cook, found them and called the estate manager who telephoned the police. The ladies refused to go to hospital, but a doctor visited them. They were not seriously hurt, badly swollen wrists were the main problem.

Hampshire Police never solved the crime, but described the ladies as "incredibly courageous".

Miss Gaskell died in 1991. Conholt Park was purchased by Paul van Vlissingen, a Dutch millionaire. He set about modernising the estate, and introduced several breeds of rare animals: European bison, llamas, highland cattle and white deer can all be seen in the park grounds. Mr. van Vlissingen died in 2006, the property is owned by a Trust.

The Conholt Park Aircraft Crash

This occurred on the 22nd November 1948 at 17.08. A Lancaster tanker, G-AHJW "Jig Willie" was on charter to British Airways. It had completed 40 sorties into East Berlin, as part of the Berlin Airlift. (The Russians attempted to starve West Berlin into submission by closing all road and rail routes across East Germany into the city, so the allies flew everything in). The aircraft took off from Wunsdorf (West Germany) at 14.56 for a flight to Tarrant Rushton to undergo periodic maintenance. It crashed off-course by some 24 miles to the north. The official report states: "The probable cause was aircraft striking trees while being flown at low altitude in conditions of poor visibility. The reason for the deviation from track cannot be determined but it seems probable that the aircraft was being homed on the Netheravon Beacon".

On the ground debris from the 'plane hit one cottage, injuring a woman (Mrs Whitlock) who was inside. She was taken to hospital, but later released. Her husband and three children who were also in the cottage were unhurt. The 'plane narrowly missed four other nearby cottages.

On board the Lancaster were two flight crews, one travelling as passengers, and three flight refuelling captains. The last message from the aircraft was to Hurn airport that it was at 2,000 feet and descending. The pilot Captain R.M. Heath, Navigation Officer A.J. Burton, Flight Engineer K. Seabourne (the crew) and passengers Captain W. Cusack, Captain C. Taylor, Radio Officer D. Robertson, and Navigating Officer M. Casey were all killed. The crew's Radio Operator, Vincent Stanley, was thrown out of the escape hatch. He was badly burned, but survived. There is a memorial stone to the dead in St. Mary's Church, Andover.

At the end of 2006 it could be said that Vernham Dean has reached the end of an era. All the major local building projects are complete. The church has been repaired; there is a new Village Hall, Sports Pavilion, and the school has a new set of classrooms. Although the school still needs a hall, that is outside the remit of the village; Hampshire County Council will decide when that is built, and pay for it. The Berrydene playing fields are well tended and well used, as is the play equipment for the children. The Sports Pavilion was renamed 'The Mac East Pavilion' in honour of Mac East, a long-time supporter of the football team and tireless worker at the playing fields, he was also a parish councillor and contributed to many other village activities. To this day his Welsh flag flies proudly on the flagpole every St David's Day.

Several local sports organisations continue to thrive: the Boys' and Men's Football Clubs do well but cricket never seems to be very popular here, those interested tend to go to Linkenholt. The Ladies Netball team, the Vernham Vixens, still plays regularly. Many of the sports teams include players from outside the village but contain a core of villagers. The Test Valley Tour cycling event often starts on the Berrydene. One villager runs his own motor racing team, Tilling Motor Sports, several villagers form part of his support team. Some villagers take part in coarse and game shooting.

There is still – just – a village shop and post office and although only open a few hours each week, it is an important part of village life. The pub, The George, is well patronised and used by locals and visitors alike. It serves food at lunchtime and in the evenings. The Pub Quiz team has been in existence for many years. Darts have also returned. A travelling cinema brings recent films to the Village Hall once a month.

The annual fete is well supported, as is the firework display in November, both being held on the Berrydene. At Christmas a number of special events are held, usually selling local and seasonal produce. Christmas 2006 saw the introduction of a Christmas Carnival, with floats, carol singing around the village, refreshments and entertainment around the pavilion, complete with artificial snow. The Theatre Group continues to perform to packed houses and performs a pantomine yearly at Christmas and usually a spring production also.

The Parish Council meets in the Village Hall to discuss local matters, and parishioners are encouraged to attend. At least one church service is held each week in the village church, St. Mary the Virgin, and also in the local Gospel Hall. St. Mary's is used for baptisms, weddings and funerals. There is a local junior choir which sings at some services although the senior choir disbanded a few years ago. Sunday School is in the form of The Star Club, which meets most weeks in the Village Hall and there is a Friday Club for children in the Gospel Hall.

Prescriptions are delivered to villagers each Thursday when a local doctor holds a surgery in the Village Hall. The WI meets on a regular basis in the hall, and meetings are well supported. The Georgians, an older citizen's social group, is now disbanded, but many of its former members attend events organized by the British Legion in Hurstbourne Tarrant. There is a Conservation Group which organises and carries out general conservation work and surveys, and helps look after wild plants and animals in the village

The village school is well supported; many pupils come from outside the village. It is not full to capacity, some year groups are full, and others have vacancies. Most local children go on to The Clere School when they leave the village school, the school bus leaving from The George car park for Burghclere each morning. The Little Fingers Play Group operates in the Gospel Hall. They, the Friends of the School, the Friends of the Church and other fund raising groups organise social events: dances, discos, dinners, clay-pigeon shooting, quiz nights, auctions of promises, race events – the list is quite lengthy.

Several local people earn their living in the village as builders, plumbers, gardeners, etc. Some work from home, many others commute to Andover, Swindon, London or Pisa. Quite a few villagers are retired. Two music teachers work in the village and horse riding for children is available. There is a Bed and Breakfast business in the centre of the village.

There are a number of local organisations doing voluntary and charitable work. The Playing Fields Association looks after the care and maintenance of the Berrydene and also organises the fete and fireworks display. The Village Hall Committee similarly looks after the Village Hall, officially called the 'Millennium Hall'. Other groups not already mentioned include the Holy Dusters – people who clean the church each week, the Flower Arranging Volunteers, and Neighbourhood Watch.

Vernham Dean has its own monthly magazine, Focus, which is the social diary of the whole village, edited, published, printed and distributed by a team of locals.

Vernham Dean – Vernham Street – Vernham Row – no more than an easy walk from each other and comprising, in the 21st century, perhaps, something which attracts so many people: a peaceful, beautiful village and a vibrant community.